Curriculum Studies in Post-Compulsory and Adult Education

A study guide for teachers and student teachers

Mary Neary

PhD, BEd, (Hons), Cert. Ed., RNT, RCNT, RGN, RMN, RNMH

Lecturer in Post-Compulsory Education,
Professional Tutor to PGCE Courses and Visiting Professor to Finland
School of Social Sciences
University of Wales
Cardiff CF10 3WA

Nelson Thornes
a Wolters Kluwer business

Published in 2002

Reprinted in 2003 by:
Nelson Thornes Ltd
Delta Place
27 Bath Road
CHELTENHAM
GL53 7TH
United Kingdom

07 08 / 10 9 8 7 6 5

A catalogue record for this book is available from the British Library

ISBN 978 0 7487 6442 6

Illustration on page 170: Steve Ballinger

Page make-up by Acorn Bookwork Ltd, Salisbury, Wiltshire

Printed and bound in Croatia by Zrinski

Contents

ACKNOWLEDGEMENTS

I express my thanks and appreciation for the help and advice given to me by the following: Dr. J. Salisbury, School of Social Sciences, Cardiff University, for her work on the hidden curriculum; Mr. K. Squires, University of Huddersfield; Dr. J. Moon, formerly at School of Education, Cardiff University; Mrs S. Whyman and Mrs J. Swift – a big 'thank you' to Sheila and her sister Jackie for sorting out my mess and to Jackie for all her help with developing my computer skills. I also wish to thank all the PGCE Course Team, at the School of Social Sciences, Cardiff University, for their support and advice, and particularly Trevor Welland, Course Director, for his work on evaluation and reflection.

I am also grateful to Donna Young, Principal Lecturer and Quality, Equality and Development Coordinator, School of Nursing and Midwifery at De Montfort University, Leicester, for giving permission to publish the mission statement in Appendix 4 and other examples of course documentation; to Professor John Furlong of Cardiff University for permission to reproduce the GCE A/AS level course specifications (WJEC/CBAC) in chapter 5 and the extracts from the PGCE course guides in Appendices 1 and 2; to Mrs Marjorie Hobbs of Llancarfan for the use of her old school journals from which the poem on p.viii is extracted, and to all the staff in the Faculty of Education at Huddersfield University.

This book is dedicated to the PGCE Course Team
at Cardiff University.

Before Prayers

Eileen wrote very fluently and happily, but at great length, on several topics. 'Before Prayers' has many delightful lines.

Some talk of work with earnest tone –
'Rose, when did John come to the throne?
What date did Metternich fast flee
To countries far across the sea?
When did the Greeks their freedom gain?
What years did Alexander reign?
I can't think of a single date!
Now – was it forty-six or eight?'

And some there are who vainly seek
To solve what seems some hopeless Greek,
Yet really is Geometry –
Prove A+B+C+D
Do equal half of O P Q –
The angle Z the only clue.

Some, too, with many a shrug and sigh
Repeat the Latin for 'I try,
I love, I work' – the conjugation
Of war and peace and sword and nation.

And so the minutes speed along:
The chatt'ring girls wish to prolong
Their cheerful talk and laughter gay,
But time still holds the greatest sway,
And all too soon the great bell clangs.
Snapped is the feeling gay which hangs
O'er all the form, and for a while
They cease to speak and laugh and smile,
And silently with reverent face
They troop into the Hall apace.

Eileen Nichols (Walthamstow High School Magazine, 1930)

Preface

The purpose of this book

The purpose of this book is to provide practical information about curriculum studies in the form of a concise set of notes. It is not meant to be an exhaustive treatment; the teacher and the student will need to read more widely about curriculum studies, especially issues to do with finance, colleges as businesses and as partnerships with industries, commerce, etc.

The aims of this book

1 To guide the student and teacher through the different aspects of curriculum studies by using a problem-solving approach (Study Problems) and recommended reading at the end of each chapter.
2 To help the student and teacher undergoing a Cert. Ed. or PGCE course, ILT members in higher education and degree courses in education; these courses may be one-year full-time or part-time courses, commonly called 'in-service' or B.Ed. courses. The book is also suitable for students undertaking Masters degrees in education or any other similar teacher education courses to develop a better understanding of and gain a practical approach to curriculum planning and development, including the concepts related to curriculum models, curriculum change, curriculum evaluation, curriculum research and curriculum innovations.
3 To help professionals who are involved in the teaching, education and training of, for example, nurses, police, mentors and those in the prison service, to develop their understanding of curriculum issues.

The book can also be used as a reference textbook that students can dip in and out of, according to their learning needs.

At the beginning of each chapter, the reader will find learning outcomes to which they should return once they have read the chapter and ask themselves 'What have I learned from this?'

This book has been designed to enhance 'flexible learning'. This allows learners to study in their own time, place and pace. It is not designed just to be another means for 'open learning' but for conventional college-based learning systems where 'flexibility' of time, place and space have been introduced. Essentially, developing flexible learning processes from traditional teaching processes is largely a matter of putting into print not only the content of a course or syllabus, but also the support which would be offered to the student or learner by teachers. Race (1989b) and Neary (2000) support the view that we 'learn by doing' and that the key aspect of the development of flexible learning resource material is the interaction between learners and materials. The most important aspects of the support and interaction which can be built into flexible learning resources are:

- the task and exercises whereby learners gain competence
- the feedback learners receive on their progress by tutors and educators

- the knowledge they gain by sharing with their peers
- the guidance learners are given regarding their use of textbooks, references and resources.
- details of the assessment criteria which will be indicative of successful outcomes.

The exercises in this book have been designed in such a way that learners can work on their own, work with a fellow learner and colleague, assess each other and are encouraged to assess their own individual progress. There is no separate answer section, learners will discover the answers to the study problems in each section as they read through each chapter. When the learner needs to revisit or move to another chapter this is indicated. My rationale for this learning and assessment strategy is to introduce the learner to the heuristic approach of self-directed learning.

Learners can learn from the most prolific recourse available to them – each other. For years there has been some reluctance to work with fellow learners; this may have stemmed from the days when collaborating with fellow learners used to be regarded as 'cheating'. However, today we have a much healthier view regarding teamwork, in the form of group work and workshops. There will be mature learners who will still retain the feeling that they should work independently, and this can lose for them the 'value of finding out where they're at' from fellow learners. However, one must respect the individual styles of all learners (Race 1991)

The ultimate aim of this book is to promote learning with or without the presence of a teacher or tutor, but the handover of control is best done one step at a time with thorough monitoring of each move towards learner autonomy. You may be a learner preparing to become a teacher, or you may be on a degree course in education. You may even be a very experience teacher or head of a department in a variety of educational settings, for example, nursing, law, teacher training. You may even be an experienced university lecturer, preparing for membership of the Institute for Learning and Teaching in Higher Education (ILT). You may be an FE college teacher undertaking an FE teacher qualification as required from September 2001 (FENTO 2001).

Students will need help and support from time to time. It is at these times that students are advised to ask their tutors and/or their peers for help.

FURTHER READING

Brookfield, S. (1984b) 'Self-directed adult learning: a critical paradigm'. *Adult Education Quarterly* 2: 59–71.
Race, P. (1982) 'Help yourself to success: improving polytechnic students' study skills'. In F. Percival and H. Ellington (eds), *Aspects of Educational Technology XV: Distance Learning and Evaluation*. London, Kogan-Page.

Introduction: The Changing Culture of Post-Compulsory Education

1

Learning outcomes

To be achieved through the process of self-directed study, teacher/mentor support and sharing learning with fellow students

By the end of this chapter you will be able to:

- explain the political influences related to curriculum development
- discuss the changing culture of education in post-compulsory education.

The Changing Culture and Political Influences

Whilst it is not my intention to delve into the controversy over the National Curriculum, I refer to it here as an example of its dominance over the last decade of educational politics, involving a series of interlocking issues.

Once a government has legislated for a curriculum, it raises complex questions: What should the curriculum consist of? What should its intellectual bases be? How should these decisions be reached? How do decisions about the curriculum relate to decisions about educational policy in general? And how do these issues relate to the traditions of education and wider culture of the country and institutions in question? These are the same questions asked by Barber (1996) when examining the issues related to the National Curriculum.

Our interest here is in examining the emergence of curriculum issues in post-16, vocational, professional and adult education. Lecturers and teachers feel bewildered by the changes taking place in the organisation of education and training. Choice is fine, but how can one make sensible choices when the different options and routes are unknown, or when one's knowledge is based on systems of education that have been replaced?

We have seen over the last decade how the changing context is closing the gap between education, training and employment. Pring *et al.* (1999) suggest however that there is a need for a sharper focus on personal development, a greater concentration upon standards, a redefinition of the partnership to include employers, parents and learners, and a dominant position given to central government in stipulating outcomes. A good example of such a partnership is the scheme set up in the University of Greenwich and described by Robson *et al.* (1995). They argued: 'Any form of professional or vocational training (including the training of teachers) can be viewed quite instrumentally in terms of its function of supplying the workforce for that profession' (p.79).

What is emerging is a reappraisal of the purposes that education should serve and therefore of the ways it should be organised. Just as in other professions and occupations there has recently been a concerted attempt to promote and enhance the employers' role, so in education employers have increasingly become more influential and more involved in the training of their existing and prospective employees.

We may remember that in 1984 Sir Keith Joseph referred to the need to convince those 'whom we serve' – parents, employers and the public, all of whom pay tax and rates. He highlighted the way forward as:

- clearly defined standards of performance to meet agreed learning objectives
- higher levels of performance against those standards across the ability range
- a curriculum for all reflecting breadth, relevance, differentiation and balance
- concentration on practical capabilities and preparation for life and the workplace
- reform of the post-16 curriculum towards more criterion-referenced assessments
- central validation of teacher training to ensure preparation for these reforms.

It was these proposals that helped to shape the Education Act of 1988, which it is argued was the most radical reform of the management of education since 1944 (Pring *et al.* 1999).

VALUES AND CULTURAL ISSUES

The structure and methods of education must help to sustain the traditional values of society, but they must also respond adequately to current cultural, social, industrial and technological issues, and to future change (Thwaites and Wysock-Wright 1983). I shall not attempt to define here the traditional values of British society, partly because in any event they gradually evolve over time and partly because ideological differences, and the contrasts within a pluralist society, seem somewhat sharper now than in recent decades. It is believed that most adults in our society possess a common instinct to what is good and best in communal behaviour and that they wish their feeling to be carried forward to the next generation, therefore the educational system must be structured to enable it to keep abreast of change in society at large. The rate of change will be such that every individual of whatever capability will need access to educational opportunities throughout their life, and the programmes of education designed to develop future teachers must highlight values and cultural issues in their curriculum.

Experience of education, work and leisure will not relate to life stages of growth, maturity and ageing, and according to Thwaites and Wysock-Wright (1983) there will be much more interleaving to enable people to retain or update their interests, or develop new ones, both personal and professional. With greater life expectancy but a shorter working life, a shorter working week and changing employment opportunities, occupation and the work ethic will decline in importance for many individuals, to be replaced by greater time spent on family and personal matters. The immediate priority is to make available to all throughout the country educational opportunities that are at present available only to some. This will require the switching of resources between and across educational sectors to set up an educational system available to all ages, all cultural groups and at all levels of educational achievement. The concept of the availability of education throughout life has to be implanted in the minds and experience of younger age groups so that they are willing returnees to learning, which we now call lifelong learning. If the concept of lifelong learning is to take hold this means that individuals could be moving in and out of colleges and universities throughout their lifetime. In the future they may not even have to attend the educational institutions, but will be able to access education by various routes, such as computer-based learning.

There is a continuing debate concerning the role of further education in higher education provision. Some FE practitioners argue that colleges should concentrate on providing high-quality vocational education and training and that they should not turn themselves into universities (*TES* 9 February 1996). Huddleston and Unwin (1997) suggest that it is likely that much growth will have to come via the FE rather than the HE route given lifelong learning target 2, i.e. by the year 2000 30 per cent of the workforce to have a vocational, professional management or academic qualification at NVQ Level 4 or above.

Lifelong learning and the learning organisation act as clarion calls for people to rise up and pledge themselves to the altar of human resource development (HRD). Huddleston and Unwin (1997) argue that the language of HRD now permeates colleges where once it was restricted to the world of industry and to my own previous profession in the National Health Service. However, a warning: educationalists prefer to see teachers and support staff in colleges as people rather than as human resource, as the terminology sits uncomfortably with the inclusive and democratic notions underpinning a true learning organisation. Education, knowledge and learning are the issues of the day.

Fullan (1996) introduces us to the 'learning society' and, quoting Drucker, says that

> *the centre of gravity has shifted to the knowledge worker, and even the enterprise has to become a learning institution, a teaching institution. Organisations (and societies) that build in continuous learning and continuous teaching in jobs at all levels will dominate the 21st century. The development of a learning society is a societal quest not just because education cannot do it alone, but because we are talking about a learning society, not just a learning school system. The commitment and practice of learning must find itself in all kinds of organisations and institutions if it is to achieve any kind of force in society as a whole. (Drucker, cited in Fullan 1996, pp.135–6)*

Essential prerequisites are constant and easy access to information on educational opportunities and to a national network of educational guidance and counselling services. This individual aspiration and potential can be realised to the benefit of the community and society at large.

The perception of education's role and place in society will alter, and indeed is changing as I write, and the significance of education in the lives of individuals will be enlarged. If society is not to fragment, nor industry decline, a necessarily expanded contribution of education in the life of all members of society must be acknowledged and relentlessly pursued (Thwaite and Wysock-Wright 1983). History has shown us something of such pursuits, and at this point I offer a brief overview of post-compulsory education from 1917 to 1999. More recent developments are considered in subsequent sections.

A BRIEF OVERVIEW OF POST-COMPULSORY EDUCATION, 1917–99

It is outside the remit of this book to examine in depth the history of the British education system. However, this brief chronology is intended to help the reader understand the ongoing dynamic process and how successive Education Acts have promoted change. Readers who wish to enhance their knowledge in this area will find Armitage *et al.* (1999, pp.217–30) and Huddleston and Unwin (1997) very useful, from which the following is adopted.

1917: School Certificate introduced

1918: Education Act (Fisher Act)
The school leaving age was raised to 14, with most pupils staying in all-age elementary schools. Fees were abolished. Central government would meet not less than half the costs of educational provision. Young workers should have a right to day release. Many other measures 'allowed' but not compelled by the Act fell when funding was cut by one-third in 1922 (the 'Geddes axe'). Introducing his Education Bill on 10 August 1917, H.A.L. Fisher, the architect of the 1918 Act, argued that 'education is one of the good things of life' and that the 'principles upon which well-to-do parents proceed in the education of their families are valid; also *mutatis mutandis* for the families of the poor' (cited in Armitage *et al.* 1999).

1922: R.H. Tawney's **Secondary Education for All** published

1926: Evening Institutes established
The precursors of adult education institutes and colleges, these, along with the technical schools, provided most of the technical education available in the inter-war period.

1926: Hadow Report, **The Education of the Adolescent**
The Hadow Committee recommended a broad and balanced secondary school curriculum which prepared learners for diverse occupational groups. It called for the establishment of 'modern' or 'central' schools and 'grammar' schools for pupils with different gifts. Hadow subsequently headed committees that reported on the primary school (1931) and the nursery and infant school (1933).

1938: Spens Report
The *Report of the Consultative Committee on Secondary Education* was strongly supportive of the idea of 'technical high schools' which would not be narrowly vocational but equal in status to grammar schools. The basis for the post-war tripartite system was now set. Spens also suggested changes to the curriculum, the School Certificate and the matriculation system.

1939–45: Day release expands from 42,000 to 150,000 during the Second World War

1940: Department of Education publishes its 'Green Book', **Education after the War**

1942: Beveridge Report
This set out plans for a comprehensive system of social security 'from the cradle to the grave'.

1943: Norwood Report
In a report about examinations appeared proposals for a system of selection through intelligence testing for entry into a tripartite secondary education system made up of modern, technical and grammar secondary schools.

1944: McNair Report
McNair proposed three-year training courses for teachers. The report suggested that training for technical teachers should commence after rather than before they started to practise as teachers.

1944: Education Act (Butler Act)
This made provision of primary, secondary and further education a duty. A clause allowed for the possibility of compulsory (part-time) further education for all young people up to the age of 18. It was, however, only to become compulsory on a day to be decided. The school leaving age was to be raised to 15.

1945: Percy Report
Entitled *Higher Technological Education*, the report looked at how universities were responding to the needs of industry.

1945: Emergency Training Scheme introduced
The aim of this was to increase the supply of teachers. After much criticism it ended in 1951.

1951: General Certificate of Education (GCE) introduced
The GCE replaced the much criticised School Certificate.

1956: White Paper **Technical Education**

1957: Willis Jackson Report, **The Training of Technical Teachers**

1959: Crowther Report, **Fifteen to Eighteen**
The report looked at the different educational needs of a technological age. It noted that over 40 per cent of LEAs had no technical schools. For those who got 'incurably tired' of school the report argued for a fresh start in a technical college or some other quasi-adult institution. Specialisation in depth was necessary in the sixth form but not on the basis of vocational usefulness. Crowther recommended that the school leaving age be raised to 16. By 1980 it

was hoped that half of 16–18 year-olds should be in full-time further education.

1960: Further Education Staff College founded at Coombe Lodge, Blagdon, near Bristol

*1963: Robbins Report, **Higher Education***
The report 'assumed as an axiom' that courses of higher education should be available for all who were qualified by ability and attainment to pursue them and who wished to do so. Robbins set out a vision of how higher education could expand. He suggested an increase from 8 per cent of the school-leaving population to 17 per cent by 1980. The report resulted in the setting up of the Council for National Academic Awards (CNAA) and made the training of teachers a responsibility of the HE sector. Teacher training colleges were renamed colleges of education. Colleges of advanced technology (CATs) became university institutions.

1964: Certificate of Secondary Education (CSE) introduced and Council for National Academic Awards (CNAA) established

1964: Industrial Training Boards (ITBs)
These boards were established by the Minister of Labour as a consequence of the Industrial Training Act of the same year. The ITBs were meant to improve the quality of training and thus tackle the problem of real craft skill shortages. Administered by employers and trade union representatives the ITBs covered most of the large industrial employment sectors. Within seven years there were 27 ITBs covering employers with some 15 million workers.

1969: Open University founded

1970: Education (Handicapped Children) Act
A hundred years after the great Elementary Education Act, children categorised as 'severely subnormal' and considered 'uneducable' were brought out of junior training schools and into the education system.

1970: First tertiary college founded in Devon
The development of tertiary colleges had been argued for by several influential figures including Tessa Blackstone.

1971: Open University enrols its first learners

1972: James Report
This report suggested three stages of teacher training: a two-year Diploma in Higher Education followed by a year of professional studies based in school. This would lead to the award of the BA (Ed.).

1972: School leaving age raised to 16 from September

*1972: White Paper **Training for the Future** (Department of Employment)*
This White Paper highlighted failures in the 1964 Industrial Training Act and

called for the phasing out of the training levy and for a new role for ITBs. The Training Opportunities Scheme (TOPS) was established.

1973: Technician Education Council (TEC) and Business Education Council (BEC) established

These bodies were established as a result of the 1969 Haslegrave Report to plan, coordinate and administer technical courses and examinations.

1973: Russell Report, Adult Education: A Plan for Development

As the title suggests Russell argued for an expansion of non-vocational adult education, particularly because of the unmet needs of 'school leavers and young adults, older adults, the handicapped and the disadvantaged'. Russell set the tone for much of the subsequent debate about adult education.

1973: Manpower Services Commission (MSC) established

The MSC was established under the Employment and Training Act (1973) to supervise employment and with sufficient powers to plan training at national level. The MSC assumed its responsibilities on 1 January 1974.

1973: Haycocks Report (Haycocks I) on the training of full-time FE teachers

The report made major recommendations for improved training. In Circular 11/77 The government welcomed the proposals and supported the in-service training of 3 per cent of staff at any one time. The report was followed in March 1978 by Haycocks II on adult education and part-time teachers and in August 1978 by Haycocks III on the training of FE teachers for 'education management'.

1976: Great Debate

Prime Minister James Callaghan delivered a speech, 'Towards a national debate', on 18 October 1976 at Ruskin College, Oxford. This speech has generally been regarded as a landmark in the history of post-war education.

1977: Holland Report, Young People and Work (MSC)

The aim of the Holland Report was 'building a better workforce more adapted to the needs of the eighties'. It proposed work experience and work preparation courses for unemployed young people. They would be paid a weekly allowance. It also proposed the setting up of the Youth Opportunities Programme (YOP), which began in 1978.

1977: Further Education Unit (FEU) established as a curriculum development and dissemination body for further education

The FEU was originally called the Further Education Curriculum Review and Development Unit. Although it was a quasi-autonomous body, the FEU was funded by the Department of Education and Science (DES).

1978: Warnock Report, Special Educational Needs

Warnock abolished the various categories of handicap then in use and suggested a wider, more individualised concept of special needs which was to be enshrined in the 1981 Education Act.

Education in context: 1979–90
Prime minister 1979–90: Margaret Thatcher (Conservative)
Secretaries of State for Education and Science: from May 1979, Mark Carlile; from September 1981, Sir Keith Joseph; from May 1986, Kenneth Baker; from July 1989, John MacGregor
Key political and economic events/issues: monetarism (controlling inflation by controlling the money supply); Thatcherism (the manifestation of monetarism and other policies in the Thatcher government); privatisation (denationalisation of industry and government); 1982 Falklands War; 1984 miners' strike; 1987 stock market crash; 'There is no such thing as society' (Margaret Thatcher); 1989 fall of Berlin Wall, collapse of Communist regimes in eastern Europe

---

1979: *A Basis for Choice* (FEU)
This report emphasised the need for a 'common core' curriculum which stressed transferable skills and flexibility through participating in 'learning experiences' rather than narrow skills-based teaching.

1981: *A New Training Initiative* (NTI)
The MSC produced two documents, *A New Training Initiative: A Consultative Document* in May 1981 and later in December *A New Training Initiative: An Agenda for Action*. These documents set the training agenda for the decade. Skills training for young people and adults was covered.

1982: *17+ A New Qualification* (DES)
This document set out the basis for the introduction of the Certificate of Pre-vocational Education (CPVE) for learners who had not yet chosen their vocation.

1983: *Technical and Vocational Education Initiative (TVEI)*
Announced by Mrs Thatcher in November 1982, the TVEI was to be the largest curriculum intervention ever by a government. The scheme was under the control of the MSC. It was a broad and experimental scheme aimed at preparing 14–18 year olds for the world of work and developing personal qualities such as enterprise and 'problem solving' skills.

1983: *Youth Training Scheme (YTS)*
The YTS replaced the YOP. In 1988 there were over half a million contracted YTS places and an average of 37,000 learners in training.

1983: *Business and Technology Education Council (BTEC) formed through the merger of BEC and TEC*

1984: *White Paper Training for Jobs*
This made clear the government's intention to make the MSC the 'national training authority'. A report: *Competence and Competition* by the National Economic Development Office (NEDO)/MSC saw the competitive success of

Japan, Germany and the USA was seen as being related to their investment in education.

1985: Further Education Act
Allowed colleges to engage in commercial activities related to areas of expertise and generate more funding. Governors were made responsible for the college budgets.

1985: Certificate of Pre-Vocational Education (CPVE) introduced
The CPVE was never successful even with less able pupils and take-up was poor.

1986: National Council for Vocational Qualifications (NCVQ) established
Only 40 per cent of the workforce held relevant qualifications. Despite the 'tremendous expansion in training', this was still a much lower proportion than in other countries. The NCVQ's primary task was to reform and rationalise the provision of vocational qualifications through the creation of the National Vocational Qualification Framework. The NCVQ introduced through the awarding bodies (RSA, CGLI, etc.) competence based NVQs that were based in the workplace and not just work related.

1987: Enterprise in Higher Education Initiative (EHEI)
Seen as the higher education equivalent of TVEI this initiative had a budget of £100 million. The aim was to see every person in HE developing 'competencies and aptitudes relevant to enterprise'.

1988: General Certificate of Secondary Education (GCSE) replaces the GCE and CSE

1988: Education Reform Act (ERA)
This Act, which followed from Kenneth Baker's so-called Great Education Reform Bill, sought to revitalise the 'producer dominated' education system. ERA brought in the National Curriculum for schools with core subjects (English, mathematics, science and religious education) to be studied by all. Several cross-curricular themes were also identified: environmental education, education for citizenship, careers education and guidance, health education, and economic and industrial understanding. It also had a strong emphasis on moral renewal, seeking to promote the spiritual, moral, cultural, mental and physical development of pupils and of society. The Act delegated financial responsibilities from local authorities to schools. It took polytechnics out of local authority control and replaced the National Advisory Body for Public Sector Higher Education with the Polytechnics and Colleges Funding Council. It required that half of the membership of the governing bodies of FE colleges represented employment interests.

1988: MSC absorbed into the Department of Employment (DoE), becoming the Training Commission for a short time and then the Training Agency

*1989: Confederation of British Industry (CBI) publishes **Towards a Skills Revolution***

This advocated common learning outcomes for all learners over 16. This document set out the employers' agenda for lifelong learning.

1989: Kenneth Baker calls for a doubling of the numbers of learners entering higher education in a speech at Lancaster University
Baker said that numbers should increase to 30 per cent. This was achieved by the mid-1990s.

1989: YTS replaced by Youth Training (YT)

1990: Core Skills 16–19 published by the National Curriculum Council (NCC)
The NCC published the core skills after consultation with the FEU, the School Examinations and Assessment Council (SEAC), the NCVQ and the Training Agency (TA). It proposed six core skills in two groups:
Group 1: 1. Communication; 2. Problem solving; 3. Personal skills; Group 2: 4. Numeracy; 5. Information technology; 6. Competence in a modern language
The first group was to be developed in all post-16 programmes and in every A- and AS-level syllabus. The NCC also recommended the use of Individual Action Plans (IAPs) and the incorporation of National Curriculum themes in the post-16 curriculum with the addition of scientific and technological understanding and aesthetic and creative understanding.

1990: *A British Baccalaureate: Ending the Division Between Education and Training* published by the Institute for Public Policy Research (IPPR)
This proposed a unitary 'advanced diploma' delivered through a tertiary college system.

1991: Training and Enterprise Councils (TECs) established
There are 82 TECs. They are limited companies governed by local industrialists and are charged with identifying local training needs and organising training to meet these needs. They operate government training schemes such as YT. They were announced by the government in 1988.

*1991: White Paper **Education and Training for the 21st Century***
In this review of the education and training system for 16–19 year olds, equal status was demanded for academic and vocational qualifications. Young people 'should not have their opportunities limited by out of date distinctions between qualifications and institutions'. The paper argued that:

> *Colleges lack the full freedom which we gave to the polytechnic and higher education colleges in 1989 to respond to the demands of learners and the labour market. The Government intend to legislate to remove all colleges of further education ... and sixth form colleges ... from local authority control ... Our policies over the last decade have not done much to enrich that preparation – for life and work. (cited in Armitage et al. 1999)*

1991: National Education and Training Targets (NETTs) recommended by the CBI in World Class Targets (1991) and set by the government
There was a major review of the targets in 1995.

1992: Further and Higher Education Act
The polytechnics were granted university status. The binary division was subsequently ended when polytechnics became universities in 1993. The CNAA was to be abolished and separate funding councils to be set up for FE and HE.

1992: Education (Schools) Act creates the Office for Standards in Education (Ofsted)

1992: General National Vocational Qualifications (GNVQs) introduced
Unlike NVQs, these qualifications would be based in schools and colleges rather than the workplace. Level 3 (later 'Advanced') GNVQ was to be 'equivalent' or 'comparable' to A levels. By 1997 learners with GNVQs had a greater chance of obtaining a university place than A-level learners.

*1993: Department for Education's (DfE) **Charter for Further Education***
This set out rights and expectations and ended with how to complain about 'courses, qualifications and results' (pp.24–9 give 23 addresses and telephone numbers). All colleges were required to produce their own charters.

1993: Incorporation of colleges
The 1992 Further and Higher Education Act was implemented on 1 April. Colleges were taken out of the control of the LEAs and became independent business corporations. Some had turnovers which put them in the *Financial Times* list of big companies. One college had a turnover of almost £50 million.

*1994: White Paper **Competitiveness: Helping Business to Win***
Michael Heseltine set the theme of national competitiveness and called for improved careers guidance for young people.

1994: Teacher Training Agency (TTA) established
The Agency was established in September, under the directorship of Chief Executive Anthea Millett, 'to improve the quality of teaching, to raise the standards of teacher education and training, and to promote teaching as a profession, in order to improve the standards of pupils' achievement and the quality of their learning'.

1994: New contracts dispute at its height
The FE colleges experienced over three years of action over the introduction of new contracts for lecturers and the abandonment of the so-called 'Silver Book' which set out conditions of service.

1994: Report of the Commission on Social Justice
This report contained the genesis of what would become the 1997 Labour government's views on education and social policy for the 1990s and beyond.

1995: Further Education Development Agency (FEDA) formed
Launched on 7 April, FEDA inherited the staff of the FEU and the Further Education Staff College at Blagdon. Its main function was to 'help FE institutions provide what their student and other customers want and need'. As 'an

independent body promoting quality in FE', FEDA intended 'not just to promote best practice but also embody it' (DfEE/FEDA 1995, p.1). Its key aims were to promote quality in teaching and learning, and to provide quality education.

1995: Department for Education and Department for Employment merge in July to become the Department for Education and Employment (DfEE)

*1996: Ron Dearing's **Review of Qualifications for 16–19 Year Olds***
This was Dearing's second much publicised report (Dearing II). Dearing II went for stability and did not recommend a unified system to replace the three existing tertiary qualifications, NVQs, GNVQs and A levels. It did suggest the incorporation of 'key skills' in all three qualifications and the relaunch of YT, modern apprenticeships and the National Record of Achievement. It also suggested that Advanced GNVQs be renamed Applied A levels.

Dearing's first report (Dearing I), *The National Curriculum and its Assessment* (1993), was a response to industrial action by teachers throughout the country concerned about the burden of assessment and the narrowness of the National Curriculum. Dearing I reduced time spent on the National Curriculum by 20 per cent and reduced the number of attainment targets and their related statements (SATs). It included a vocational option at Key Stage 4.

1996: European 'Year of Lifelong Learning'

1996: Lifetime Learning (DfEE)
A consultation document drawing on previously published work including *Competitiveness: Forging Ahead: Education and Training* (1995). The Labour Party published *Lifelong Learning*, a consultative document (1996).

1996: Awarding bodies combined
In 1996, BTEC and London Examinations formed Edexcel. In 1998 City and Guilds, the Associated Examining Board and the Northern Examinations and Assessment Board formed the Assessment and Qualifications Alliance (AQA).

1996: New Labour leader Tony Blair's 'Education, Education and Education' speech to the Labour Party conference on 1 October, 20 years after Callaghan's Ruskin College Speech
The speech was published in the *Times Educational Supplement* of 4 October (p.6) and an extract follows.

> *The three main priorities for Government are education, education and education ... At every level we need radical improvement and reform. A teaching profession trained and able to stand alongside the best in the world and valued as such ... There should be zero tolerance of failure in Britain's schools. The Age of Achievement will be built on new technology. Our aim is for every school to have access to the superhighway, the computers to deliver it and the education programmes to go on it. With the University for Industry for adult skills, this adds up to a national grid for learning for Britain. Britain the skill superpower of the world.*

*1997: Report of Helena Kennedy's Committee of Enquiry into widening participation in education, **Learning Works***
Kennedy initially suggested redistributing resources and removing the bias towards undergraduates and school sixth forms. Seventy-five per cent of the five million learners in England are supported by £3.5 billion of funding through the 'Cinderella' service of FE colleges, whereas the university sector with 25 per cent of the student population receives 75 per cent of the available funding. The report revealed the 'shocking fact' that 64 per cent of university learners come from social classes 1 and 2, and only 1 per cent from social class 5. The general direction of the many recommendations of the report is a lifetime entitlement to education up to A-level standard, with free teaching for people from deprived backgrounds or with no previous qualifications: 'The government should ... give priority in public funding with post-16 learning to general education and transferable learning, including key skills, at and leading to level 3: the costs of ensuring that all can succeed to (NVQ) level 3 must be recognised' (p.43).

*1997: Dearing Report, **Higher Education in the Learning Society** (National Committee of Inquiry into Higher Education)*
One of the nine 'principles' governing the report (Dearing III, Dearing 1997) was that 'learning should be increasingly responsive to employment needs and include the development of general skills, widely valued in employment' (Summary Report, p.5). Dearing III was hailed as the most comprehensive review of higher education since the Robbins Report. Dearing III made 93 recommendations. These include: a system by which learners pay fees covering up to 25 per cent of the cost of tuition; the establishment of an Institute for Learning and Teaching (ILT) in higher education to accredit training programmes for HE staff and to look at computer-based learning; the promotion of student learning as a high priority; and a review of research which may allow some institutions to opt out of the competitive funding system based on the Research Assessment Exercise (RAE). In his introduction Dearing sees 'historic boundaries between vocational and academic education breaking down, with increasingly active partnerships between higher education institutions and the worlds of industry, commerce and public service' (Summary Report, p.2).

1997: Government announces the abolition of student grants and the introduction of fee payments of up to £1000 per annum
The power to do this was given through the Teaching and Higher Education Bill (see below).

1997: NCVQ/School Curriculum and Assessment Authority (SCAA) merge to form a new national curriculum advisory body, the Qualifications and Curriculum Authority (QCA)
The QCA's powers are a cause of concern to the awarding bodies.

*1997: **Learning for the 21st Century***
In November, Professor Bob Fryer produced this report for the National Advisory Group for Continuing Education and Lifelong Learning. The report

consolidated much of the thinking about lifelong learning that had appeared since the Report of the Commission on Social Justice.

1997: Teaching and Higher Education Bill
This bill was the first of a series of responses by the government to Dearing III. It gave the Secretary of State powers to interfere in university affairs and was seen by some as a major attack on academic autonomy.

1998: General Teaching Council (GTC) formed
A GTC was established in Scotland as a result of the Wheatley Report on local government (1963). A voluntary GTC (England and Wales) has been in existence since 1988 and has sought support from the various professional bodies and attempted to secure legislation. The Teaching and Higher Education Bill (1997) established a statutory GTC which will not be a 'teachers' GTC but will have a broad membership. Teachers in schools may now register with the GTC.

1998: The Learning Age: A Renaissance for a New Britain (DfEE)
The expected White Paper on lifelong learning appeared as a Green Paper. It promised to bring learning into the home and workplace.

1998: Higher Education for the Twenty-first Century: Response to the Dearing Report
This paper set out as a priority reaching out to groups underrepresented in higher education. It argued for a better balance between teaching, research and scholarship. An Institute for Learning and Teaching in Higher Education was to be established to accredit programmes of training for HE teachers. Work experience was to become a feature of higher education courses and the aim of employability was stressed.

1998: University for Industry established
This university, established after discussions with 'learning organisations' such as Ford, Unipart and Anglian Water, is not a physical but a virtual university, a network providing access to training.

1999: Institute for Learning and Teaching (ILT) launched
The ILT was launched as a result of recommendations in the Dearing Report on higher education (Dearing 1997). This envisaged the formation of the ILT to establish higher education teaching as a profession in its own right. The ILT began public activities with a series of launch events in June and July 1999 in York, London, Cardiff, Belfast and Edinburgh. The ILT offices in York were formally opened by Baroness Blackstone, Minister of State for Education and Employment, on 23 June 1999.

The ILT's principle activities are:

- accrediting programmes of staff development in higher education
- developing individual routes to membership
- providing support for those engaged in facilitating, learning and teaching
- stimulating innovation.

The Institutional Accreditation programme included:

- Accreditation of institutional programmes in learning and teaching. The half-year target was to accredit 20 programmes. By the end of March 33 programmes had been accredited at 31 institutions; by September 58 programmes had been accredited against a target of 35. The majority of these programmes were accredited as a result of an agreement to grant accreditation to programmes that had received recognition from SEDA (the Staff and Educational Development Association).

- Agreements with other professional bodies to provide further routes to membership based on accreditation carried out by those bodies. On 30 June 2000 an agreement was concluded with the United Kingdom Central Council for Nursing, Midwifery and Health Visiting (UKCC) and the four National Boards for Nursing, Midwifery and Health Visiting to allow teachers of health and social care who have recorded a teaching qualification on the UKCC Professional Register to apply directly for ILT membership. The ILT is currently working with the British Psychological Society to set up a similar accreditation agreement.

The formation of productive relationships with other professional bodies is an important aspect of establishing the ILT as a professional body. Links have been formed with a wide range of professional bodies and are providing valuable opportunities both to learn from their experiences and to provide new routes to membership.

The target for membership numbers through the initial entry route to membership was 500 by 31 March. The number of applications processed through this route was 492 at 31 March with a total of 446 accepted. The total number of applications received via all routes was 837, against a target figure of 900 for the first six months of the recruitment year. By 30 September a total of 2888 applications had been received and 2483 applicants had been accepted, against a target of 2153.

Continuing Professional Development (CPD)

Work is now under way on developing the ILT Continuing Professional Development (CPD) framework. In 2000, the ILT's Transitional Council established a CPD Working Party, chaired by Dr Joanna de Groot, Vice-Chair of the Transitional Council. Its remit is to:

- explore what constitutes credible CPD activity (including activities that constitute the membership requirements for other professional and statutory bodies and subject associations) and seek staff views
- research and report on appropriate mechanisms for recording CPD
- consider appropriate strategies for analysis and evaluation of individual CPD records
- recommend suitable methods and timescale for the review and evaluation of the proposed CPD framework.

Curriculum 2000

September 2000 saw the introduction of Curriculum 2000. This was the beginning of something big. A levels get 'airbrushed', GNVQ's become more streamlined. Why? According to the Secretary of State, David Blunkett, it will give greater choice to learners, as well as offering a more flexible approach – the 'pick and mix' qualifications.

There have been many debates surrounding British qualifications over the last few years. Only recently, education and qualifications have changed, with the introduction of more vocational courses such as NVQ and GNVQ. New education agencies have arisen, many disappearing or augmenting. The many examination boards have been reduced to four, these being AQA, Edexcel, OCR (resulting from the merger of the Oxford and Cambridge boards and the RSA) and the WJEC (Welsh Joint Education Committee). Education is again undergoing a major transition in the form of Curriculum 2000. This new transition will see A levels getting a facelift, as well as the GNVQ being remodelled. Some politicians and educationalists argue this is for the best. Others see potential problems occurring, especially the 'watering' down of A-level quality ('dumbing down' effect).

Curriculum 2000: an overview

The 'new' Curriculum 2000 proclaims to offer a broader 'mix and match' qualification for a rapidly changing work environment. David Blunkett has stated that the new curriculum reforms are paramount in raising educational standards within the UK. The reforms promise to widen choice, be more accommodating (i.e. more flexible) and encourage learners to study a greater breadth of subjects. Some see this as an attempt to emulate the qualifications of the rest of Europe, i.e. the baccalaureate, although in a more watered-down version. Learners, however, are assured that they will be able to combine both academic (i.e. A-level) subjects and vocational studies (i.e. GNVQ). Learners will also be required to study key skills. These will involve numeracy, communication and information technology. The Curriculum 2000 reforms are predominantly directed towards the 16–19-year-old market. This follows on from the Dearing Report of 1996, which recommended that the post-16 curriculum should be more flexible in its approach as well as offering a greater breadth of skills and subject areas.

Curriculum 2000 and A-level qualifications

The new A level will involve six curriculum units. The first three will form an AS level. This may be used as a 'stand alone' qualification, i.e. half an A level, or students can progress to a full A level.

All A-level syllabuses have changed. Gone are the days of the long essay questions. Now there are structured questions that are specific, to elicit 'straight to the point' responses. Students who wish to obtain an A-level qualification will have to sit a synoptic paper. This covers key elements of all units and will account for 20 per cent of a full A level. The rest of the marks (for example in psychology) are made up of 20 per cent for coursework and 60 per cent for other exams. The A levels will be assessed both internally and externally; learners can only sit an assessment unit once, but can resit the whole A level more than once.

Curriculum 2000 and GNVQ qualifications

The new GNVQs will be known as vocational A levels. The change to the 'new' GNVQ will reduce the assessment burden of the present system. The new GNVQ will consist of six mandatory units and six optional units. Assessment will be made clearer. Learners will be informed of what they need to know and what they have to do, and their educational attainment will be clearly tracked. Units will no longer be subdivided. This makes the work easier to teach and mark (good news for teachers), as well as being clearer and thus less ambiguous for the learners.

'Pick and mix': A levels and GNVQ

To reinforce the 'flexible' approach to learning, learners will be able to mix GNVQ and A levels. This, it is argued, will give the individual both broader skills and academically-based qualifications.

Learners in their first year at an FE college could take the following combination:

Year 1   3 AS levels + Single GNVQ + key skills *or*
           4 AS levels + key skills
Year 2   Single GNVQ + 2 A levels *or*
           3 A levels

Curriculum 2000 and key skills

The most dramatic change, especially within post-compulsory education, has been the introduction of key skills. The new Curriculum 2000 will see the introduction of key skills. These will require the student to gain a good working knowledge of maths, gain adequate awareness of communication and acquire a general standard of information technology skills. These will be mandatory for both A-level and GNVQ candidates. They will be certified and be recognised by the UCAS university tariff system, for university entrance.

Student knowledge of Curriculum 2000: a survey

Many of the statements made by the government and their agencies seem very glossy and inviting. They build up a fantastic image of Curriculum 2000, almost placing it on a pedestal. A kind of magical elixir that will cure all educational shortcomings and may also alleviate employment problems. However, what about the learners themselves? What do they actually know about the curriculum changes? Why do learners study A levels opposed to GNVQs, and vice versa? It is all very well making dramatic statements of what Curriculum 2000 will achieve but it will be a pointless exercise unless learners are aware of what they can do, and where the 'new' qualifications will lead them. To answer such questions one student undertook a survey at a college while undertaking the PGCE teacher training course.

The college was based in South Wales. The student, Meurig Tiley, was particularly interested to know why A-level learners choose A levels and why GNVQ learners choose their particular course. He was interested in the learners' knowledge of the different qualifications on offer at a further education college. The survey involved 20 learners, 10 each of A level and GNVQ.

Results of the survey

Some interesting results were found from this survey. Table 1.1 shows the answers given by both A level and GNVQ learners. It is interesting that 30 per cent of learners were unaware of other courses. Few learners knew that A level and GNVQ courses were changing. An interesting finding was that 30 per cent of learners were unclear as to what they wanted to do. This certainly may highlight potential problems in how learners choose their courses. It may be the case that learners are be 'pushed' into classes to make up the numbers and thus their 'needs' may not be given priority.

Table 1.1

Responses by both A level and GNVQ learners to general information questions

Why did you choose your current course?	No (%)	Yes (%)
I did not know what other courses were offered	70	30
I would like to go into higher education	40	60
I would like to go into further training	75	25
I did not know what to do	70	30
I wanted to gain practical skills for a job	55	45

Table 1.2 shows the responses to the general questions made by A-level learners. Out of the ten learners asked, 60 per cent wanted to go into higher education; although 90 per cent did not want to go into further training. Very few of the learners wanted to gain practical skills. In fact, only 20 per cent answered yes to this question.

Table 1.2

Responses by A level learners to general questions

Why did you choose your current course?	No (%)	Yes (%)
I did not know what other courses were offered	80	20
I would like to go into higher education	40	60
I would like to go into further training	90	10
I did not know what to do	70	30
I wanted to gain practical skills for a job	80	20

Table 1.3 indicates the responses made by the GNVQ students to the general questions of the survey. Interestingly, 80 per cent of students did not want to go into higher education. However, 60 per cent did want to go into further training. Many of the GNVQ students wanted to gain practical skills (70 per cent).

Why did you choose your current course?	No (%)	Yes (%)
I did not know what other courses were offered	90	10
I would like to go into higher education	80	20
I would like to go into further training	40	60
I did not know what to do	70	30
I wanted to gain practical skills for a job	30	70

Table 1.3

Responses by GNVQ learners to general questions

Table 1.4 highlights the A-level learners' responses on their knowledge about GNVQ courses. Some startling results emerged: out of the ten students asked 70 per cent knew very little about GNVQs. Consequently, 70 per cent would not have considered undertaking such a qualification. The A-level learners still saw A levels as an entry to higher education (70 per cent), and saw GNVQs as an entry to further training (70 per cent).

Question	No (%)	Yes (%)
Would you have considered doing a GNVQ course?	70	30
Do you know much about GNVQ courses?	70	30
Do you see A-levels as an entry to academic subjects?	30	70
Do you see GNVQ courses as an entry to further training?	30	70

Table 1.4

Responses by A level learners on their knowledge about GNVQ courses

Table 1.5 shows the responses of GNVQ students on their knowledge about A-level courses. Interestingly, 90 per cent of students would not consider undertaking an A-level course. Again the knowledge of another course, i.e. A levels, was sparse. Only 20 per cent of the students asked knew about A levels and that they were another option available. The GNVQ students saw the GNVQ as an entry to further training (80 per cent) and A levels as an entry to academic subjects (60 per cent).

Question	No (%)	Yes (%)
Would you have considered doing A levels?	90	10
Do you know much about A level courses?	80	20
Do you see A levels as an entry to academic subjects?	40	60
Do you see GNVQ courses as an entry to further training?	20	80

Table 1.5

Responses by GNVQ learners on their knowledge about A-level courses

This survey highlights that there is still a divide between A-level and GNVQ courses: that A levels are seen as academic and GNVQs as practical and a prerequisite for further training. It seems to be the case of never the twain shall meet. Maybe Curriculum 2000 is the answer to this problem. The new qualifications, especially the 'pick and mix', may break down the barriers and allow learners to experience both academic and vocational qualifications. However, the most worrying aspect from this survey was that students were unaware of other courses being offered by the college. It is difficult for students to make an informed choice without knowing what all the options are. The government, along with FE colleges, really do need to publicise Curriculum 2000. They need to target particular individuals – future learners – and explain exactly just what GNVQ and A levels are, and how the new curriculum will change them.

The government's decision to change and refine A levels and GNVQs may be a good thing. However, one cannot help thinking that such a change is not a purely altruistic act. Whose interests will be furthered by the changes to Curriculum 2000: industry or learners?

Adult Learning Inspectorate (ALI)

As part of the Learning and Skills Act 2000, a new Adult Learning Inspectorate has been created, with responsibility for the inspection of provision for those aged 19 and over and also of work-based learning for those aged 16 and over.

The Adult Learning Inspectorate inspects the delivery of courses and qualifications that will be funded through the LSC. It can be expected to have considerable influence over the quality of provision of all post-16 education and training that is fully or partly funded through the public sector.

Occupational standards

The FE sector developed occupational standards for teaching and supporting learning in further education in England and Wales in 1998/9. The development work was carried out by the then Further Education Development Agency (FEDA) working on behalf of the Further Education Staff Development Forum (FESDF). The work of the FESDF was taken up by the Further Education National Training Organisation (FENTO) in 1999. FENTO has developed the application of the standards and has carried on to develop standards for college management. Work is continuing in that standards for support staff are currently under development.

The two sector stakeholders currently responsible for standards and qualifications are FENTO and the Qualifications and Curriculum Authority. Their responsibilities and sphere of influence are described below.

Qualifications and Curriculum Authority

The Qualifications and Curriculum Authority (QCA) controls the design and specification of the occupational standards that underpin many qualifications, including national vocational and related qualifications. Scotland and Wales both have equivalent organisations, namely the Scottish Qualifications Authority (SQA) and ACCAC. QCA is powerful and influential in that, acting on behalf of government, it can fund the development of national occupational standards, and it is the authority that gives ultimate approval to qualifications that are based on the standards.

Any changes and developments that the FE sector proposes to make to its occupational standards must receive QCA approval, as must proposals from awarding bodies to offer qualifications based on the occupational standards.

DEVELOPMENTS IN POST-COMPULSORY EDUCATION: 2001 AND BEYOND

Further Education Sector Workforce Development Plan (2001)

Published by FENTO in April 2001, this consultation paper firstly presents a summary of information that was previously reported in FENTO's January 2001 publication, *Skills Foresight for Education in the United Kingdom*. It identifies serious shortages of staff, for example IT specialists, lecturers in engineering, construction and accounting, and course or programme managers and leaders. While the excellent skills of many in the sector are acknowledged, a key purpose of FENTO's work is to promote action to address 'skills gaps' in the existing FE workforce.

Illustrations of the proportion of colleges that suffer from some of these skills gaps are given in Tables 1.6, 1.7 and 1.8.

Skill	% identifying gap
Teaching the disaffected	35
Performance management	35
Supporting on-line learners	34
Generic management skill	21
Pedagogy (generic teaching skills)	20
Research	20

Table 1.6

Examples of skills gaps as identified by colleges

Skill	% identifying gap
Performance management	34.6
People management	31.3
Using IT for management	23.3
Generic management skills	20.6
Business development	18.9
Financial understanding	17.9
Strategic management	17.9
Commercial awareness	16.4

Table 1.7

Percentage of colleges identifying skills gaps in college managers

Skill	% identifying gap
Providing support on-line	33.9
Business development	24.3
Supporting ICT	23.5
Languages	17.2
Learning centre management	17.0
Supporting the disaffected	16.8
Pedagogy	15.7
Inclusive learning	15.6
IT for personal use	13.3
Customer service	13.2
Careers guidance	11.1
Basic skills	10.7
Key/core skills	9.8

Table 1.8

Percentage of colleges identifying skills gaps in support staff

Another series of changes that are impacting on the sector is linked to the devolution of governmental power and responsibility for education. Hence Northern Ireland, Scotland and Wales are actively developing their own structures that will establish policy, administer funding and promote and assure quality in further education. In England the establishment of the Learning and Skills Council to replace the Further Education Funding Council and Training and Enterprise Councils is having a similar effect.

The changes are beginning to work through so that in most cases it is possible to identify the structures and organisations that will be in place to maintain further education for the foreseeable future.

Action points in the development plan

Overcoming skills shortages and recruitment difficulties
The outcome of the proposed actions would be to reduce recruitment difficulties and remove skills shortages. The targets that are proposed are an immediate reduction of 20 per cent in reports of recruitment difficulties and a 50 per cent reduction over three years.

Addressing skills gaps
The outcome identified is that the skills levels of the FE workforce will rise so that it is better equipped to develop the nation's workforce. The target proposed is for reports of skills gaps to reduce by 50 per cent over four years.

Action on management development
The outcomes are identified as:

- improvements in college performance arising out of the new initiatives for the training of principals and senior managers
- an improved supply of trained junior managers.

The targets require that baselines are established in the first year and that there is a 25 per cent improvement in the numbers of qualifications accompanied by a halving in the levels of skills gaps in four years.

Information and learning technology (ILT)
The outcome expresses the vision of an FE workforce that is fully equipped to maximise the efficiency and effectiveness gains that should arise out of using ILT. The target is to achieve a 15 per cent per annum growth in the numbers of FE staff who are specifically qualified to use ILT within their programme delivery.

Developing support staff and lecturers
The FE sector employs 400,000 staff of whom 56 per cent are lecturers or teachers and a further 13 per cent are employed in roles that directly support learners. Many lecturers are exceptionally well qualified, as they possess higher-level technical qualifications in their chosen areas of expertise and graduate or postgraduate qualifications as teachers. However, weaknesses do exist in the overall profile of qualifications as, for example, 12 per cent of course and programme managers and 28 per cent of part-time lecturers are not qualified as teachers.

The action points specifically refer to the need for all support staff to become professionally qualified to carry out their roles. The targets are for qualifications to be available for all the main support staff roles by September 2002 and for 20 per cent of support staff to be qualified by the end of 2004.

Overcoming barriers to training and development
The outcome is that participation in training and development will be considered as the norm for all categories of the FE workforce. The target links this aspiration to the issue of mandatory qualifications so it is for all staff to be participating in CPD within three years.

Research and data collection
This action point recognises the need for quite extensive data collection in order to facilitate monitoring of the sector and its performance. It seeks to engage the stakeholders in all four countries in working to an agreed data collection plan that optimises the timely availability of valuable information while minimising the demands placed on college administrative systems. The target is for a fully coordinated data collection strategy to be fully operational within three years.

This consultation version of the *Further Education Sector Workforce Development Plan* does not end with a conclusion, but with a proforma which you are invited to use to make your response, and which is available on the FENTO website (www.fento.org).

New mandatory qualifications

The fact that a significant proportion of lecturers are not well qualified as teachers is explained in part by the tradition of allowing qualified status to be optional in up to 20 per cent of general FE colleges. A second factor is that a high proportion of FE teacher training is 'in service', so that many lecturers and teachers remain unqualified for the first two to five years of their employment. Finally there are problems in attracting staff who are sufficiently skilled and qualified in their specialist fields without the added complication of demanding teaching qualifications. FENTO's role in the steps being taken towards mandatory Qualified Teacher Further Education (QTFE) status for FE teachers in England is to set national standards for teacher training for the FE sector. At the same time improvements in pay and conditions are being offered to attract and retain more lecturing staff in an attempt to overcome some of the skills shortages

Initial Teacher Training (ITTFE)

In England the regulations have changed so that, with effect from September 2001, new lecturers who are unqualified have to embark on an endorsed programme of teacher training.

The assumption is being made that there will be adequate provision of Initial Teacher Training (ITTFE) and it seems likely that this will be the case. Nevertheless, FENTO will need to monitor the availability of training courses.

Funding existing and additional demand for teacher training and allowing time for trainees to follow their programme of study, and to receive the requisite level of support from within the employing college, will also present challenges to the sector.

The outcome is simply that all staff should be professionally qualified for their roles. The targets are for all staff to be participating in formal programmes of CPD within three years and for the reduction in the proportion of unqualified staff to proceed at a rate of 20 per cent per annum.

Universities and higher education institutions

The higher degrees, Bachelor of Education (BEd), Post-Graduate Certificate in Education (PGCE) and Certificate in Education (Cert. Ed.) qualifications are awarded by universities and higher education institutions (HEIs). (See Appendix 1 for an example of a PGCE course guide.)

Most, but not all, of the 30 HEIs that validate teacher training FE qualifications deliver the courses themselves, but approximately ten also validate courses delivered in FE colleges, usually on the basis of franchised arrangements. Of these the largest validates courses at nearly 40 locations. Seven HEIs operate solely as validating bodies, having no role in qualification delivery.

There has not been any obligation for universities to submit their FE teacher training courses for external quality assurance, although some may have chosen to do so. FENTO's new role in endorsing qualifications will introduce an element of mandatory external quality assurance and will ensure full coverage of the standards within teacher training for FE.

FE colleges as teacher training institutions

City and Guilds is the biggest awarding body provider of teacher qualifications for FE, and almost all its qualifications are delivered in FE colleges.

City and Guilds qualifications (notably the 730 qualification) have provided the alternative to university awards for a long time in FE. They have been popular as a part of the development of part-time lecturers and have, in recent years, been developed so that they give exemption from the early stages of Cert. Ed. and PGCE courses. Information provided by City and Guilds indicates that there are more than 500 centres that offer the 730 qualification in England alone.

There are other awarding bodies that award teacher training qualifications. These include Edexcel and OCR.

Colleges that offer teacher training qualifications are subject to the quality assurance requirements specified by the awarding body, but as in the case of the universities, awarding bodies are not obliged to submit their systems to external quality assurance.

General Teaching Council (GTC)

In the interests of completeness it is relevant to note that England's GTC has no remit in relation to teachers in FE.

Overcoming barriers

Among the barriers to training and development are the factors of cost, time and culture. The moves to make teaching qualifications compulsory, and to earmark funding from central government for staff development, should go a long way towards addressing these problems. Care will have to be taken to ensure that the benefits are not limited to the full-time lecturer workforce at the expense of the large numbers of part-time staff, student support staff and management trainees.

Learning and Skills Council (LSC)

The Learning and Skills Council is the new body with responsibility for the publicly funded part of full- and part-time education and training, other than higher education, for the over 16s. It has replaced the Further Education Funding Council and Training and Education Councils in England only. Its budget will be in the order of £6 billion, a considerable proportion of which will be spent in FE.

The LSC's mission is 'to raise participation and attainment through high-quality education and training which puts the learner first'. Its vision is that 'by 2010, young people and adults in England will have knowledge and productive skills matching the best in the world' (FENTO 2001).

In the light of these priorities, FE can expect to benefit from the support of the LSC. FE will also be challenged to operate in ways that the LSC sees fit. As was demonstrated in FENTO's Skills Foresight research, FE readily recognises the power and influence of the major public sector funding body.

There can be no doubt that, in pursuit of the vision of young people and adults having knowledge and productive skills that match the best in the world the LSC and FE share a common interest. Together they must rapidly ensure that the teaching and learner support staff in the FE sector are the best in the world.

Further illustrations of the LSC's priorities are given in their interim targets for the period to 2004. They demonstrate a continuing commitment to attainment of qualifications at Levels 2–4. Importantly for FE they attach much more importance to basic skills and they are explicit in their commitment to raising and measuring quality and effectiveness in education. The targets are:

- To raise the achievement of *young people aged 19*, measured by the proportion attaining a Level 2 qualification and the proportion lacking the basic skills of literacy and numeracy
- To raise the achievement of *young people aged 21*, measured by the proportion attaining a Level 3 qualification, and the proportion lacking the basic skills of literacy and numeracy
- To raise the achievement of the *entire adult population*, measured by the proportion attaining a Level 3 qualification and the proportion lacking the basic skills of literacy and numeracy
- To raise *participation post-16*, measured by the proportion of 16–18 year olds engaged in education and training
- To raise the *quality and effectiveness* of the education and training we support, measured by external inspection grades and by structured feedback from learners, employers and training providers.

In pursuit of quality and excellence the LSC is likely to place considerable emphasis on the strategic development of provision, typically based on partnership and collaboration between the providers of learning opportunities. Investment in the development of lecturers and teachers has to be the other key strategic priority.

Current initiatives include distribution of the *FE Standards Fund*, which was introduced in 1999–2000 and was originally managed by the FEFC, and is set to continue for 2000–1 and 2001–2. The LSC will now be responsible for the fund, which aims to support colleges in improving and sharing good practice.

There are six categories under which colleges can apply for funding:

- college improvement
- improving teaching and learning, with specific reference to:
    basic skills quality initiative
    part-time teachers
    information and learning technology skills for teachers
    curriculum
    new teacher posts
    retraining
    professional updating
    staff mentoring
- training and development for principals and senior management teams
- the good governance programme
- dissemination of good practice
- the achievement fund.

National Institute of Adult Continuing Education (NIACE)

The National Institute of Adult Continuing Education is a registered charity whose formal aim is to promote the study and general advancement of adult continuing education, which it interprets to mean advancing the interests of adult learners and potential learners.

NIACE operates in England and Wales (within Wales a specialist committee, NIACE Cymru, oversees the organisation's work). It is a membership organisation, with individual members and more than 260 corporate members across the full range of providers, policy makers and users of adult learning opportunities.

NIACE is committed to supporting an increase in the total numbers of adults engaged in formal and informal learning in England and Wales, and to take positive action to improve opportunities and widen access to learning opportunities communities which are underrepresented in current provision.

A special feature of NIACE is said to be that its work crosses the sectoral boundaries of post-school education and training. It works in all fields of UK education and training, including local authority organised provision, the FE college sector, higher education in universities and HE colleges, employment-led learning involving both employers and trade unions, learning in the voluntary sector and learning through the media, especially broadcasters.

Basic Skills Agency (BSA)

The Basic Skills Agency is the national agency for basic skills in England and Wales. It is supported and funded by the government but is run as an independent, non-profit-making charity.

The BSA's mission is to help raise basic skills in England and Wales. It aims to reduce the number of children, young people and adults with poor basic skills through promoting the work of the agency, and to develop effective, quality and diverse learning opportunities through innovative approaches that raise the standards of basic skills.

The General Teaching Council for Wales

The General Teaching Council for Wales is an independent self-regulating professional body for teachers in Wales and came into being under the Teaching and Higher Education Act 1998.

All teachers are required to register with the council in order to teach in a maintained primary, secondary or special school in Wales. They are currently encouraging teachers in the FE sector with Qualified Teacher Status (QTS) for teaching school age pupils to register, however, current legislation does not allow them to register teachers with an FE qualification.

The Council is responsible for advising the National Assembly for Wales and other bodies on a wide range of teaching issues including standards of teaching and teacher conduct, the role of the teaching profession, training and career development and recruitment to the profession. They also have powers relating to the investigation, hearing and disciplining of teachers' accused of serious professional misconduct and incompetence.

University for Industry (UfI)

The UfI is taking forward the government's vision of a University for Industry, by stimulating and meeting demand for lifelong learning among businesses and individuals. Working as a public–private partnership in England, Wales and Northern Ireland, The UfI aims to put individuals in a better position to get jobs, improve their career prospects and boost business competitiveness.

New Deal

New Deal for people aged 18–24

New Deal is a joint initiative between the Department for Education and Skills (DfES) (formerly the DfEE) and the Department of Social Security (DSS). Full-time education or training is one of the four options available if an unsubsidised job cannot be found during the first few months of New Deal. The education or training must help to provide the skills and qualifications required by the person in order to enter employment. Those who enter full-time education and training under New Deal for 18–24 year-olds are guaranteed the equivalent of the Jobseekers Allowance. Help can be given towards the cost of books or materials.

New Deal for people aged 25+

Full-time education and training may be selected as the most appropriate programme of help. It provides the chance to retrain in skills, whilst remaining on the Jobseekers Allowance. While most courses are short, it is possible to follow full-time education or training for up to a year. The education and training undertaken must be vocational, and must help the participant to find work. It could involve a short course to boost existing skills, or training for new skills. An example is given below.

INFORMATION LEARNING TECHNOLOGY (ILT) STANDARDS (MARCH 2001)

Key Role A: Learning Facilitation

Plan to use ICT as part of the learning programme

Learning facilitators need to be able to identify how ICT can best support the achievement of learning objectives, taking into account learners' abilities and learning styles and the college facilities available. They can either acquire ILT materials, after having established their suitability for use, or amend existing ILT materials to make them appropriate to the learning objectives and context, or develop new ILT materials using their own and others' expertise. Learning facilitators must be aware of the law of copyright and how this may restrict their use of ILT materials.

This requires learning facilitators to have a *generic knowledge* of:

- learning theories and how they affect teaching and learning
- how to select appropriate teaching methods on the basis of learning theory
- ways of learning and appropriate learning strategies
- the use of differentiated learning materials
- the relationship between learning styles and the required outcomes of learning programmes
- the range of ILT available to support learners and learning facilitators
- the principles and processes of continuing professional development
- the range of analytical tools and techniques
- colleagues, specialists and others who can provide advice, guidance, information or support,

and how to consult with them.

Evaluate learning gained through using ICT

Learning facilitators need to use ICT effectively to facilitate learning within the physical environment of the college and its associated learning outlets. They therefore need to evaluate the contribution of ICT to the achievement of learning objectives, recommend improvements and incorporate these in their practice.

This requires learning facilitators to have a *generic knowledge* of:

- curriculum requirements and their implications for learning programmes using ICT
- formative and summative assessment techniques
- evaluation strategies and methods
- how to analyse information on teaching and learning using ICT and ILT and extract what is relevant to modify future learning strategies
- how to evaluate learning programmes based on the use of ICT and ILT in terms of efficiency, effectiveness and equity.

EXPECTATIONS AND EDUCATIONAL ACHIEVEMENT

Countries which achieve higher standards in education and training, such as Germany, France, Japan and Singapore, would appear to have one fundamental thing in common: as nations they place great emphasis on educational achievement, engendering high educational aspirations amongst individuals. They tend to have a 'learning culture', whereby parents and teachers have high expectations of their children's educational achievements, the education systems are designed to provide opportunities and motivation for learners of all abilities, and the labour market and society in general reward those who do well in education. Education has played a particularly important role in the historical development of these countries as modern nation states. Education was a critical factor in the industrialisation of each of these countries, and it was also critical to the process of political and economic restructuring after the Second World War. For these and other historical reasons these societies place an exceptionally high value on education both for its potential contribution towards national development and for its enhancement of individual opportunities (Green and Steadman 1995). High expectations in these countries are also institutionalised within the education system. Curriculum development and pedagogical research have been more systematically organised and focused than in countries such as Britain. The importance of systematic curriculum development and evaluation cannot be overemphasised.

It could be argued that Britain is trying to redress the balance, particularly with vocational courses in which preparation for adult life includes training in the skills required for a job. These skills are pitched at different levels, are either highly job specific and do not require much thought in their application, or are generalisable and applicable to a range of employment. The more generalised the skills and the more judgement required in their application, the more blurred is the distinction between education and vocational training. The blurring of the distinction is to be seen in the National Targets for education and training, which the CBI specified in 1988 and which the government endorsed and handed over to the TECs to achieve (see Tables 1.9, 1.10 and 1.11).

Up to age 19	GCSE	Grade	GNVQ/NVQ
85%	5	C or above	Intermediate or Level 2
75%			Level 2
35%			Advanced or Level 3
Age 21	**GCE A level**	**GNVQ/NVQ**	
60%	2	Advanced or Level 3	

Table 1.9

National Target for 2000: Foundation learning

% of workforce achieving qualification	NVQ	GNVQ	GCE	
60%	Level 3	Advanced	2 A level	
30%	Vocational	Professional	Management	Degree level
Plus:	70% of organisations employing 200 and above			
	35% of organisations employing 50 or more			
	to be recognised as Investors in People (NACETT 1995)			

Table 1.10

National Target for 2000: Lifetime learning (AUT 1999, p. 23)

Table 1.11		
The government's dream (AUT 1999, p. 23)	1960s	One in twenty UK learners entered full-time HE
	1998	One in three for the UK – 34% as a whole
		45% in Scotland and Northern Ireland
	1980–present	For each HE lecturer in UK the number of learners has doubled

Government's dream: Wants at least 50% of school leavers to participate in HE by 2010. This equates with a further 100,000 full-time undergraduate places in Britain.

THE GROWTH OF POST-COMPULSORY EDUCATION

Vocational courses have been based in the past in FE colleges, with learners given day release from work. However, we need to examine the aims and scope of FE colleges and realise their diversity. There are 556 FE colleges in the UK (452 in England, 51 in Scotland, 29 in Wales and 24 in Northern Ireland). This education sector is growing, with approximately 21 per cent full-time and 28 per cent part-time learners from all age groups. The FE sector has always had a policy of all inclusiveness in its provision. That is, it has provided own-selective education for anyone over 16 who wished to benefit from extended education or vocational training. This provision now includes everything from basic education to undergraduate and professional programmes (except nurse education – more about this later). Colleges now see themselves as providing for the needs of the local community as well as for a growing regional, national and, for some, international student clientele. Huddleston and Unwin (1997) suggest that not all is well, as there are still changes taking place and there exist some conflicts between staff and management about contracts, employment conditions, funding bodies and resources which are leading to high levels of stress and increased staff demoralisation. Perhaps there is a place in curriculum studies for stress management!

FE colleges now cater for more 16+ learners than the universities and sixth forms put together, with over three million learners in 1996 (FEFC 1996b); the majority of learners are mature adults who attend part-time courses. For some learners FE represents a second-chance education: it is estimated that about a third of FE learners are studying for academic qualifications, while about a half are studying for vocational qualifications. The growth in higher education has been achieved in part by learners progressing through the FE sector by the access route or by franchising arrangements, whereby colleges offer an undergraduate programme in collaboration with an HE institution. The FE and tertiary colleges cater for anyone over 16 and offer a very broad range of programmes. The specialist designed colleges are those mainly catering for adult provision. In addition to FE colleges, the FEFC also funds further education in HE institutions and some 500 external institutions, mainly adult education centres (Huddleston and Unwin 1997). Colleges still provide some courses for adults which do not lead to vocational qualifications; these are mainly leisure and recreational classes. Colleges may also mount 'full cost' courses where learners or their employers are prepared to pay the real cost of a course. These include company-specific training programmes, short courses for business, seminars and workshops. These courses are often provided by a separate business or enterprise unit within colleges. The planned growth for the FE sector will not be achieved through FEFC funding alone, so colleges will need to be more pro-active in identifying new markets and in attracting new fundings from new sources. For further information in this area see Hodkinson (1996) and FEU publications 1979–99. Whatever the future for post-compulsory education there is one area we all need practical help with: the curriculum.

FURTHER READING

Anderson, D., Brown, S. and Race, P. (1997) *500 Tips for Further and Continuing Education Lecturers*. London: Kogan Page.

Armitage, A., Bryant, R., Dunnill, R. *et al.* (1999) *Teaching and Training in Post-Compulsory Education*. Milton Keynes, Open University Press.

Ashcroft, K. and Foreman-Peck, L. (1994) *Managing Teaching and Learning in Further and Higher Education*. London, Falmer Press.

AUT (1999) *Higher Education in the New Century*. London, AUT.

Benn, C. and Chitty, C. (1997) *Thirty Years On: Is Comprehensive Education Alive and Well or Struggling to Survive?* Harmondsworth, Penguin.

Brookfield, S. (1984b) 'Self-directed adult learning: a critical paradigm'. *Adult Education Quarterly* 2: 59–71.

Castling, A. (1996) *Competence-based Teaching and Training*. London, Macmillan.

Curzon, L.B. (1997) *Teaching in Further Education: An Outline of Principles and Practice* (5th edition). London, Cassell.

DfEE/FEDA. (1995) *Mapping the FE Sector*, London, Further Education Development Agency.

DfEE/Scottish Office/Welsh Office (1995) *Lifetime Learning: A Consultation Document*. London, DfEE.

Edwards, R. (1993) 'Multi-skilling the flexible workforce in post-compulsory education'. *Journal of Further and Higher Education* 17(1): 44–51.

Green, A. and Steadman, H. (1995) *Education Provision, Education Attainment and the Needs of Industry: A Review of the Research for Germany, France, Japan, the USA. and Britain*. London, National Institute for Economic and Social Research.

FENTO (2001) *Further Education Sector Workforce Development Plan*. Consultation version, April. London, FENTO.

Hodkinson, P. (1996) ' "Careership": the individual, choices and markets in the transition into work'. In J. Avis, M. Bloomer, G. Esland *et al.* (eds) *Knowledge and Nationhood*. London, Cassell Education.

Hodson, A. and Spours, K. (1997) *Beyond Dearing, 14–19: Qualifications, Frameworks and Systems*. London, Kogan Page.

Huddleston, P. and Unwin, L. (1997) *Teaching and Learning in Further Education: Diversity and Change*. London, Routledge.

Jarvis, P. (1995) *Adult and Continuing Education: Theory and Practice* (2nd edition) London, Routledge.

Kolb, D.A. (1984) *Experiential Learning: Experience as the Source of Learning and Development*. Englewood Cliffs, New Jersey, Prentice-Hall.

NACETT (1995) *Report on Progress towards the National Targets*. London, NACETT.

Payne, J. (1995) *Routes beyond Compulsory Schooling*. England and Wales Youth Cohort Study. Sheffield, Employment Department.

Petty, G. (1998) *Teaching Today* (2nd edition). Cheltenham, Stanley Thornes.

Race, P. (1993) 'Never mind the teaching – feel the learning'. SEDA Paper No. 80, ch. 1, Birmingham: SEDA Publications. Summarised at http://www.lgu.ac.uk/deliberations/ eff.learning/happen.html (accessed 5 February 2001).

Reece, L. and Walker, S. (1992) *Teaching, Training and Learning: A Practical Guide*. Sunderland, Business Education Publishers.

Robson, J., Cox, A., Bailey, B. *et al.* (1995) 'A new approach to teacher training: an evaluation of a further and higher education partnership'. *Journal of Further and Higher Education* 19(2): 79–91.

Sandberg, J.A. (1994) 'Educational paradigms: issues and trends'. In R. Lewis and P. Mendelsohn (eds), *Lessons From Learning*. IFIP TC3/WG3.3 Working Conference 1993, Amsterdam, pp. 13–22.

Schneider, D.K. and Block, K. (1995) *The Learning and Teaching Environment: in the World-Wide Web in Education*. ANDREA. (A Network for Distance Education Reporting from European Activities), Vol. 2, No. 5, 12 June. Available at http://tecfa.unige.ch/tecfa/research/CMC/andrea95/andrea.html (accessed 10 February 2001).

Walklin, L. (1991) *The Assessment of Performance and Competence: A Handbook for Teachers and Trainers*. Cheltenham, Stanley Thornes

CURRICULUM CONCEPTS AND RESEARCH

2

Learning outcomes

To be achieved through the process of self-directed study, teacher/mentor support and sharing learning with fellow students

By the end of this chapter you will be able to:

- write your own definition of the curriculum
- discuss the classic definitions offered by British and American writers from the 1960s to the present
- describe the elements of the curriculum
- explain the importance of curriculum research and change.

THE CONCEPT OF CURRICULUM

The word derives from the Latin *currere*, which means 'to run', and its associated noun which has been translated as 'a course'. The word is used to refer to following a course of study.

Modern writers on the curriculum define the curriculum in terms of the whole situation (Jarvis 1995). Many attempts have been made to produce a satisfactory model of the teaching and learning process in curriculum terms.

As professionals working in the post-16 education sector, we teach and train through many different courses and one thing we have in common is that we all have some kind of curriculum through which we aim to help our learners to learn. A student on a PGCE course said to me some time ago: 'In this place I find on all sides people talking and writing about "curriculum" but I'm not sure what they mean by the term – and I'm pretty certain they mean differing things by it.'

I took the opportunity to ask a PGCE student cohort of 120 the question 'What is a curriculum?' The following are some of the student responses.

- Something to do with planning a course.
- What the teacher intends to cover on the course.
- A group of 'modules' we will learn from.
- The college's formal planning for learners.
- A group of courses we can choose from.
- It's all the learning experience planned by the college or university.
- It is what the teacher wants us to learn from a series of lectures and practical skills.
- The teaching methods and structure of the course.

The first task then is to consider:

1   What is a curriculum?

2   What does 'curriculum' mean?
3   What definition would you offer?

These questions are worth pondering, especially in relation to individual profession, activity, work context, learning environment, and when faced with material about the curriculum offered in this book. We must not assume there is a 'correct' or 'final' answer.

To help this reflection it is worth considering the following related questions.

Study problem

1   How do we distinguish between those activities that are part of the curriculum in an educational institution and those that are not?
2   Disagreements here may reflect different concepts of 'curriculum' or of 'education' (different ideologies). Is there any way of showing that some are right and some are wrong or do we just have to 'agree to differ'?
3   How would you differentiate the following terms: curriculum, course, timetable, syllabus, programme? Can you suggest others?
4   Are there clear, hard-and-fast distinctions to point to or a web of overlapping and interrelated users?
5   What is your response to this claim by John Wilson? Schools, he suggests, might set out to encourage a
    Spartan attitude by keeping the school dormitories cold or a sense of beauty by placing the school in glorious mountain scenery. Here it would be linguistically absurd to say that cold dormitories or mountains were 'in the curriculum'. (Wilson 1969, p.66)
    Do you agree? Why, or why not? Try to relate the comment to the full range of activities and circumstances of your own institution – for example, is the condition of the building and furniture part of the curriculum?
6   Would you say that the college or university 'has a curriculum' in exactly the same way that a primary school or secondary school might be said to 'have a curriculum'?

In order to gain some sense of what a curriculum is we need to revisit some of the old classics of the 1960–1970s so let us look at some of these now.

What do the 'experts' say?

The authors of the (many) books on curriculum issues of the last few decades usually offer some definition. Here is a selection for your consideration.

We appear to be confronted by two different views of the curriculum. On the one hand the curriculum is seen as an intention, plan or prescription ... On the other, it is seen as the existing state of affairs in schools. (Stenhouse 1975)

A curriculum is the formulation and implementation of an educational proposal, to be taught and learned within a school or other institution and for which that institution accepts responsibility at three levels, its actual implementation and its effects. (Jenkins and Shipman, 1976a)

All the opportunities planned by teachers for pupils. (Nicholls and Nicholls, 1978)

All the learning which is planned and guided by the school, whether it is carried on in groups or individually, inside or outside the school. (Kerr, 1968)

That the curriculum consists of content, teaching methods and purpose may in its rough and ready way be sufficient definition with which to start. These dimensions interacting are the operational curriculum. (Taylor, 1968)

Study problem

Drawing on your own experience try to work out lists of those activities that are part of the curriculum, those that are not and those that you consider are borderline or doubtful. What do you consider are (or should be) the criteria of differentiation? Discuss your views with others to find out whether or not there seems to be general agreement on the placing of activities and on the criteria.

Ask yourself: Is it clean and unambiguous? Is it possible to offer a form of words which covers everything we might want to talk about under the heading of 'curriculum'? Figure 2.1 may help to clarify.

To help you answer these questions study chapter 5 on curriculum design.

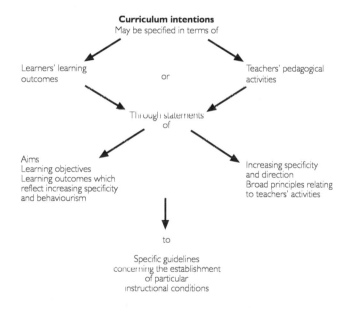

Figure 2.1

Curriculum intentions (adapted from FEU 1982, p.19)

TEACHING AS PART OF CURRICULUM

Teaching is also concerned with the curriculum, but the intention or aim differs in that teaching aims to bring about understanding and insight.

Therefore, whilst the subject matter may be the same, the aims and the methods differ. The ways in which the knowledge is held by the learner are also different and cannot be described as part of teaching.

It has, in analysing teaching, been helpful to establish criteria or standards by which we may judge whether or not to describe the activity as teaching. Peters (1966) was one of the first to use this technique to illuminate the concept of education. He suggested that the content of education and the methods of transmission provide two possible criteria. There may also be a case for a third criterion concerning the way in which we hold knowledge:

1 The content to be transmitted to the learner must be worthwhile.
2 The methods by which these worthwhile activities or subjects are transmitted must help develop the learner's powers of independent judgement.
3 The knowledge learnt must not only be understood but the learner must be able to relate their knowledge to other areas of knowledge.

Peters (1966) regards education as initiation: initiation into the worthwhile activities of society. The educated person is transformed by what they know – they have not arrived at a destination, but 'travel with a different view' (p.34).

Study problem

Using one of the lessons you teach, list the different kinds of knowledge you are trying to achieve. Then match these to the appropriate method. Ask yourself: 'Should I be trying to achieve any other kinds of knowledge?' and 'Should I be using any other methods of bringing about learning?' Does imparting knowledge form part of the curriculum, or does the teaching strategy form the curriculum? (Teaching strategies will be considered in chapter 3.)

ANALYSIS OF 'CURRICULUM'

Wilson's (1969) analysis of the curriculum is more differentiated and stringent than those considered so far. He dismisses much talk about curriculum as part of the hot air and fantasy that he sees as characterising much (or most) talk about education. I am not suggesting that you should accept his views, and indeed there are many educationalists who do not accept them, but they are worth considering seriously and deserve a considered acceptance or rejection.

Wilson suggests that 'curriculum' is only properly used for planned, sustained learning which is taken seriously, which has a distinct and structured content and which proceeds via some kind of stages of learning. He sees the following as among the immediate implications of this analysis:

Now if we reflect on this – fairly stringent – set of conditions in relation to what may be quite large numbers of pupils (or at any rate some learners), it immediately becomes apparent that to ask 'What sort of curriculum should they have?' may beg many questions. For we might well think that such learners should not do very much in the way of serious, sustained, structured learning at all or we might not think them capable of very much. We need rather to ask something like 'How much of 'what we do with' these learners should be curricular at all?' or 'How much do they need a curriculum as against, say, pastoral care, hobbies, 'interests', and so on?

Wilson's notion of 'serious, sustained, structured learning' is given further elaboration in his hierarchical categorisation of activities, only the fourth (and highest) of which he considers to be curriculum activities in the 'stringent' sense of his analysis. These should now be looked at carefully.

John Wilson's hierarchy of activities

1 *Least demanding, there is the situation where the learners do not do things in any serious sense at all – we do things to them. We hug them, give them sweets, listen to them, smile at them, and so on, or – a rather thin kind of 'doing' – the learners breathe, eat, sleep, daydream, walk about, perhaps vaguely watch television. No learning is involved here at all.*

2 *More demanding are situations in which learners do things in a stronger sense; that is, they engage in what fairly may be called 'activities' which have some kind of structure, may involve taking means to ends, thinking, concentrating, achieving, appreciating, organising, or, in general, confronting the world. They may play games, keep pets, enjoy music, and so forth. Here, though there may be some learning involved, the activities are not activities of learning. We do not usually play games in order to learn, and in fact we may not actually learn much or anything when we play. Keeping pets is not an activity of learning, and to like keeping pets is not to like learning.*

3 *More demanding still are situations which are avowedly learning situations. These extend beyond the normal sense of 'curriculum', as we have seen earlier. One may learn to play chess as a hobby, learn about foreign countries when visiting them, learn the guitar, and so on. There are of course plenty of borderline cases between this category and (2) above, but the basic distinction is clear enough – it is a distinction between the points or purposes of the two types. In (2), a person tries to keep a pet or play football, in (3), he/she tries to learn about how to keep pets or how to play football.*

4 *Most demanding of all are learning situations which are still further removed from what we may call 'natural' interest than the examples of learning situations in (3). People may in some sense 'naturally' take to learning games, musical instruments, boat building, or how to win friends and influence people; these connect, though often in obscure ways, with standard and immediate interests which are often readily identifiable. This is not true, I think, of (for example) higher mathematics or physics, serious philosophy, the study of Anglo-Saxon literature, or the complexities of the Athenian tribute lists during the Peloponnesian War. It is true, however (or more true if such a phrase be allowed), of some of the things which the orthodox literature describes, badly, as 'forms of thought'; for instance, the appreciation of the arts, involvement in religion, and some aspects of morality and 'personal knowledge' (Hirst and Peters, 1970, p.62). This I take to be the concealed truth behind common remarks to the effect that some activities are more 'abstract', 'intellectual' or 'highbrow' than others*

(and, as the last word shows, this notion has some application to the appreciation of the arts). If I had to specify what this is a hierarchy of, I should have to say something like this: it is ordered in relation to the degree that an average person has to put himself/herself – that is, his/her 'natural' desires and impulses and interests – in the background, in the interests of his/her subject matter. What is more 'demanding' about the more sophisticated items in the hierarchy is that the person has to pay more and more attention to realities outside himself/herself, and submit to more and more discipline, that is in so far as he/she has not yet learned to invest emotionally in these more sophisticated items. Of course some people, and a few learners, invest in them at an early stage; but I am claiming, empirically, that this is rare.

Taking this view seriously would involve a radical reappraisal of the current state of affairs in both theory and practice, as this paragraph makes clear:

Many learners (even in the UK and certainly throughout the world), I would guess, are not suited by any very sophisticated curriculum or even perhaps by anything one could seriously call a 'curriculum' at all. Of course this is just a guess; but certainly it will be true of some learners. Their particular needs are often more basic; to be socially viable, to be able to love, and to be given a chance to pursue whatever genuine and worthwhile interests they do happen to pick up from us. This is not, of course, an argument for not taking however much 'curriculum' we think suitable for them with the utmost seriousness (rather than watering it down so that it ceases to be serious learning at all). It is rather an argument for making much sharper distinctions here. If a learner looks like being, or can be encouraged to be, genuinely interested in literature or history, then we can thank our lucky stars and set him/her seriously to work; if he/she is not, we try something else, or admit that his/her more basic needs have been so ill-met that serious learning is not for him/her – and then we must try to cater for these needs much more directly. Nothing is gained by diluting literature into trashy books 'relevant to the modern worlds', or diluting history into 'environmental studies'; then we must give them love or discipline in as straightforward a way as possible, not via 'relevance' or other desperate attempts to engage their interest. And if they can manage to meet the demands of serious learning, we must keep the demands serious.

Study problem

1   Even though Wilson's view of the curriculum was written in the 1960s it is still worth considering. How does it square with your own professional practice? With the state of affairs in your own college? How much influence does Wilson's concept have on your college's curriculum development?
2   Form a group with fellow learners and discuss the following statements.

The curriculum:

A   encompasses the entire educational environment

B   is the sum of learning activities and experiences that a student has under the auspices of the college

C   is all the learning planned and guided by the school/college (Kerr 1968).

DEFINING THE CURRICULUM

Defining the term 'curriculum' to everyone's satisfaction is probably an impossible task. But we need to agree on some sort of working definition, if only because rational discussion of issues raised during later stages of curriculum studies courses depends to some extent on what is meant by 'curriculum'.

> *Definitions of the word curriculum do not solve curricular problems: but they do suggest perspectives from which to view them. (Stenhouse 1975, p.1)*

More recently Armitage *et al.* (1999) suggest that 'due to the business of teachers and maximum numbers of learners the curriculum is all too often simply whatever course we happen to be teaching at the time' (p.160).

Different perspectives

We seem to be confronted by at least two different views of the curriculum – one which emphasises plans and intentions (e.g. a set of intended learning outcomes or a written statement of syllabus content) and one which emphasises activities and effects (e.g. accounts of what teachers and learners actually do in classrooms or of the knowledge and skills acquired by learners, whether intended or not). Jenkins and Shipman (1976a) appear to favour a description which embraces both views:

> *A curriculum then is concerned with pre-requisites (antecedents, intentions), with transactions (what actually goes on in classrooms as the essential meanings are negotiated between teachers and taught, and worthwhile activities undertaken), and with outcomes (the knowledge and skills acquired by learners, attitude changes, intended and unintended side effects, etc.). (p.5)*

Study problem

Listed below are nine classic definitions of 'curriculum' from the 1960s to the present day used by different American and British writers. Which view of the curriculum is being emphasised in each case? Enter the appropriate code numbers in the boxes provided. I make no apologies for introducing the well-worn 'classic' when discussing the meaning of curriculum. I will refer to the more recent 'definitions' as we develop our arguments throughout this book.

Code to use

1 = curriculum as a plan of learning outcomes

2 = curriculum as a plan of learning activities

3 = curriculum as activities that are geared to the attainment of specified learning outcomes

4 = curriculum as activities which are not necessarily related to planned learning outcomes

Some definitions may need to be classified under more than one heading.

1	2	3	4

Definitions of 'curriculum'

The curriculum is now generally considered to be all of the experiences that learners have under the auspices of the school.

Curriculum is a sequence of content units arranged in such a way that the learning of each unit may be accomplished as a single act, provided the capabilities described by specified prior units in the sequence have already been mastered by the learner.

A curriculum is a group of courses and planned experiences which a student has under the guidance of the school or college.

The term curriculum is, of course, used very variedly, but I shall take it to mean a programme of activities designed so that pupils will attain by learning certain specifiable ends or objectives.

Curriculum is that body of value-goal-orientated learning content, existing as a written document or in the minds of teachers, that, when energised by instruction, results in change in pupil behaviour.

The curriculum is all the learning which is planned and guided by the school, whether it is carried on in groups or individually, inside or outside the school.

The curriculum can be regarded as all planned learning outcomes for which the school is responsible.

A curriculum is an attempt to communicate the essential principles and features of an educational proposal in such a form that it is open to critical scrutiny and capable of effective translation into practice.

A curriculum is the planned and guided learning experiences and intended learning outcomes, formulated through the systematic reconstruction of knowledge and experience, under the auspices of the school, for the learner's continuous and wilful growth in personal-social competence.

If, as Jenkins and Shipman (1976a) suggest, a curriculum is 'the formulation and implementation of an educational proposal', how does the study of curriculum differ from the study of the teaching–learning process? How can we distinguish between 'curriculum' and 'instruction'? Consideration of this problem has led Johnson (1967) to suggest that a curriculum is, in fact, no more than a structured series of intended learning outcomes:

> Accepted usage identifies curriculum with 'planned learning experiences'. This definition is unsatisfactory, however, if 'curriculum' is to be distinguished from 'instruction'. Whether experiences are viewed subjectively in terms of the sensibility of the experiencing individual or objectively in terms of his/her actions in a particular setting, there is in either case no

experience until an interaction between the individual and his/her environment actually occurs. Clearly, such interaction characterises instruction, not curriculum ... a useful concept of curriculum must leave some room for creativity and individual style in instruction. In other words, decisions regarding the learning experiences to be provided are the result of instructional planning, not of curriculum development. The curriculum, though it may limit the range of possible experiences, cannot specify them ... it is here stipulated that curriculum is a structured series of intended learning outcomes. Curriculum prescribes (or at least anticipates) the results of instruction. It does not prescribe the means, i.e. the activities, materials or even the instructional content, to be used in achieving the results. In specifying outcomes to be sought, curriculum is concerned with ends, but at the level of attainable learning products, not at the more remote level at which these ends are justified. In other words, curriculum indicates what is to be learned, not why it should be learned. (p.6)

The notion that instruction is separate from curriculum is reflected clearly in MacDonald's view of curriculum as 'those planning endeavours which take place prior to instruction' (cited in Tawney 1976).

Here is a list of definitions given by PGCE (FE) student teachers:

- The curriculum is the content of a course offered by the education institute.
- The curriculum is made up of the syllabus and content of a course.
- The curriculum is every planned experience to ensure learning outcomes are achieved.
- The curriculum is a structured plan of lessons, assessments and evaluation strategies.
- The curriculum is a structured programme of teaching and learning.

One student offered the difference between course, syllabus, timetable and curriculum and likened it to a restaurant:

Restaurant = curriculum	= everything in the college including the building
Menu = course/programme =	the choice on offer
Meal = timetable =	what actually is delivered

Consider another analogy:

A curriculum is like a house. An architect consults his/her clients to find out what the functions of the rooms are to be, how the space is to be used. He/she will also consider the money available, the character of the site, the climate, and from this a model and design will be drawn up. It is the physical structure which will be more or less permanent. However, the architect can build into the structure degrees of flexibility of use, according to his/her clients' requirements and needs.

From this we could argue that the curriculum is all-inclusive, i.e. the building, resources, staff, finance, planned programmes, courses and planned learning outcomes, assessments, examinations, etc.

Taba (1962) has observed that the very breadth of some definitions tends to make them non-functional, whereas 'excluding from the definition of curriculum everything except the statement of objectives and content outlines and relegating anything that has to do with learning and learning experiences to "method" might be too confining to be adequate for a modern curriculum' (p.9). She appears to favour a definition that lies somewhere between the two extremes. It should be noted, however, that in describing a curriculum as 'a plan for learning', Taba (1962, p.11) seems to imply that the means by which such plans are put into action could lie outside the curriculum.

So, although many writers over the years have tried to establish an adequate definition of curriculum, the basic dilemmas remain – between plans and happenings, between content and method, between intended learning outcomes and planned learning experiences.

In order to help you to decide how you want to use the term 'curriculum' and to enable you to be more discerning when you observe its use by other people, you might like to think about the following questions.

Study problem

1. How do you account for the differences among various writers in defining 'curriculum'?
2. Is the difficulty in reaching agreement on a single definition of 'curriculum' likely to impede the study of curriculum problems?
3. To what extent are all of the observable interactions between teacher and student in a college part of the curriculum?
4. How can we distinguish between 'the curriculum' and those voluntary activities commonly referred to as 'extra curricular'?
5. Do you accept that 'curriculum' is the criterion for instructional evaluation'?

By way of summary, write down what you would regard as a satisfactory working definition of 'curriculum'.

ELEMENTS OF THE CURRICULUM

A simple way of looking at the curriculum is to divide it up into a series of basic elements or phases. Much of the thinking about curriculum is dominated by such a notion; for example:

The rationale developed here begins with identifying four fundamental questions which must be answered in developing any curriculum and plan of instruction. These are:

1. *What educational purposes should the institution seek to attain?*
2. *What educational experiences can be provided that are likely to attain these purposes?*
3. *How can these educational experiences be effectively organised?*
4. *How can we determine whether these purposes are being attained?*

All curricula, no matter what their particular design, are composed of certain elements. A curriculum usually contains a statement of aims and specific objectives; it indicates some selection and organisation of content; it either implies or manifests certain patterns of learning and teaching, whether because the objectives demand them or because the content organisation requires them. Finally, it includes a programme of evaluation of the outcomes. Curricula differ according to the emphasis given to each of these elements, according to the manner in which these elements are related to each other, and according to the basis on which the decisions regarding each are made. (Taba 1962, p.10)

Wheeler (1967, p.30) suggested that:

The curriculum process consists of five phases:
1 The selection of aims, goals and objectives.
2 The selection of learning experiences calculated to help in the attainment of these aims, goals and objectives.
3 The selection of content (subject matter) through which certain types of experience may be offered.
4 The organisation and integration of learning experiences and content with respect to the teaching–learning process within school and classroom.
5 Evaluation of the effectiveness of all aspects of phases 2, 3 and 4 in attaining the goals detailed in phase 1.

(Evaluation is discussed in more detail in chapter 7).

In many aspects, these simple models are giving way to rather more sophisticated alternatives even though they were popular in the 1960s, but they continue to be useful. In talking about factors influencing the curriculum in adult education, for example, dividing the curriculum into a number of elements certainly helps to establish which particular aspect of the curriculum is being discussed.

Study problem

Read the following extracts and try to decide which particular element of the curriculum is being most strongly reflected or emphasised in each case. Enter the appropriate code letters in the boxes provided:

Code to work with
A = aims and objectives
C = content and subject matter
E = evaluation and assessment
M = methods and learning experiences
S = structure and organisation

In some cases you may find classification difficult. What do you think are the reasons for these difficulties? At the completion of this exercise, consider whether you want to make any amendments to your working definition of 'curriculum'.

A C E M S

We wish to suggest that the most important qualities needed for success in a business career are not so much particular skills but the imagination, breadth of interest, understanding of the world outside work and of the pressures which social and economic changes exert, and the ability to derive full satisfaction from life as well as the ability to adapt to rapid social changes and to learn new skills throughout working life.

The reasons for this mismatch between higher education provision and student demand are many and complex; but they include the unique combination of freedom and curricular choice in English and Welsh education (whether the choice be that of the student, the parent or the teacher), and early specialisation; the bad image of productive industry, and of the engineering profession, in the schools (normally for the wrong reasons); and the influence which the members of the school teaching profession may have upon the educational and career choices of their students.

Good teaching produces, amongst other things, a situation in which there is every encouragement for a student to find things out for himself/herself ... the lecture situation should be used with caution, and the tutorial should be used as an essential complementary function in which the powers of the learners themselves to apply, and analyse and synthesise be developed.

I regard it as an essential characteristic of an educated nation that it should understand, support, and take pride in, the means whereby it earns its living ... I see two main approaches in education to achieve this aim. One is to introduce into schools the teaching about industrial society as part and parcel of our culture ... the second approach that I would like to see is a correction to the imbalance in higher education that has been produced by an over-expansion of full-time study.

It is an accepted aim of the system that it should attract and keep in further education the maximum number of young people able to benefit ... The proportion who successfully complete a full course is not the sole criterion of success. Some who have failed will be better equipped as a result of the tuition they received while making the attempt. But, where possible, prognosis should be used to ensure that learners are placed on the right course to ensure qualification.

It is of great importance for young people to find employment suited, as far as possible, to their personal needs, abilities and potentialities, and to make a choice of career on the basis of informed advice ... Occupational guidance and education must be seen as an integral part of the curriculum especially from the age of 13 onwards.

Many students, of considerable innate ability, who fail to make progress with ordinary academic education, could develop their powers to the full by a more 'practical' approach. Minds that move more easily from the practice to the theory, or that reason better in non-verbal ways, are not necessarily inferior. If there is not to be waste of talent there should be more provision for them.'

The outstanding characteristic of further education colleges in Britain is the extreme fragmentation of their curriculum. It derives from the demarcations of the craft system in industry but it has developed across the whole range of college work. For example, student engineers, plumbers, bricklayers, typists, nurses and many others pursue similar studies in part of their curriculum but the plumbers, for example, generally share their classes only with plumbers, and so on.

The forces which help to shape the curriculum in post-16 education arise from a wide variety of sources (see chapter 1 for the history). The above extracts are intended to illustrate this, originating (in alphabetical order) from the Association for Liberal Education, the Central Advisory Council for Education (Crowther Report), the Chairman of the Schools Council, the Confederation of British Industry, the Joint Committee for ONC/OND, a Minister of State for Education, the National Advisory Council on Education for Industry and Commerce (Haslegrave Report) and the principal of a large college.

You might like to try to guess which statement can be attributed to each of these sources.

THE HIDDEN CURRICULUM

Dr Jane Salisbury, of Cardiff University, reminds us that there are two theoretical approaches to the analysis of the hidden curriculum within the sociology of education: the functionalist and the neo-Marxist.

Neo-Marxists are by far the most prolific writers on the hidden curriculum. Philip W. Jackson is generally acknowledged as being the first person to use the term in life in classrooms (1968, pp.10–33) and is of the functionalist tradition. He identified three features of classroom life as forming the core of the hidden curriculum. Pupils, he claims, must come to terms with these if they are to have a satisfactory passage through the school institution. The other main proponent of the functionalist view of the hidden curriculum is Robert Dreeben (1968, p.65); the work of Philip Cusick (1973) is also essentially concerned with the hidden curriculum. All three writers' works are premised on a consensual understanding of both society itself and of the school's role in relationship to it.

Although the concept of the hidden curriculum originated in the consensualist school of thought it has been the conflict theorists who have developed it within the sociology of education. Many of those who contribute to the debate on the unwritten purposes or goals of school life do not use the term 'hidden curriculum'. This is noticeably the case in Bowles and Gintis's work *Schooling in Capitalist America* (1976). These writers suggest that schools reproduce the existing social relations of capitalist society by reproducing the consciousness necessary for such relations. The particular social relations they deem important in the reproductive process are principally the hierarchical division of labour between teachers and learners, the alienated character of learners' school work itself, and the fragmentation in work – reflected in the institution- alised and often destructive competition among learners through continual and ostensibly meritocratic ranking and evaluation (Lynch 1989, p.3).

Emile Durkheim (1964), one of the founding fathers of the discipline of sociology, was very positive about the functions of education.

Study problem

Consider Durkheim's view that education is a major socialising device:

> *Education is the influence exercised by adult generations on those that are not yet ready for social life. Its object is to arouse and to develop in the child a certain number of physical, intellectual and moral states which are demanded of him by both the political society as a whole and the special milieu for which he is specifi- cally destined ... It follows from (this) definition ... that education consists of a methodical socialisation of the young generation. (p.10)*

Other thinkers and writers share the idea that schooling prepares young people for the society in which they live but they stress the inequalities of that society. Michael F.D. Young, editor of the now classic text *Knowledge and Control* (1971), argued that academic curricula in this country involve assump- tions that some kinds and areas of knowledge are much more worthwhile than others.

Young and the other contributors (for example Keddie, Bourdieu, Bernstein, Bernbaum) changed the direction of the sociology of education by asking some fundamental questions:

- What knowledge counts?
- Whose knowledge is it?
- Do learners have access to different kinds of knowledge?
- What other learning (outside the official curriculum) occurs in educational institutions?

Study problem

Consider some of the 'probing' questions listed above.

Like all formal organisations, schools and colleges have relationships and values which are not officially laid down in rule books and syllabuses. The idea of the 'hidden curriculum', or what Hargreaves (1989) calls the 'para curri- culum', suggests that learners learn many values and forms which teachers are not consciously trying to teach them.

> *The functions of (the) hidden curriculum have been variously identified as the inculcation of values, political socialisation, training in obedience, and docility, the perpetuation of the class structure – functions that may be characterised as social control ... I use the term to refer to those non- academic but educationally significant consequences of schooling that occur*

systematically but are not made explicit at any level to the public rationales for education. (Vallance 1974, p.51)

Study problem

Consider Vallance's description of the hidden curriculum.

You have been introduced to the concept of the hidden curriculum. You now need to read Goodson and Ball (1984) and Higham *et al.* (1996), after which you and a fellow student should discuss the 'hidden curriculum' in your college. For example: Describe, via reflection and 'interrogation of experience' of various educational settings, the hidden curricula of your own education.

CURRICULUM RESEARCH, CHANGE AND INNOVATION

Curriculum research

'Curriculum research' is often used as a general term for enquiring into the many and varied aspects of curriculum study. It may be concerned with very practical issues or with fundamental theoretical issues; it may be conducted on a large, wide-ranging scale or it may be small scale and localised.

In a system in which curriculum decisions are made centrally, the problem is seen as finding the right curriculum to prescribe. In a system where curriculum decisions are delegated to the individual colleges, the college becomes the focus of curriculum development, and a process of continuous organic development becomes possible. The curriculum from year to year should be modified as part of a continuous process of adjustment and improvement. We therefore need to extend the range of choice open to curriculum developers and teachers. How do we do this?

Study problem

On your own or with a fellow student:

1   Devise a way in which curriculum research can be carried out.
2   Consider how curriculum research meets the needs of: the following:
     learners
     employers
     the community.

Stenhouse (1975, p.124) suggests a model which he likens to a supermarket – he suggests we place competing products on the shelves. The college then has a choice among those products. We may opt for curriculum A or B. Each will have its own identity, though it may offer alternatives within itself. Another possibility is that the principles on which a product is built are so clear that it is open to teachers both to criticise the curriculum in terms of its principles and as a result improve it in practice, or to extend the range of materials and teaching strategies by building on the curriculum offering, in light of these principles.

Many argue that teachers' participation in research is a key factor and that

- research should be carried out within the reality of the particular college and particular classroom
- the research role of the teacher and the curriculum planning team members should complement one another
- the development or maintenance of a common language is a prerequisite.

Study problem

Consider the following questions:

- Can the teacher sustain the multiple role of teacher, assessor, researcher, curriculum planner, curriculum developer and evaluator?
- What is the availability of time for research work?
- What form should the research take?
- How wide should the span of research be?
- How far can research be open in its findings?

Once you have considered the above questions, look at the ABC of curriculum by James Eaton (Figure 7.1, p.170) and ask the above questions again!

General areas of curriculum research

1 Needs
Enquiries are conducted into the processes and products of existing and proposed curricula to see how well they fit the needs of learners, employers and the community. Problems encountered include distinguishing between present perceived and actual needs.

2 Curriculum process
Research is conducted into the various stages of the curriculum process such as development, dissemination, evaluation, etc.

3 Learning processes
Although psychology has, in the past 50 years, provided us with much information about how people learn, we still need more information about this, particularly with regard to certain subjects and skills. We also need to know more about group interactions in the learning process.

4 Context
We need to know more about the various effects of organisational systems (administrative systems, schedules, physical environment, political influence, etc.) on the student's learning experiences.

5 Knowledge

The above issues are very important but perhaps even more important and fundamental are questions concerning the nature of knowledge itself, such as:

- What is knowledge? (what do we mean when we claim that we 'know' something?)
- Can knowledge be divided up in any way?
- Can existing subject divisions be justified?
- What is the distinction between theoretical and practical knowledge?
- Is knowledge determined or influenced by social factors?
- How does the application of knowledge to practice create an effective 'practicum'?

6 Values

We appear to be witnessing a crisis in the consensus regarding the school and the further education curriculum. Therefore investigation is needed into the implications for the curriculum of different value systems.

7 Teaching methods and strategies for assessment of learners learning

We are witnessing new instructions in these areas which need to be researched in order to judge their effectiveness.

Some problems in curriculum research

1 Clarification of concepts.
2 Following a physical science model may be very restrictive and indeed produce misleading 'results', while more 'interpretative research' may be regarded as too subjective and biased (refer to chapter 7 for more detail).
3 Research may be seen as threatening towards those institutions and individuals being investigated.
4 Presentation and communication of research results (e.g. problems of esoteric language, statistics, etc.).
5 Researchers are sometimes seen, perhaps correctly, as having a vested interest in curriculum change.

Research and the teacher

The relatively recent shift in emphasis in educational research from quantitative to qualitative methods has led to suggestions that practising teachers should be involved in research. Such research is not without its problems, but it can be a counterbalance to traditional quantitative methods and to the case studies approach. 'Personally orientated action research' was advocated by many researchers; this emphasises the strong links that do and should exist between theory and practice i.e. 'the practicum', but there is a danger that the subjectivity of such an approach may make communication difficult. Research can and does lead to curriculum change.

Curriculum change

The history of education is a story of change: learners and teachers have changed, so also have institutions (e.g. polytechnics have become new univer-

Figure 2.2

A curriculum change cycle

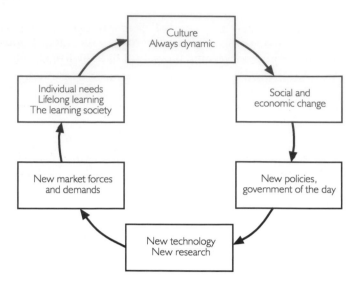

sities, FE colleges offer degree courses, nurse education has moved into universities, etc.), together with access, books, educational technology and examinations. The curriculum (formal and informal, explicit and 'hidden') has therefore changed. Sometimes curriculum developments have led to institutional and other changes; more often, curriculum developments have lagged behind other changes.

Reasons for curriculum change

These are numerous and complex, as depicted in Figure 2.2. Different reasons may dominate at different times. Among important reasons are:

- technological change leading to different skills being required by industry and commerce
- social change (associated with technological change) leading to different expectations and aspirations
- changes in educational technology making possible different patterns of learning and enabling different subject matters to be studied
- demands from individuals/individual need
- recommendations made as a result of research studies and commissioned government reports.

Very often these reasons will overlap. An important point to note is that, in one sense, education (certainly in the formal sense) is concerned with preparation for the future and therefore curriculum change involves an element of prediction about what measures will satisfy future needs. Furthermore, curriculum change inevitably takes place over a period of time during which the original reasons for the change may themselves alter.

Change may be inevitable, but is not always for the better. It needs to be directed; there is a need for constant evaluation.

Change agents

Almost any individual, group of individuals, or association connection with education, can initiate and promote curriculum change. The change agents, as we have already seen in chapter 1 and will consider again in chapter 8, may include national government, professional organisations and associations, headteachers, individual teachers, advisory bodies, charitable foundations, publishers, etc. They may, of course, act together or separately; they may cooperate on a formal or an informal basis. The effectiveness of different groups as change agents will depend on circumstances, particularly the timescale over which curriculum change is viewed.

Any proposed curriculum change will almost certainly encounter resistance. This may be because of opposition to change (in the case being considered) or because of disagreement with the direction of change (i.e. the need for change is agreed, but not the nature of the change). As well as a lack of *will* on the part of individuals and associations to go along with change, there may be a lack of *means* which leads to a retarding of, if not actual resistance to, curriculum change. (This may be particularly true of 'top down' curriculum development strategies). Most of the change agents listed in the previous paragraph can also resist change.

Some writers see curriculum change as being largely influenced by social and more recently by technological innovations (Huddleston and Unwin 1999). Others have seen educational theorists (philosophers?) as playing an important role. The influence of theory, as opposed to that of practical matters, on the curriculum may be difficult to measure and may well occur over a long period of time, but it could be argued that our present secondary school curriculum owes something to Plato and that our primary schools owe something to Dewey.

The ethics of curriculum change

To change the curriculum (or some aspect of it) is to experiment. Experiments do not always work. Educational experiments involve learners who will only pass our way once. Learners can be harmed (perhaps for life) if an experiment fails in what it set out to do or if an experiment or innovation results in learners receiving a widely differing experience from that of their contemporaries or predecessors. Change agents therefore have a great responsibility to clarify their aims, to make value judgements explicit, to gain the consent of others involved and to monitor and evaluate the changes.

As has been seen, 'vested interests' can inhibit change. However, it is possible for 'vested interests' to push particular changes. This may be for educational, political or personal or even financial reasons. Consider the role of publishers in this respect.

Any curriculum change involves a 'cost'. It may be a financial cost, but more importantly there may well be costs to individuals and institutions in terms of additional preparation, study of documents, organisational change, etc. Such factors may be hard to quantify but they are undoubtedly important. Thus, not only do we need to ask whether, as a result of change, curriculum B is better than curriculum A, we also need to consider the cost of change from A to B. This is not to argue that we should resist change. Curriculum change is inevitable. It is argued that we need to consider carefully the claims for and the results of any change, and that we should attempt to direct change. How we do this will depend on our basic value positions.

Consider for example the introduction of nurse education reforms in the

1990s and after many research projects, the most recent one being *Fitness for Practice* (1999), its redrafting again in the 2000s, under the heading *First Wave*, costing millions!

Study problem

People and organisations resist change:

- List the reasons for this.
- Discuss the differences or similarities.
- How would you bring about change to your present curriculum without creating conflict among your fellow workers?
- Do we need change and why do we need it?
- Has the curriculum changed in your college? If so, why?

The resistance

Resistance may be particularly great when people feel that they have some investment in the original design, or when their response has become a habit. Schon (1971) calls this 'dynamic conservatism'. He suggests that resistance is particularly strong when a change is perceived to threaten a 'stable state', and we all need stability in our lives. However, at the same time we need to be able to adapt to change: growth is change; our own needs and expectations change; the society around us is changing continually. Without change we become bored or ineffective and even inefficient. Many of us have experienced change in our careers, home life, etc., and we know that for some this can be very stressful. In a world where change seems to be exponential, we may find that we are needing new ways to adapt (Hutton 1989). Schon (1971) suggested that we need to have a stable process rather than a fixed outcome. The stable state is maintained in the situation not by controlling the outcome but by using a process. What can be fixed is the knowledge that one has about the 'conditions' and 'stance'. Conditions are those facts which may be known, such as physical characteristics, culture, resources available, relationships and history. Stance is the attitudes, values, beliefs, assumptions and expectations. Hutton (1989) suggested that the conditions and stance are the knowledge we have and which we draw upon as we proceed. They provide us with some basis for making choice. Choice, she claims, implies some alternative. Sometimes people come to decision-making without recognising that alternatives exist.

Strategies for curriculum change

To some extent each curriculum change, actual and proposed, will involve a different strategy. Nevertheless, certain general approaches can be described.

1 Top-down strategy

This is involved when a curriculum change is introduced by a central body (not necessarily national government) and applied across all (or at least many) educational institutions. It corresponds to Havelock's (1973) 'Research, development and diffusion' perspective. Teachers are required to receive and to implement ideas. It can be rather costly because large-scale planning is involved. Some examples include Nuffield science schemes, the School Mathematics project, and nurse education (Project 2000 and First Wave 2001).

Study problem

Before you go any further, consider the advantages and disadvantages of the top-down strategy.

You may have included the following:

Advantages

- It can be based on thorough and extensive research.
- Dissemination of information is relatively easy.
- Large samples can be used for analysis.
- It can draw on a wide range of subject-matter expertise (not just teachers).
- Teachers may be assisted by well-produced materials.

Disadvantages

- Teachers may not be committed to it (feel it is imposed).
- It can develop a 'momentum' of its own (because of its large scale and 'vested interests').
- It assumes that similarities between schools/colleges are greater than differences.
- The corresponding organisational changes needed may not be implemented.
- It is often confined within traditional subject boundaries.
- It can be very costly.

2 Grass-roots strategy
Here the emphasis is on a decentralised approach; the curriculum change originates at the 'periphery' of the education system rather than at the centre. It involves a local response to a particular problem and is often on a small scale. The teacher often acts as both a producer and a consumer.

Study problem

Before you go any further, consider the advantages and disadvantages of the grass-roots strategy.

You may have included the following:

Advantages

- Teachers are the initiators of ideas and materials and therefore more likely to use them than if they came from outside.

- It can involve a flexible response to local needs.
- It can fairly easily be changed as needs change.
- It is less expensive.

Disadvantages

- It can be amateurish and piecemeal.
- It is not easy to coordinate.
- Research is more difficult.
- Teachers may not have the expertise required to produce and test materials.
- It may leave learners exposed to the idiosyncrasies of teachers.
- The body of knowledge concerning curriculum change that is built up cannot necessarily be applied elsewhere, and therefore it is difficult to generalise from such local experience.
- Innovative teachers may feel very isolated.

Both these strategies have considerable drawbacks as strategies for producing major curriculum change. The grass-roots approach really requires some central (or regional?) coordination if it is to result in other than many unrelated (but perhaps useful) projects. The top-down approach often encounters resistance. It has been observed that it is usually more successful when the project materials are reasonably discrete so that teachers can be selective (Nuffield science projects are examples here). Thus change occurs, but it may not be the type or extent of change that was originally intended.

3 Network support strategy
In this the focus is on the institution rather than on the project itself. At perhaps a regional level a supporting network of centres is set up. These will involve material resources and expertise which can be called upon by teams of curriculum innovators from schools.

Study problem

Before you go any further, consider the advantages and disadvantages of the network support strategy.

You may have included the following:

Advantages

- Teachers can initiate curriculum change while receiving help with the production and dissemination of materials.
- Coordination of efforts can result in mutual assistance and in the avoidance of duplication of effort.
- If the school/college is the focus of change (rather than an individual teacher or a national body) more consideration may be given to the whole curriculum rather than to change within subjects or groups of subjects.
- Research should be easier than when teachers work in isolation.

Disadvantages

- Teachers may not be able to obtain just the help they need at a particular time and place.
- The 'teacher-consultant' relationship may be difficult to establish and maintain.
- It may need complex organisation.

Abercrombi, N. and Urry, J. (1983) *Capital, Labour and the Middle Class*. London, Allen and Unwin.

Apple, M.W. (1982) *Education and Power*. London, Routledge and Kegan Paul.

Apple, M.W. (1988) 'Facing the complexity of power: for a parallel list position in critical education studies'. In M. Cole (ed), *Bowles and Gintis Revisited*. Lewes, Falmer Press.

Armitage, A., Bryant, R., Dunnill, R. *et al.* (1999) *Teaching and Training in Post-Compulsory Education*. Milton Keynes, Open University Press.

Bennis, W.G., Benne, K.D. and Chin, R. (1985) *The Planning of Change*. New York, Holt.

Bowles, S. and Gintis, H. (1976) *Schooling in Capitalist America*. New York, Basic Books.

Bruner, J.S. (1971a) *The Process of Education*. Cambridge, Massachusetts, Harvard University Press.

Bruner, J.S. (1971b) *Towards a Theory of Instruction*. Cambridge, Massachusetts, Harvard University Press.

Burgess, R.G. (1986) *Sociology, Education and Schools*. London, Batsford.

Chin, R. and Benne, K.D. (1976) 'General strategies for effecting changes in human systems'. In W.G. Bennis, K.D. Benne and R. Chin (1976) *The Planning of Change*. New York, Holt.

Cusick, P. (1973) *Inside High School*. New York, Holt, Rinehart and Winston.

Dreeben, R. (1968) *On What Is Learned in School*. Reading, Massachusetts, Addison Wesley.

Duke, C. (1992) *The Learning University*. Buckingham, Open University Press in association with the Society for Research in Higher Education.

Everhart, R.B. (1983) *Reading, Writing and Resistance*. Boston, Routledge and Kegan Paul.

Gleeson, Dennis (ed.) (1990) *Training and Its Alternatives*. London, Oxford University Press (chs 7, 8 and 11).

Goodson, I.F. and Ball, S. (1984) *Defining the Curriculum*. Lewes, Falmer Press.

Haffer, A. (1986) 'Facilitating change'. *Journal of Nursing Administration* 16 (4): 18–22.

Hammersley, M. and Hargreaves, A. (1983) *Curriculum Practice: Some Sociological Case Studies*. Lewes, Falmer Press.

Hammersley, M., Scarth, J. and Webb, S. (1984) 'Developing and testing theory: the case for research on student learning and examination'. In R. Burgess (ed.), *Issues in Educational Research: Qualitative Methods*. Lewes, Falmer Press.

Handy, C. (1990) *The Age of Unreason*. Boston, Harvard Business School Press.

Hargreaves, A. (1989) *Curriculum and Assessment Reform: Modern Educational Thought*. Milton Keynes, Open University Press.

Higham, J., Sharp, P. and Yeomans, D. (1996) *The Emerging 16–19 Curriculum*. London, Fulton.

Hirst, P. and Peters, R.S. (1970) *The Logic of Education*. London, Open University and Routledge and Kegan Paul.

Jackson, P.W. (1968) *Life in the Classroom*. New York, Holt, Rinehart and Winston.

Jones, J.E. and Woodcock, M. (1985) *Manual of Management Development*. Aldershot, Gower.

Kember, D. (2000) *Action Learning and Action Research: Improving the Quality of Teaching and Learning*. London, Kogan Page.

Kember, D. and Kelly, M. (1993) *Improving Teaching through Action Research*. Green Guide No.14. HERDSA, New South Wales.

Lawn, M. and Barton, L. (eds) (1981) *Rethinking Curriculum Studies*. London, Croom Helm.

Maccia, E.S. (1972) 'Conceptual structures for curriculum inquiry'. Paper presented at a meeting of the American Educational Research Association, Chicago, April.

McRobbie, A. (1978) 'Working-class girls and the culture of femininity'. In Women's Studies Group *Women Take Issue* London, Hutchinson.

Peters, R.S. (ed.) (1966) *Ethics and Education*. London, Allen and Unwin.

Race, P. (1989b) *Forward Thinking: How Do We Learn? Why Are You at College?* Teaching and Learning Higher Education Series 13, Aberdeen, CICED.

Robinson, J.E., Such, S, Walters, C. *et al.* (1996) 'Researching in further education: an illustrative study from Suffolk College'. In M. Young *et al.* (eds), *Colleges as Learning Organisations: The Role of Research*. Unified 16+ Curriculum Series No. 12. London, Institute of Education

Schofield, H. (1972) *The Philosophy of Education* (chs 3 and 9). London, Unwin.

Schön, D.A. (1971) *Beyond the Stable State: Public and Private Learning in a Changing Society*. New York, Norton.

Spender, D. and Spender, E. (eds) (1980) *Learning to Lose: Sexism and Education*. London, Women's Press.

Vallance, E. (1974) *Conflicting Conception of Curriculum*, Berkeley, California, McCutchan.

Wilson, J. (1969) *Thinking with Concepts*. Cambridge, Cambridge University Press.

Young, M. *et al.* (1996) *Colleges as Learning Organisations. The Role of Research*. Unified 16+ Curriculum Series No. 12. London, Institute of Education.

CURRICULUM MODELS AND DEVELOPMENTS IN ADULT EDUCATION

3

Learning outcomes

To be achieved through the process of self-directed study, teacher/mentor support and sharing learning with fellow students
By the end of this chapter you will be able to:

- discuss briefly curriculum theory
- describe the traditional curriculum models
- explain how curriculum planners can get the balance right between the product and process models
- discuss the philosophy of adult learning
- describe curriculum developments in adult courses.

CURRICULUM PROCESSES AND EFFECTS ON PLANNING

The relative importance which we attach to different aspects of the processes of curriculum planning and implementation will depend on our overall view of the nature of the curriculum and the students.

In recent years there have been some significant changes in emphasis. These include:

- a recognition of the need for change in subject content because, in a period of rapid technological change, new skills and knowledge are required
- a recognition of the need to define the content of the curriculum more precisely so that assessment procedures can be made fairer and more reliable
- a recognition of the importance of learning processes as well as learning products (i.e. teaching/learning strategies are important in their own right and not just as a means to an end)
- a greater emphasis on the active participation of the learner in the learning process (this has developed from an emphasis on classroom 'activity' to various forms of individualised learning and then to the idea of learner negotiation of the curriculum)
- a greater emphasis on the total context in which teaching and learning take place.

These changes in emphasis should not be regarded in isolation. Many college schemes were concerned with updating subject content, but in doing so they also became concerned with changes in teaching/learning strategies.

In some of the 'new' teaching and learning schemes the emphasis has shifted away from content towards learning processes, experience and the role of the learner. Also, structural and administrative changes in further and higher education have resulted in a changing context for the curriculum. An example would be the development of work-based projects.

It should be noted that the relative emphasis given in curriculum planning to factors such as content, processes, context, the role of the learner, have a number of important implications. These include philosophical problems concerning means and ends and more practical problems concerning the freedom and professionalism of teachers. Barber (1996) reminds us of the existence of traditions in curriculum theory. He refers to four.

1 The liberal-humanist tradition

The most important approach over the last two centuries has been this tradition. Barber states that exponents of this view have agreed that

> *western thought has developed a sophisticated understanding of people and the universe which they inhabit. This understanding is divided into series of disciplines, such as science and philosophy, which examine specific aspects of human experience and which have developed their own traditions and approaches to explaining the world and arriving at the true, the good and beautiful or the nearest possible approximation. (Barber 1996, p.12)*

This was a knowledge-centred curriculum based on subjects and had a powerful influence in the independent and grammar school sectors. This tradition was only suitable for the more able learner and was argued to be not sufficiently relevant to real life. Relevance in the modern world demands, among other things, knowledge and understanding of science, technology and a range of work-related skills which the liberal-humanist tradition failed to provide.

2 The progressive tradition

Dewey (1916) saw the liberal humanism as too teacher centred so he developed a middle road. This places the learner at the centre of the educational and learning process and its purpose is to unlock the potential of the learner. This tradition helps the learner to learn through discovery. Learning for the learner is an active process, and this process is as important as the outcome. It is argued that the learner learns from their own direct experience and intuition; this also fits very comfortably with the principles and theories of adult education, whereby teachers become facilitators of learning and respond to the learners' needs as they become apparent. Critics on the political right argue that this system provides no stable common course of study and that it is based on naive assumptions about learners' learning and institutions; it results in a lack of discipline. However, this tradition has played an important part in shaping education and has helped to promote confidence among learners. It has encouraged effective work in groups and creativity and indeed has influenced the debate about the National Curriculum.

3 The technocratic tradition

This approach to curriculum development assumes that the curriculum can be set down in specific objectives or outcomes. Barber (1996) argues that once established it is possible to work backwards from them and to work out how to achieve them. Assessment of learners' learning involves testing whether they have achieved the specific objectives. Many critics have suggested that this system does no more than 'ticking the boxes', which was well demonstrated in Neary's study (1996a) on continuing assessment in nurse education, where it became a bureaucratic nightmare. We are reminded (in chapter 6) that learning is not solely about outcomes. Many learners and teachers can describe learning experiences which were not planned or the objective of the original activity, which Neary (2000) calls 'the unpredictable learning outcomes' (p.136).

4 The cultural-analysis tradition

Here the chief task of the education institute is to transmit elements of a culture from one generation to the next; the curriculum is seen as a cultural artefact which emerges from a social negotiation between generations. Dewey described it as follows:

> *The first office of the social organ we call the school is to provide a simplified environment. It selects the features which are fairly fundamental and capable of being responded to by the young. Then it establishes a progressive order, using the factors first acquired as a means of gaining insight into what is more complicated ... it is the business of the school environment to eliminate so far as possible the unworthy features of the existing environment from influence upon mental habitudes ... As a society becomes more enlightened, it realises that it is responsible not to transmit and conserve the whole of its existing achievements, but only such as make for a better future society. The school is the chief agency for the accomplishment of this end.*
> *(Dewey 1916, p.20)*

The question is who decides the content of the curriculum. Is it a job for social negotiation? How will the decision be made? Will the curriculum in practice reflect the views of a particular class or group within society? Barber (1996) argues that 'if we agree with the idea of a social negotiation, involving all the relevant interests, the tough "power" questions remain' (p.15). Any negotiation over the shape of the curriculum or content is likely to be controversial. It may not be suitable or appropriate for an era of very rapid, social, economic, technological and cultural change.

Armitage *et al.* (1999) remind us of another model, i.e. instrumentalism, a curriculum delivery of a specific product such as the development of a skilled workforce. This ideology has become an increasingly important element in UK government policy. With the election of labour government in 1997 this model is at the heart of government policy. The instrumental curriculum sees knowledge in factual terms and is clearly teacher/trainer led. Learners are preparing themselves for their roles in the workplace and in society as a whole. The present government sees a highly educated workforce as essential in meeting growing international competition and values high levels of numeracy, literacy, science and technology as relevant to achieving this goal.

TWO MODELS FOR CURRICULUM DEVELOPMENT

1 The product model

This is also referred to as the behavioural objectives model. The use of behavioural objectives became widespread in the late 1960s because of:

- the vagueness of many syllabuses
- the need to specify practical skills more precisely
- the need to make assessment techniques more precise
- the influence of the ideas of behaviourism.

It should be noted that such an approach is not entirely new. Aspects of the approach, such as a tight specification of what the learner should be able to do, can be found in a few science syllabuses of the 19th century. Earlier in the 20th century there was the work of Bobbit in America. The main development of the approach began with the work of Tyler (1949). Later work (e.g. by Davies, Gronlund, Mager, etc.) appeared to satisfy an apparent need for education to become more 'technological' and precise. The theoretical work by Bloom (1965) on 'domains' of learning provided a basis for this and is very much in use today.

It is assumed that the main features of the behavioural objectives model are familiar. Of course it is important to note that there are many variations on the basic model. Consequently some curricula based on this approach are more flexible than others. This model is interested in the product of a curriculum. It is closely associated with Tyler (1949), who argued that it is the dominant model of the 20th century. Tyler organised his model around four fundamental questions, which must be answered when developing any curriculum; as part of your own learning try answering the following questions.

Study problem

1   What are the aims and objectives of the curriculum?
2   Which learning experiences meet these aims and objectives?
3   How can the extent to which these aims and objectives have been met be evaluated?
4   How can these learning experiences be organised?

Who plans, designs, develops and evaluates the curriculum?

These questions require careful thinking, including the element of needs analysis for both learners and employers, and task analysis by the curriculum planners.

The advantages of the use of behavioural objectives in curriculum planning may include:

- avoidance of vague, general statements of intent
- making assessment more precise
- helping to select and structure content

- making teachers aware of different types and levels of learning involved in particular subjects
- guidance for teachers and learners about skills to be mastered.

However, the behavioural objectives approach has encountered considerable criticism. For details of this see for example the work of Eisner (1969), MacDonald-Ross (1973) and Wesson (1983), and chapters 5 and 6 of this book. Among the possible drawbacks are:

- At 'lower levels' behavioural objectives may become trite and unnecessary.
- It is difficult to write satisfactory behavioural objectives for 'higher levels' of learning (even in science and technology).
- The 'affective domain' cannot be considered adequately in terms of specific behaviours.
- The 'affective domain' cannot be assessed adequately.
- Behavioural objectives will discourage 'creativity' on the part of both learner and teacher.
- Behavioural objectives are 'undemocratic' in that they aim to make the result of learning predetermined by outside control.
- Use of behavioural objectives may imply a false division between 'cognitive', 'effective' and 'psychomotor' domains.

But the most serious criticism levelled against the use of behavioural objectives is that such an approach to curriculum planning will inevitably enshrine the psychology, and indeed the philosophy, of behaviourism (associated particularly with Skinner). To many people behaviourism is an unacceptable view of human nature. The curriculum is too subject and examination bound.

Further reading and reflection will show that there are strong arguments for and against the use of this approach. It may be argued that an intermediate position can be adopted in which the psychology and philosophy of behaviourism are rejected but in which some use is made of objectives in, for example, the planning of practical lessons.

2 The process model

This is seen by several writers as an alternative to the behavioural objectives model. According to Stenhouse (1975) the issue is 'can curriculum and pedagogy be organised satisfactorily by a logic other than that of the means-end model?' (p.26).

As its name suggests the process model focuses on:

- teacher activities (and therefore the teacher's role)
- student and learner activities (perhaps the most important feature)
- the conditions in which the learning takes place.

Study problem

On your own, focus on your own curriculum and list your role as (1) a teacher, (2) a learner in a process model.

In defining the nature of the learning experiences, rather than the specific learning outcomes to be achieved from them, the process model appears to emphasise means rather than ends. However, it can be argued that prescription of learning activities provides the appropriate means of achieving the broad intentions of the curriculum.

Such an approach to curriculum planning may well lead to the idea that, if learning activities are more important than prescribed content, the learner should have a part in deciding the nature of those activities (see the section on the negotiated curriculum, chapter 5, pp.111–15). It also leads to a more individualised atmosphere in which it is assumed that the learner makes a unique response to learning experiences.

At present the process model is mainly associated with curricula designed to teach social and life skills. However, it could be argued that, because all education should be concerned with social and life skills, on these grounds alone the process model has a contribution to make in other subject areas.

Among the advantages of the model are:

- the emphasis on the active roles of teachers and learners
- the emphasis on learning skills
- the emphasis on certain activities as important in themselves and for 'life'.

Possible disadvantages include:

- the neglect of considerations of appropriate content
- difficulty in applying the approach in some areas.

Bruner (1971a) stated that knowledge is a process not a product, and went on to claim that curriculum content lies in the structure of the field of knowledge, and the subject matter to be taught is worth knowing and is usable beyond the situation which it is taught. Neary (1996a) suggested that the process model leads to both professional and personal development of autonomous practitioners and encourages lifelong learning.

Raht (1971) suggested the following criteria for a process model of the curriculum.

1 opportunities for the learners to make informed choices and be allowed to reflect on the consequences of their choice
the assignment of active rather than passive learning roles
3 the engagement of learners in the inquiry into ideas, and application of intellectual processes, or current problem, either personal or social
4 the involvement of learners with real objects and models
5 the involvement of learners in activities that may be completed successfully by learners at several different levels of ability
6 the involvement of learners in examining a new setting, an idea, an application of an intellectual process, or a current problem which has been previously studied
7 the examining of topics or issues that citizens in our society do not normally examine and that are typically ignored by the major communication media
8 risk-taking, not of life or limb but the risk of success or failure
9 the rewriting, rehearsing and polishing of initial efforts
10 the application and mastery of meaningful rules, standards, or disciplines

11 the opportunity to share with others' planning, the implementation of a plan, or the results of an activity.

This list of criteria alters fundamentally the traditional learner–teacher relationship and traditional climate that exists within classrooms, as it moves from the classical approach to teaching and learning to one which encourages independence and responsibility and concentrates on learning rather than teaching. This leads us into the examination of the role of the teacher in relation to the process model, i.e. the facilitator.

Teacher v. facilitator

The process model calls for learner-centred education (see Figure 3.1) based on active discovery, in contrast to the essentially passive, conformist, 'accumulation of stored knowledge'. The humanist approach to education marked out by Roberts and Norman (1990) place emphasis on feeling and thinking, on the recognition and importance of a learner's personal values, on interpersonal communication, and on the development of 'positive self-concepts'. Therefore the aim of the teacher (educationalist) should be 'the fully functioning person ... a person who is dependable in being realistic, self-enhancing, socialised and appropriate in his behaviour ... a person who is ever changing, ever developing, always discovering himself and the newness in himself ...' The outstanding quality of the successful teacher is empathy – the ability to see someone else's problems through one's own eyes, and to communicate that understanding with clarity and ease.

The teacher needs to be aware of the personality differences in their learners. For example, is one learner more suited to the Syllabus-Bound (SYLBS) classification and another more in tune with the Syllabus-Free (SYLFS) classification? The terms are largely self-explanatory. SYLBS learners tend to accept the system, are very much examination orientated and like to know exactly what is required of them in assignments. SYLFS learners by

Teacher	Facilitator	**Figure 3.1**
Focuses on teaching	Focuses on learning	Characteristics of a teacher and facilitator
Teacher centred	Student centred	
Control	Sharing	
Superior–subordinate relationships	Partnership	
Director	Participant	
Knowledge given	Knowledge available	
Treats all the same	Perceives individual learning needs	
Focuses on groups	Focuses on individual	
Closed learning environment	Open learning	
Controls parameters of learning	Lets learner set parameters	
Narrow horizon	Wider horizon	

Skills required of a facilitator

1 Identifying learning needs and styles of students
2 Devising coping strategies for dealing with mixed-ability classes
3 Devising methods of assessing how much learning has taken place
4 Devising remedial methods for lack of learning and extra learning for those who want more
5 Techniques for teaching in small groups or one to one
6 Role change from paternalistic to partnership

contrast find the confines of the syllabus very limiting and wish to explore much more widely. They are happy to find things out for themselves and take responsibility for learning. Rowntree (1981) called this a methodology-oriented course, and it fits very comfortably with the principles of adult teaching and learning.

Assessments in a process model

In the process model, everything is directed at improving the process of learning, and even assessment plays a central role in this. Instead of appearing at the end of the learning process, merely as a check on the success, it becomes part of the process, appearing at all points during the programme, and is thus used to feed back helpful information to the learners as they go along (diagnostic and formative assessments). This also has a major significance for attendance patterns. The contract sessions offered in the process model are designed to offer vital processes and experiences for which no amount of reading or note-copying would be a proper substitute. Learners' attendance at a process course has therefore to be more extensive than at a course based on the product model. Models of assessment that fit comfortably in a process model are contract assignments, learning contracts and continuous assessments. Here the teacher is cast in the role of critical appraiser of the learners' work, with the emphasis on developing self-appraisal and self-assessment in the learners (Neary 1998 and 1996a).

Stenhouse (1975) states that 'the worthwhile activity in which teacher and learner are engaged has standards and criteria in it and the task of appraisal is that of improving learners' capacity to work to such criteria by critical reaction to work done. In this sense, assessment is about the teaching of self-assessment' (p.95).

Use of terms

While it is important to consider the relative merits and drawbacks of various approaches to curriculum planning it is also important to avoid using terms such as 'process' and 'product' as mere slogans. The commonsense view that both are important should not be lightly discarded. 'Ends' and 'means' are inextricably linked and especially in adult education. It is argued by some that the process model fits comfortably with the concept of andragogy (see the box below). In the sphere of adult learning however there are many authors who are opposed to this concept.

The andragogical model

1 The need to know   Adults adopt a more questioning approach.
2 Learner's self-concept   Adults are responsible for all of their actions.
3 Learner's experience   Adults have a greater range of life experiences to bring to the learning environment.
4 Readiness to learn   Adults learn because they wish to. Internal locus of control.
5 Orientation to learn   Adults are life centred in their orientation to learn.
6 Motivation   Adults are generally internally motivated

Adapted from Knowles (1980) and Darbyshire (1993)

THE ANDRAGOGY/PEDAGOGY DEBATE

If we are to develop a curriculum for adults, we need to understand the concept of adult learning. Andragogy is defined as 'the theory and practice of the education of adults' (Knowles 1980, p.43). Authors such as Knowles draw strict distinctions between the way children and adults learn. However, there are others who are less purist and suggest that both children and adults respond better to a more eclectic approach with styles associated with both pedagogy and andragogy. The andradogy/pedagogy debate continues to fuel much discussion

Knowles believes that adults are different from children in three important areas – biologically, legally and psychologically. These differences impact on the way they learn.

Darbyshire (1993) believes there is little or no evidence to support the stark differences between the way adults and children learn as stated by Knowles. The term adult has been used to describe a whole range of people aged from 16 upward. Generalisations can be very dangerous as individuals need very different support and therefore some will respond to a pedagogical approach and others to an andragogical approach. A 40-year-old learner may need a very structured pedagogical approach even though they are classified as an adult learner. Likewise a teenager may respond better to an andragogical style of teaching where they are studying more independently. This idea is supported by Huddleston and Unwin (1997). Children working on school projects are often self-directed and enthusiastic; this refutes the andragogy/pedagogy debate.

Andragogy relies on the learner engaging in self-directed learning. There is no guarantee that this will occur, and some learners respond better to a more structured format no matter what their age.

Burnard (1996) suggests that andragogy principles apply more to employed adults. Those who are unemployed may be more motivated by external factors to learn. This suggests that there may be social class implications. It could also be argued that in the current employment market where there is increasing uncertainty employed adults may also learn in response to external motivators.

Milligan (1995) suggests that the andragogical approach uses a range of teaching styles, such as group work, problem-solving activities, discussion and experiential learning; all of these methods are expensive in terms of staff, equipment and resources. These teaching styles may be difficult to adopt when teaching large numbers of learners. A session involving open discussion and disclosure of personal details requires the learners to feel comfortable with the group; if they are not the learning could be unsuccessful. This again requires small numbers to be most effective. The small group-size issue has been cited as a limitation of andragogy by Boud (1981). As learner numbers increase the ability to use small groups is reduced. Learners may perceive the abdication of the educator. Some learners wish to be taught by the educator rather than adopt a more active problem-solving approach (Neary 2000).

Some institutions and learners maintain a culture of authoritarian dictatorship. This approach relies upon the educator teaching from the front with very little interaction from the learners. This is not synonymous with an

Figure 3.2

A comparison of the assumptions of pedagogy and andragogy

	Pedagogy	Andragogy
Concept of the learner	The role of the learner is, by definition, a dependent one. The teacher is expected by society to take full responsibility for determining what is learned, how it is to be learned, and if it has been learned.	It is a normal aspect of the process of maturation for a person to move from dependency towards increasing self-directedness but at different rates for different people and in different dimensions of life. Teachers have a responsibility to encourage and nurture this movement. Adults have a deep psychological need to be generally self-directing, although they may be dependent in particular temporary situations.
Role of learners' experience	The experience learners bring to a learning situation is of little worth. It may be used as a starting point, but the experience from which learners will gain the most is that of the teacher, the textbook writer, the audio-visual aid producer, and other experts. Accordingly, the primary techniques in education are transmittal techniques – lecture, assigned reading, audio-visual presentations.	As people grow and develop they accumulate an increasing reservoir of experience that becomes an increasingly rich resource for learning for themselves and for others. Furthermore, people attach more meaning to learning they gain from experience than to leaning they acquire positively. Accordingly, the primary techniques in education are experiential techniques – laboratory experiments, discussion, problem-solving cases, simulation exercises, field experience and the like.
Readiness to learn	People are ready to learn whatever society (especially the school) says they ought to learn, provided the pressures on them (such as fear of failure) are great enough. Most people of the same age are ready to learn the same things. Therefore, learning should be organised into a fairly standardised curriculum, with a uniform step-by-step progression for all learners.	People become ready to learn something when they experience a need to learn in order to cope more satisfyingly with real-life tasks or problems. The educator has a responsibility to create conditions and provide tools and procedures for helping learners discover their 'needs to know'. Learning programmes would be organised around life application categories and sequenced according to the learner's readiness to learn.
Orientation to learning	Learners see education as a process of acquiring subject-matter content, most of which they understand will be useful only at a later time in life. Accordingly the curriculum should be organised into subject-matter units (e.g. courses) which follow the logic of the subject (e.g. from ancient to modern history, from simple to complex mathematics or science). People are subject centred in their orientation to learning.	Study problem (see p.67).

andragogical approach. Many law and medicine degree courses still adopt this style of teaching, yet all of these learners are adults.

Some educators may feel threatened by the fact that some control is relinquished and that responses cannot be anticipated from the learners. (See Figure 3.2 for a comparison of assumptions.)

Study problem

On your own or with a fellow student, read carefully all the completed boxes in Figure 3.2 and using the principles of andragogy fill in the blank box. Once you have done this discuss the outcome of your work with other like-minded friends.

The use of a purist andragogical approach may be detrimental to some learners who have not developed an abstract learning style. This would be particularly relevant for individuals who have learning difficulties. The concept of andragogy was developed in America and is therefore based upon American culture. There is potential for problems to occur when the andragogical approach is used in a different culture. The language does not translate comfortably across cultures.

As Havinghurst and Orr (1956) conclude,

People do not launch themselves into adulthood with the momentum of their childhood and youth and simply coast along to old age. Adulthood has its transition points and its crises. It is a developmental period in almost as complete a sense as childhood and adolescence are developmental periods.

FACTORS IN CURRICULUM DEVELOPMENT

As we have seen, many new curricula involve a greater emphasis on teaching/learning activities than on specification of detailed content. However, in many subject areas the selection and structuring of content is still regarded as important. In 'traditional' curricula there is a tendency to assume that what is to be taught is self-evident and that the sequencing of the content is dependent on the logical structure of the subject matter. This may be true of some scientific and technological subjects.

Even within these subjects, however, there are arguments for pursuing a psychological rather than a logical approach. This involves starting with the learners' interests and working back (or down) to the underlying logical structure of the subject. Basic concepts are often highly abstract and difficult; learners' early interests often lie in obvious applications of the subject. In science teaching this is not an easy problem to resolve (for example, in chemistry 'real life' substances such as wood or glass have very complex structures). Learning the 'language' of the science or technology is another aspect of this problem of where we should start.

According to Dewey (1916), 'The logical (or scientific) order is an ideal to be achieved not a starting point from which to set out' (p.10).

TEACHING METHODS AND STRATEGIES

Many curriculum planners and developers have asked me if they should include teaching methods and strategies in their planning. My advice to them is always to include these as a guideline which will help teachers to make an informed, rational and logical choice about the teaching strategies they may employ when implementing the curriculum for their specialist subject area. The following strategies and methods are more appropriate to helping adults to learn because these methods also offer teacher support and encourage self-assessment. It is not my intention to go into detail about the everyday teaching strategies that most experienced teachers use in their day-to-day teaching, such as chalk and talk and lecturing. We know these better as didactic methods.

Didactic methods

Many teachers resort to the use of didactic methods simply because they perceive these methods as being the best way to 'teach' a curriculum rigidly imposed by an examining board or other outside agency. Learners are expected to learn precisely what the teacher transmits and later to regurgitate the knowledge in their examination booklets; this method results in an examination-bound curriculum, where learners have very little understanding of what they repeat and soon forget once the examination is over. We refer to this as rote learning.

Socratic method

A series of carefully planned questions are asked by the teacher with the intention of leading learners towards the statement of a principle or truth, a conclusion. This is a problem-solving or decision-making approach to learning, using step-by-step questioning. Searching questions that encourage insight, contemplation and active and creative participation by all, are more valuable than simple closed (yes/no) questions which do not challenge the learners intellectually. It is argued that this method is more suited to adult learners.

Facilitative methods

As discussed on page 63 (see the section 'Teacher v. facilitator'), these methods are learner centred and are designed to encourage a high level of participation, with learners accepting considerable responsibility for their individual learning outcomes, which is at the heart of the principles of adult learning.

Choosing appropriate teaching methods

Differences between groups of learners and their learning characteristics affect the choice of teaching and learning methods to be employed. The curriculum planner/developer and the teacher (who may well be the same person on the curriculum planning team) need to be familiar with each of the above methods and carefully select the one that will benefit the learner's learning outcome without restricting the classroom teacher's preferred option.

Teachers are responsible for the management of teaching and learning and for the deployment of resources (which will also be considered by the curriculum planning team) to the best effect. In judging the appropriateness of methods the curriculum planners and teachers need also to consider task analysis.

Task analysis

The techniques of task analysis are guided in military and industrial training; they are particularly useful when planning how to teach people to carry out repetitive tasks in circumstances where there are clear-cut criteria as to whether or not the task has been adequately performed. Curriculum planners need to complete this process. Critical-incident analysis may be needed to help decide which tasks are really important enough to be worth incorporating into the curriculum and for teaching. The process of task analysis is reasonably simple: you analyse the content carefully, and break it down into the set of fairly minute substeps which need to be followed in order to ensure success. As a result this form of analysis should enable the curriculum team to decide on a suitable sequence of events throughout the planning and development of the curriculum.

Study problem

Task analysis helps us to produce quality courses. As an exercise in task analysis consider the following:

1 The learners: Who are they?
2 The resources: What resources are actually available?
3 The programme: What is on offer to the learners?
4 The profession/vocation which the learners are entering: Are there external requirements from professional bodies (e.g. nursing, law, teaching, etc.)?
5 The assessments/examination methods: Are these reflected in the teaching methods?
6 The curriculum model itself (see Figure 3.3): Which model is being used?

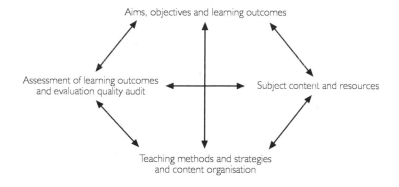

Figure 3.3

A curriculum model for modern courses

New approaches to teaching and learning

Strategies which meet all of the above examples of a curriculum model can be found in the approaches to teaching and learning listed below, which move away from the more traditional methods. These are seen as appropriate for adult learners, and curriculum planners can incorporate them into their curriculum model. However, most curriculum planners aim to get the right balance between 'product' and 'process', often resulting in an eclectic model.

- Learning contracts and contract assignments
- Becoming a reflective practitioner
- Mentorships
- Experiential learning
- Learning/professional journals

These new approaches are considered in more detail in chapter 4.

FURTHER READING

Curzon, L.B. (1997) *Teaching in Further Education: An Outline of Principles and Practice* (5th edition). London, Cassell.

Darbyshire, P. (1993) 'In defence of pedagogy: a critique of the notion of andragogy'. *Nurse Education Today* 13: 328–35.

Havinghurst, R.J. and Orr, B. (1956) *Adult Education and Adult Needs.* Boston, Centre for the Study of Liberal Education for Adults..

Jarvis, P. (1995) *Adult and Continuing Education: Theory and Practice* (2nd edition) London, Routledge.

Knowles, M.S. (1990) *The Adult Learner: A Neglected Species* (4th edition). Houston, Texas, Gulf Publishing.

Knowles M.S. (1980) *The Modern Practice of Adult Education, from Pedagogy to Andragogy.* Cambridge, Adult Education Company New York.

Linderman, E.C. (1926) *The Meaning of Adult Education.* New York, New Republic. Republished in 1989 by Oklahoma Research Centre for Continuing Professional and Higher Education.

Neary, M. (2000) *Teaching, Assessing and Evaluation for Clinical Competence: A Practical Guide for Teachers and Practitioners.* Cheltenham, Stanley Thornes.

Nottingham Andragogy Group (1983) *Towards a Developmental Theory of Andragogy.* University of Nottingham Department of Adult Education.

Reece, L. and Walker, S. (1992) *Teaching, Training and Learning: A Practical Guide.* Sunderland, Business Education Publishers.

Taylor, P. (1993) *The Texts of Paulo Freire.* Buckingham: Open University Press.

Teenant, M. (1996) *Psychology and Adult Learning.* London, Routledge.

Walklin, L. (1990) *Teaching and Learning in Further and Adult Education.* Cheltenham, Stanley Thornes.

4

Learning outcomes

To be achieved through the process of self-directed study, teacher/mentor support and sharing learning with fellow students

By the end of this chapter you will be able to:

- analyse flexible approaches to teaching and learning for adult learners
- describe the processes of using learning contracts and contract assignments, case studies, experiential learning and learning journals
- discuss the importance of becoming a reflective practitioner
- discuss the role of mentors in creating a learning environment
- describe how the above processes can be incorporated into the curriculum and lesson plan.

LEARNING CONTRACTS AND CONTRACT ASSIGNMENTS

A learning contract can be described as an individualised learning plan that has been negotiated between the personal tutor and the learner. A contract assignment is an agreed/negotiated project that is an extension of the learning contract; this assignment forms part of the continuous assessment and is both formatively and summatively assessed. Learning contracts and contract assignments can, if carefully negotiated between learner, mentor and personal tutor, fulfil the learning needs of adult learners.

The term 'contract' is a familiar one: in our adult lives we frequently enter into a contract. A contract binds two (or more) people in an agreement to carry out specific behaviours, usually within a certain period of time. It is essential before signing a contract that all parties are in agreement about goals and have a clear understanding of responsibilities of each participant. Contracts can often be renegotiated when the situation of either party alters the ability to meet commitments. These facets of a contract apply equally to learning contracts.

The process of negotiation in designing the learning contract is crucial and is known as 'contracting'. Neary (1998) suggested that the contract should be a document drawn up by the teacher and the learner in which they specify what the learner will learn, how this will be achieved, within what time span and the criteria for measuring the success of the venture. Contract assignments are an integral part of a learning contract, continuous assessment and adult learning, and should be made explicit (Neary 1992a).

We are concerned with the education and training of adults; thus the processes used should be based on andragogical principles (i.e. should be learner centred and self-directed) rather than pedagogical principles (i.e. teacher centred, as in the teaching of children) (see chapter 3). There is evidence that what adults learn on their own initiative they learn more perma-nently than what they learn by being taught (Rogers 1983; Neary 1998). Psychological research shows that a characteristic of adults is the need and capacity to be self-directed. The use of contract assignments could be a means of reconciling the requirements imposed by the present structure of adult education and the learners' need to be self-directing. However, having assumed that our (adult) learners will be mainly self-directing learners we must of course remember that there will still be some variation in their learning styles.

Freedom to learn

The use of contract assignments provides an individually negotiated degree of support and freedom and thus caters for these variations, without losing the obvious benefit to the learners of developing the ability to direct their own learning. This flexibility was discussed by Boud (1981), in relation to learning contracts, who found that some adult learners will be happier with informal discussion whilst others may prefer a more structured approach, and that the learning contract may therefore be used to create a climate of informality and ease, or to support a framework for procedure with clearly defined roles and responsibilities. Studies over the last ten years (O'Neill *et al.*1993; Davies *et al.*1994; Jowett 1995; Neary 1996a and 1998) have shown that the assessment and evaluation of this form of learning must therefore be through contract assignments and negotiated assessments.

Theory/practice gap

There is much concern about the theory/practice gap in professional education and many attempts are being made to bridge this gap. For example in nurse education we have seen the development of new 'learner support' roles such as joint appointments, preceptors, mentor/clinical facilitator roles and, most recently, practice educators. In teacher training (PGCE) we have seen the development of both college mentors and subject mentors (see Appendix 2). Contract assignments are used as a bridge between the college academic input and practice placements (see Figure 4.1), particularly in the use of projects related to teaching practice (scenario-based critical-incident analysis or activ-

Figure 4.1

Curriculum design

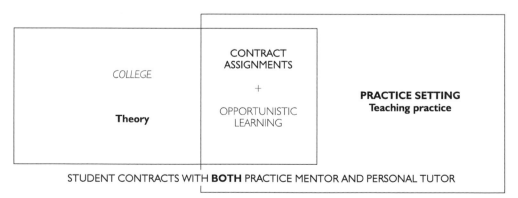

STUDENT CONTRACTS WITH **BOTH** PRACTICE MENTOR AND PERSONAL TUTOR

The end product is an integrated project which is continually assessed at various stages
Therefore FORMATIVE ASSESSMENT
The completed assignment = summative

ities), as the shared 'plan of learning' (learning contract + opportunistic learning) (see Figures 4.2 and 4.3) and the shared accountability for learning between mentor, learner and teachers would enhance communication and give written clarity to the 'practice based on theory' concept of the practicum.

Handing over control of learning

The use of learning contracts and contract assignments requires the handing over of the control of learning to the learner; this challenges the basic assumption underlying the traditional approach to professional education and thus some antagonism, and resistance to the idea, has to be expected.

Neary (1992a) argued that contract assignments, when an integral part of learning contracts and continuous assessment, shift power and control over to the learner, helping them towards independence, while Keyzer (1986) argued that 'learning contracts are explicit of the social distribution of power and the principles of social control in the educational establishment and, therefore, in the relationships held by learners and teachers in the learning programme' (p.104).

Curriculum planners need to remember that any learning and assessment programme is based on an unequal distribution of power which is initially accepted by both parties as a matter of necessity. In order to modify these power relationships in a changing assessment strategy, the first task is to identify the nature of this uneven relationship and the changes which are likely to occur as the learner is, for example, gradually directed to independence. The rate of such change might be slow at first, quickening later as confidence, experience and autonomy increase, although it need not be consistent and there are times when learners might need to be 'reeled in'. Such contingencies need to be incorporated into the design of any scheme. Many mentors or assessors take for granted their position of power in their assessment relationship with learner teachers. A particularly interesting finding of Neary's (1996b) study was the extent to which the 'taken for granted' has become explicit at early stages of the process, as the assessor sought to confirm their expertise and establish the subordination of the learner in power terms. Changes in power dynamics occur as learners move from novice to expert and to varying degrees of autonomy. Appreciating such changing power relations is the key to the design and development of contract assignments (for an example of a contract assignment see Neary 1998).

This kind of relationship can be problematic, especially in educational institutions (and they do exist) where learners are actively discouraged from questioning the 'facts' and are not taught to argue logically or to substantiate argument. These may be seen as attempts by teachers and assessors to retain power, and they have been a source of much criticism in adult education for many years. However, with the introduction of the recent education reforms and teachers becoming more confident, this is becoming a thing of the past – hopefully!

In the context of contract assignments, both the intentions and the interpretations of the mentor/assessor are intended to be made explicit. The criteria for contract assignments need to be balanced explicitly, taking into account factors which include getting to know learners better in order to diagnose their strengths and weaknesses (formative assessment), helping to recognise learning

Figure 4.2

Unit of competence from a Health and Social Care module

STANDARD OF PERFORMANCE STATEMENT: UNDER THE SUPERVISION OF A SKILLED PRACTITIONER.

Nature: Continuous assessment

Elements of competence	Related performance criteria	Date	Signature of student	Self-assessment comments	Signature of assessor	Comments
a. The recognition of common factors which affect physical, mental and social well-being of patients/clients. b. The use of appropriate communication skills to develop relationships with patients/clients, their families and friends.	1. Identifies the documents used to record the psychosocial and/or nursing/medical history of an individual. 2. Recognizes factors which contribute to the physical, mental and social well-being of a patient/client. 3. Identifies those factors which adversely affect the individual's health and well-being. 4. Discusses the effects of an altered level of functioning on an individual's role in the family unit. 5. Discusses the strategies used to assist the individual to cope with his/her altered level of functioning.					

CONTRACT ASSIGNMENT

Focus: Individualise patient/client study

To demonstrate their ability to apply theory to practice, the learner will produce an assignment on patient/client profile.

needs, and activities which help others to be better informed about the learner at the end of a set period of learning and achievement (summative assessment). The use of contract assignments is advocated by Neary (1992a and 1998) as an integral part of continuous assessment, as depicted in Figures 4.4 and 4.5. Continuous assessment can help to provide the mentor and assessor with the basis for adjusting their teaching and assessing tactics according to how a learner is developing; within this process contract assignments can, at best, provide learners with immediate feedback on their strengths and weaknesses in relation to specific requirements, and fit comfortably within the principles of responsive assessments (Neary 2000) (i.e. teaching, learning and assessing learners' competence in a situational context, such as classroom teaching practice, fieldwork, etc.). Contract assignments can also be used to help to link theory to practice (see the example from a Health and Social Care module in Figure 4.2).

Study problem

Having been introduced to the concept of contract assignments:

1   Formulate your own definition of what a contract assignment is.
2   Explain what a contract assignment is not (the definitions in the box below may help).

Learning contracts and contract assignments are:

- documents drawn up by the learners and their personal tutor or mentor, which specify what the learners will learn, how this will be accomplished, within what period of time and what the criteria of the evaluation will be
- written agreements between the concerned parties, which identify the nature of the relationship held, the expectations each individual can have of the other, the time period covered by the contract, the means whereby success can be identified and the way in which the contract is to be terminated
- explicit statements of the social distribution of power and the principles of social control in the educational establishment and, therefore, in the relationships held by learner, teacher and mentor in the learning programme.

The learning contract is extended to become a contract assignment by agreeing and negotiating an assignment which will be assessed.

Learning contracts lie along a continuum, with teacher/mentor-controlled and initiated at one end and learner-initiated and controlled at the other end. In between these two extremes lie a host of contracts which represent the degrees of power sharing negotiated by the teacher and the learner.

These contracts are not a means of negating our accountability and responsibility as a teacher or mentor, nor are they a means of keeping learners dependent on our knowledge and expertise.

Note: A written agreement can be used to formalise the contract and become part of a learner's portfolio and profile and a record of learner progress.

Study problem

Take time out and try to relate the process of using learning contracts and contract assignments to your own profession.

Study problem

Before you go any further, write down what you think learning contracts and contract assignments provide.

What learning contracts and contract assignments provide

1   The safety for learners to make decisions about their learning within the boundaries set by the curriculum framework and objectives
2   The opportunity for teachers and learners to utilise the individual's internal motivation to learn and/or change
3   A framework for supporting learners who may fail to do well because of their unstructured approach to learning
4   A vehicle by which the external needs of the organisation and the internal needs of the individual can be met
5   A means for identifying the individual's preferred learning styles
6   A means whereby the pace of learning can be adjusted to the needs of the individual
7   A vehicle for integrating theory and practice (this is extremely important for practice-based professions/occupations)
8   The basic unit for auditing the learning programme and the identification of performance indicators:
    - learners
    - teachers
    - programme
9   Contract assignments can also be used as a vehicle to
    - identify gaps in learning with reference to learning opportunities available in practice settings
    - identify new learning that learners want to achieve
    - identify learning needs to make links with previous experience and learning
    - develop a learning portfolio/journal and reflective journal.

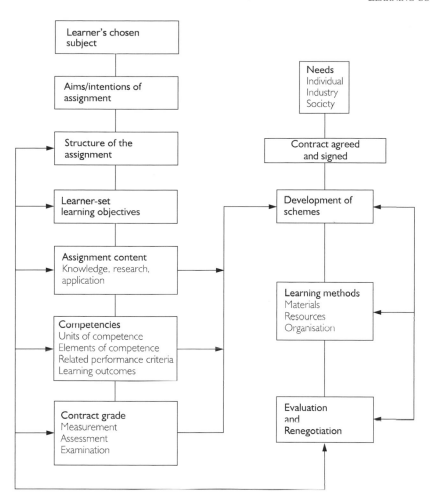

Figure 4.3

The process of contract assignment

Contract assignment steps and progression

Contract assignment is a criteria-based assessment, therefore the criteria for pass/fail must be clearly stated.

The flow chart in Figure 4.3 demonstrates the process of contract assignment and helps to give structure and guidance for planning. Figure 4.4 shows the status of contract assignments within continuous assessment and suggests the strategy for competence to be achieved. The data from Neary's study (1996a) suggests that the way forward may best be achieved in developing a scheme which assesses the learner's professional and personal growth through teaching, learning and evaluation, which becomes an integral part of learning contracts which can be incorporated into the curriculum. Figure 4.5 gives an example of assessment criteria.

Review of learning contracts and contract assignments

It is important to review learning contracts and contract assignments at regular intervals to ensure that they are meeting their objectives. The following questions may help to serve as a focus for the review process.

Figure 4.4

Contract assignments, an integral part of continuous assessment

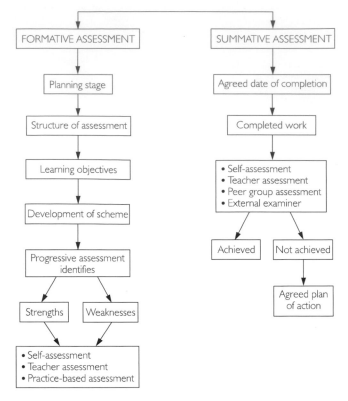

ASSESSMENT STATUS

Formative assessment: During the planning and progressive stages, learner will be assessed by clinical mentor and personal tutor

Summative assessment: Learner-completed project is assessed and agreed status given, i.e. pass/fail

Review of learning contracts and contract assignments: guidelines for practitioners, teachers and learners

1   Are the learning outcomes clear, understandable and realistic? Do they describe what the learner proposes to learn?
2   Are there any other outcomes which should be considered?
3   Do the learning strategies seem reasonable, appropriate and efficient?
4   Are there other strategies or resources which could be utilised?
5   Does the evidence of accomplishment seem relevant to the various outcomes and is it convincing?
6   Is there other evidence that could be sought?
7   Are the criteria and means for validating the evidence clear, relevant and convincing?
8   Are there other ways of validating the evidence that should be considered?
9   Are the key factors and 'dynamics' explicit in the curriculum? (see Figure 4.6).

CONTRACT ASSIGNMENT

Criteria checklist

Within the scope of the assignment, the student has/has not demonstrated:

1. an understanding of the chosen area
2. evidence of familiarity with relevant literature
3. an ability to use resources
4. an ability to present an argument, supported with wider reading
5. skills of analysis, synthesis and evaluation
6. good writing skills, consistent referencing and an accurate bibliography
7. academically sound arguments
8. that they have met their own stated and agreed objectives.

(**Tutors:** Tick words or phrases above to show which criteria have been met satisfactorily and circle words or phrases to show those criteria which have not been met satisfactorily. Use the space below to expand on these.

Taking into account the criteria, and in relation to comments made, this assignment is judged to be SATISFACTORY/UNSATISFACTORY.

Signed . . . . (Tutor) . . . .(Date)

Figure 4.5

A negotiated contract assignment

Study problem

In order to give structure to contract assignments it is useful and helpful to have a 'Contract Form' on which you and your learners can agree the following:

- aims of assignment
- rationale for study
- learning outcomes/learning objectives
- resources to be used
- dates agreed to meet learner, etc.
- criteria for success.

Have a go! Choose your own specialist area of practice, design your own form and then compare it with the two example contract forms in Figures 4.7 and 4.8.

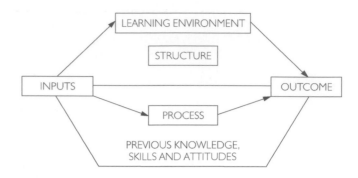

Figure 4.6

Educational courses: key factors and dynamics

Inputs
Subject content
Skills (from human and inanimate sources)
Meaningful experiences
Cultural issues
Opportunistic learning

Processes
Perceptions
Conceptualisations
Cognitive strategies
Emotional experiences
Motivation
Attitudes and values
Formative skill learning

Outcomes
Personal growth
  • increased knowledge
  • enhanced skills
Change in behaviour
Change in values
Maintenance of motivation
Academic credibility
Competent professional
  practitioners

USE OF CASE STUDIES

'Case studies' have been a part of the assessment of learners for some years at many colleges, and with a dynamic examination system and a move towards continuous assessment in most colleges, the use of this type of project is likely to increase even further. There has been frequent, informal discussion regarding the actual learning which takes place during the production and on completion of these case studies. There can be lack of creativity in the finished products, and much of the information gathered and presented is not highly relevant to the development of the learner's understanding of theory and practice. The case-study format is fairly prescriptive in its requirements and many learners put a lot of effort into producing what they perceive the teacher wants, with relatively minimal educational gain for themselves (Neary 1996a).

There are benefits inherent in the learner using case studies when studying 'real life' situations, and these benefits could be enhanced by the use of a contract assignment which enables flexibility, encourages critical analysis and allows the learner to offer intelligent (research-based) alternatives, and can be extended to become part of a practice portfolio to demonstrate a learner's 'fitness for practice' in professions such as teaching, law, nursing, etc.

Confusion and ambiguity appears to exist for learners undertaking the case study, related to what is expected from them and what they can gain from the study. Use of a contract assignment would ensure that both the learner and their personal tutor or practitioner (mentor) would agree the aims of the study, the learning outcomes, and the self- and tutor/mentor-assessment criteria; thus there would be clarity of expectations and the freedom for the learner to direct their own learning within their own contracted framework.

Figure 4.7

Example of a learning contract

CONTRACT

This is a contract signed between:

. . . . Learner

. . . . Tutor/Named Practitioner

It is agreed that . . . . Student
will undertake the professional educational study on:

. . . . (title of study)

STAGE 1   The aim of the project is:

. . . .
. . . .
. . . .
. . . .

STAGE 2   The detailed objectives are:

. . . .
. . . .
. . . .
. . . .

STAGE 3   In order to achieve the above aims and objectives, the
learner undertakes to do the following:
  (a) Identify the rationale for the above study
  (b) Identify the resources needed to complete the study
  (c) Show how this study has helped you to integrate theory
  and practice.

STAGE 4   The following resources, people and organisations will be
involved:

. . . .
. . . .
. . . .
. . . .

STAGE 5   It is agreed that the study will be assessed and evaluated by
self/the tutor/mentor/peer group in the following manner:

. . . .
. . . .
. . . .
. . . .

Figure 4.7

Continued

STAGE 6   It is considered that the work involved is suitable to be accomplished in the term period

Year 1	Year 2	Year 3

✓ tick the appropriate box

STAGE 7   The end product will be delivered to the personal tutor or mentor by the following date: . . . .
Exact dates to be negotiated with your tutors.

Signed this . . . . Day of 2002

By: . . . . (Learner)

By: . . . . (Tutor/Named Practitioner/Mentor)

THIS CONTRACT SHOULD BE RETAINED AND RETURNED WITH YOUR COMPLETED PROJECT.

Note: At each stage learners and significant others negotiate and renegotiate the outcomes. Mentors/assessors are encouraged to give feedback at the various stages of the contract process.

Figure 4.8

Example of an educational proposal

EDUCATIONAL PROPOSAL

First Meeting: Stage 1

This is an educational proposal signed between:

. . . . (Learner)

. . . . (Tutor)

It is agreed that . . . . (Learner)
will undertake the professional educational project outlined below.

Working title: . . . .
• The aim for the project is: . . . .

. . . .

. . . .

. . . .

• The rationale for the project is: . . . .

. . . .

. . . .

. . . .

• The objectives are: . . . .

. . . .

. . . .

. . . .

Second Meeting: Stage 2

NB: Responsibility for contacting/meeting personal tutors is that of the
learner. In order to achieve the above aims and objectives, the learner
undertakes to do the following:

. . . .

. . . .

. . . .

. . . .

Agreed by student and tutor on the following date . . . .

Figure 4.8

Continued

- The following resources, people and organisations will be involved:

  . . . .

  . . . .

  . . . .

- The end product of the project will be a 4000-word essay. To be included:
  - all changes to aims and objectives identified as agreed by personal tutor
  - self-assessment, e.g. what did you learn from the project?
  - plan of action for further development

- It is agreed that the study will be assessed and evaluated by the tutor in the following manner:

  . . . .

  . . . .

Stage 3
- The first draft will be delivered to the personal tutor for marking on (date) after which learners will present their final work on (date).

Third Meeting: Stage 4

- To agree the content for presentation at the learners' mini conference. The agreed date for submission is (date).

THIS CONTRACT SHOULD BE RETAINED AND RETURNED WITH YOUR COMPLETED PROJECT. YOUR CONTRACT ASSIGNMENT *CANNOT* BE MARKED *WITHOUT THIS DOCUMENT*.

Signed: . . . . Learner

. . . . Tutor

Date: . . . .

NB: Failure to submit on time = <u>fail</u>

The personal tutor and practitioner is there to help the learner to achieve the aims and learning outcomes of a satisfactory project, and to learn in the process, not to provide another difficulty for the learner to overcome.

EXPERIENTIAL LEARNING

Most traditional curricula can be regarded as very artificial creations. The incorporation of experiential learning into curricula involves learning through the use of experience of 'real' situations in order to enable the learner to develop insights, skills and attitudes related to these situations. Note the emphasis on processes rather than products here.

The experiences may be either *direct*, in which the learner is directly involved in the 'real' situation, or *indirect*, in which awareness of the 'real' situation is gained vicariously through the use of films, reports, etc., or through gaming such as role-playing.

An important aspect of experiential learning is that it values what the 'learner' brings to the educational situation. A possible disadvantage is that it may become too individualised and constricted. However, experiential learning is now rightly receiving more attention in further and higher and teacher education.

Hutton (1989) defines experiential learning as 'learning which is rooted in our doing and our experience. It is learning which illuminates that experience and provides direction for the making of a judgment as a guide to choice or action' (p.50). In Hutton's view, learning to make sound judgements is one of the major tasks for professional education: or of living in modern society, and the process of making a judgement is also a key element in learning how to learn. As part of this process Hutton searches for an approach to learning which could enable people to act and to learn.

Overview of experiential learning

The following list of points may help to clarify what experiential learning is, and what it is not.

1 Learners are involved in an active exploration of experience. Experience is used to test out ideas and assumptions rather than to obtain practice passively. Practice can be very important but it is greatly enhanced by reflection.
2 Learners must selectively reflect on their experience in a critical way, rather than take experience for granted and assume that the experience on its own is sufficient.
3 The experience must matter to the learner. Learners must be committed to the process of exploring and learning.
4 There must be scope for the learners to exercise some independence from the teacher/skilled practitioner. Teachers/skilled practitioners have an important role in devising appropriate experiences and facilitating reflection. However, the transmission of information is but a minor element and the teacher/skilled practitioner cannot experience what the learners experience or reflect for the learners.
5 Experiential learning is not the same as 'discovery' learning. Learning by

doing is not simply a matter of letting learners loose and hoping that they discover things for themselves in a haphazard way through sudden bursts of inspiration. The activity may be carefully designed by the teacher/skilled practitioner and the experience may need to be carefully reviewed and analysed afterwards for learning to take place. A crucial feature of experiential learning is the structure devised by the teacher/skilled practitioner within which learning takes place.

6   Openness to experience is necessary for learners to have evidence upon which to reflect. It is therefore crucial to establish an appropriate emotional tone for learners: one which is safe and supportive, and which encourages learners to value their own experience and to trust themselves to draw conclusions from it. This openness may not exist at the outset but may be fostered through successive experiences of the experiential learning cycle.

7   Experiential learning involves a cyclical sequence of learning activities. Teaching methods can be selected to provide a structure for each stage of the cycle and to take learners through the appropriate sequence. The cycle also allows learners the opportunities to reflect on what they have already learned.

THE REFLECTIVE PRACTITIONER

Hoyle in 1976 suggested that teachers can be categorised as 'restricted' and 'extended' professionals. He went on to describe the restricted professional as the individual who sees their work simply within the confines of their classroom, and relies on their intuition and experience rather than constant reappraisal. They may be an excellent classroom teacher but do not see their work within the wider context of society. The extended professional, he argued, was by contrast seeking to improve their practice, become well informed on educational issues and teaching methods and see college problems within the context of society at large. We cannot discount the 'classroom performer' but there is a preference for the extended professional who is also an autonomous practitioner. To be an autonomous practitioner one must be able to choose between alternatives on notional grounds; this practitioner comes to practical decisions and acts on them. Autonomy does not entail being able to act on whim, or without thought. A practitioner becomes effective and efficient through the process of reflective practice. The reflective autonomous professional is able to deliberate about alternatives in any situation. This implies seeking knowledge to inform these judgements. Some teacher practitioners may have a notional autonomy, but they are blinkered by their own prejudices or even laziness. They are not autonomous in respect of their professional practices.

A professional has had a prolonged education which equips them to deliberate among alternatives and come to reasoned judgements and decisions. The professional will have acquired and be intent on developing their specialist skills; they aspire to the highest standards of competence in their work. The professional seeks to improve their performance through seeking understanding. If the teacher acts in this way they will develop a range of experience. That experience is invaluable, not only for their own or their learners' benefit, but because if that experience can be shared with others, they will profit from it. Such practical experience is necessary to the development of theoretical understanding, which is why conversation among teachers is critical to illuminating that understanding, improving confidence and ability. The introduction of teaching, learning and assessment through reflective practice has recently become the norm in some curricula (see Appendix 3 for an example).

Learning through reflection

Reflection in relation to learning has been extensively researched by among others Boud *et al.* (1985), Kemmis (1985), and Kolb and Fry (1975), but Schön's work gives a new dimension to the topic. Reflection-in-action in the context of reflective practice is based on the concepts of Model I and Model II behaviour, where Model I is seen as the traditional client/professional relationship and Model II as the foundation of reflective practice.

Model I learning produces a view of the professional as expert, taking unilateral decisions and giving advice, where problems are seen in clear-cut terms and amenable to solution by routine methods.

Model II learning, by contrast, promotes a view of the professional as one with specialised knowledge and experience, who may be helpful and who will work with the client/patient towards finding an individual solution or amelioration for his individual problem. The experience of this, as well as continued conventional learning, will be used to help in forming solutions to future problems which have similar features but are equally individual. The concept of reflection-in-action is further assisted by other work done in conjunction with Argyrus (Argyrus and Schön 1974).

A study by Davies *et al.* (1994) (see Neary 1996a) discovered practitioners with many years' experience who are superb practitioners, respected by colleagues and learners alike, and whose learners gain a great deal from them. This situation is one familiar to most professionals. However, equally familiar is the practitioner with similar years of experience who is no more effective now than they were as a newly qualified teacher, and from whom learners learn little. This led the researchers to question why there is this difference and what factors promote it. Schön's work (1983 and 1987) the reflective practitioner highlighted the problem and led the researchers to incorporate this theoretical framework as part of their study.

Learning from experience

> *Reflection is an important human activity in which people recapture their experience, think about it, mull it over and evaluate it. It is this working with experience that is important in learning. The capacity to reflect is developed to different stages in different people and it may be this ability which characterises those who learn effectively from experience. (Boud* et al. *1985, p.19)*

Learning effectively from experience is a complex process, the outcomes of which depend to large extent on the cognitive and affective responses of the individual concerned and the context in which they are learning. We will explore this process using a model developed by Boud *et al.* (1985) analysing the experience(s) that precipitate reflection, the three stages of reflection – returning to experience, attending to feelings and re-evaluating experience – and some of the possible outcomes.

Study problem

What does the word 'experience' mean to you? It may have different meanings depending on the context in which it is used. Take a little time now to think about the concept of 'experience' and make a note of your ideas.

Watson (1991) found that the word 'experience' was used in four ways:
- exposure to an event, a situation, an emotion or information
- an event, a situation or an emotion
- the amount of knowledge gained over a period of time
- time spent in the service (practice).

Watson proposed that the word 'experience' is often used as though it were synonymous with 'learning', although how far any of the four definitions cited above lead to new understandings and appreciations depends on the nature of the experience and the response of the individual to that experience. It is, however, a common belief that the longer we live, the more experience we have and the wiser we become, but some would argue that the passing of the years does not necessarily bring gifts of understanding within one's own life. Twenty years' experience, it has been said, may be no more than one year's experience repeated twenty times.

An individual's response to a new experience will be significantly determined by past experiences. It is not only the person who is affected by an event or situation; the event or situation is also affected by the person. Dewey (1938) states:

We live from birth to death in a world of persons and things which in large measure is what it is because of what has been done and transmitted from previous human activities. When this fact is ignored, experience is treated as if it were something which goes on exclusively inside an individual's body and mind. It ought not to be necessary to say that experience does not occur in a vacuum. There are sources outside an individual which give rise to experience. It is constantly fed from these springs. (pp.39–40)

Thus, no experience occurs in isolation from what has happened before. Taking this to a logical conclusion, every experience that a person has is influenced by the cumulative effects of both their own previous experiences and those of their outer world. Dewey suggested that viewed over time, experience can be described as a dynamic continuum, where 'every experience affects for better or worse the attitudes which help decide the quality of further experiences' (1938, p.37).

Cell (1984) argued that the cumulative effect is that each experience contains something of our past and our future. This is very important, since what is learnt from an experience may be dysfunctional and lead us to act in the future in ways which may inhibit or distort our future development and growth.

So it seems fair to suggest that although all learning stems from experience, not all experience results in learning (Dewey 1938; Cell 1984; Boud *et al.* 1985).

LEARNING THROUGH REFLECTION: THE USE OF LEARNING JOURNALS

Probably all of us reflect, some more than others, and for some, being reflective can give an orientation to their everyday lives. For others, reflection comes about when the conditions in the learning environment are appropriate – when there is an incentive or some guidance. This section focuses on the practical activities that will provide a context in which reflection can be encouraged. The activities are mostly no more than situations in which various conditions which favour reflection are accentuated or harnessed in a formalised manner as, for example, in a learning journal. The activities are grouped for convenience according to these 'accentuated conditions' – though there will be much overlap.

Because the use of journals as a vehicle for reflection in educational situations is becoming common, and because the literature on writing journals is relatively abundant, the use of journals to enhance learning and practice warrants attention. There is a form of journal called a 'dialogue' journal, which is different in that it involves written conversation between two or more people, which will be the case with you and your learners.

Writing in a journal as a means to reflection

There are a number of words used in the literature as synonymous with 'journal', such as log, diary, dialectical notebook, workbook, or autobiographical and reflective writing. Sometimes a journal is also the same as a profile and a 'progress file'. Precisely defining words is fairly unhelpful here, so we use 'journal' to refer to predominantly written material that is based on reflection and is relatively free writing, though it may be written within a given structure (see the example on p.93). A journal is written regularly over a period of time rather than in a single session. Within this generalised form there are many variations, and this section is an attempt to capture the essence of the activity in its relation to reflection in order that it can be applied elsewhere. A learning journal is also known as a reflective or a professional journal.

Study problem

Why keep a learning/reflective journal? Think about your own experiences, reflect and make notes.

The purpose of writing journals

Where journals are used in formal education, Stephani suggested that the method is more suitable for courses where there are 'smaller numbers of mature learners who have a clearer sense of their own goals' (cited in Moon 1999) – as opposed to the traditional higher education situation where traditional patterns of expectation of teaching, learning and assessing may cause difficulties. These are, however, only the same problems that occur for any unusual self-managed form of learning, and some of these rigid expectations need to be overcome in any programme of study in the development towards a future functional employee.

There are many purposes for using journals. Some of the purposes relate to personally initiated writing, and some to formal educational situations. In the latter cases, in particular, a clear statement of purpose can be important for the success of the activity. Most initiators of journal writing would identify several purposes for writing a journal, and these are set out below.

To record experience
The primary purpose of journal writing may be to record experience, with the emphasis initially being on the recording rather than the reflective activity, although this may come later. Recording of experience may entail long-term or short-term recording.

To develop learning in ways that enhances other learning
This represents a group of purposes generally specified in formal learning situations. Writing a journal can, for example, encourage the valuing of personal observation and knowledge.

To deepen the quality of learning – in the form of critical thinking or developing a questioning attitude
Mortimer described the use of portfolio development with reflective commentary as a

> *means of increasing critical ability and of encouraging the adoption of a deep approach to … 'learning'. The technique that is crucial for developing critical approaches to learning is the initial noting of detail – the 'look' and the 'look again', returning to the material to reflect on it in a double-entry journal. (cited in Moon 1999)*

To enable the learners to understand the process of their own learning
The examples of the use of journals that conform to this purpose tend to be from situations where a group of individuals are being taught to teach or train another group of learners. Morrison suggested that a journal helps learners 'to self-direct and gain control of their own cognitive processes … e.g. using preferred learning styles in organising tasks' (cited in Moon 1999).

Journals enable learners to understand the limitations of their own learning styles. In this way they can be better facilitators of the learning of others, when they themselves become registered practitioners.

To facilitate learning from experience
Journal writing is about learning from experience of events, but some writers have been clearer in their specification of this purpose. For example, Boud *et al.* (1985) designed a journal so that the sequence of recording takes account of the cycle of experiential learning, with the initial recording of an event, then reflection, and an account of the subjective inner experience and further reflection and generalisation. On a broader basis, journals that accompany field

work or work experience provide a method of developing the meaning of experiences so that the learner can relate their unique experience to established theory, or develop their own theory.

As a means of assessment in formal education

Journals may be used as a form of assessment. Their use in learning will be enhanced if the appropriate assessment criteria can be identified in advance between the practitioner, the staff and the learner. A journal can accompany a submission for the assessment of prior experiential learning which can give returning (to learning) adult learners exemption from parts of a programme of learning.

To enhance professional practice or the professional self in practice

A common purpose for journal writing is to encourage the development of what is called reflective practice – reflective practice has many identities. This is often used in the professional development context, but increasingly there is a more generalised application of the term. The central issue in improving practice might seem to be the translation of the products of reflection into the real world of action so that they affect practice and something is done differently. Some journal structures seem more clearly to accord with this objective than others, in requiring the students to think about what they will do that is actually different. The issue of transfer of ideas into practice is problematic where initial education is concerned, and the journal can only facilitate appropriate attitudes towards practice and perhaps encourage the habits of reflection.

In the context of professional development, there are examples of electronic (email) journal writing as a means of communication between learners on teaching practice at a distance from their tutors.

The process of reflection

The process of reflection increases the potential learning from experience; as Boyd and Fales (1983) assert, it is 'the core difference between whether a person repeats the same experience several times becoming highly proficient at one behaviour, or learns from experience in such a way that he or she is cognitively or effectively changed' (p.100).

There are many 'models' which are aimed at helping practitioners to reflect. Heath (1998) suggests that models are meant to provide guidance, not rules, for reflection and practitioners should be encouraged to develop a flexible approach to their use, giving some thought to which parts of the model are most useful in the situation described. She goes on to advise that 'Rigid use of a model focuses attention on the model rather than practice and could inhibit depth of exploration thus deflecting the original aim of the model's author' (p.592).

Boud *et al.* (1985) identified three elements which they believe to be important in the reflective process: 'returning to experience', 'attending to feelings' and 're-evaluating the experience'. These three stages provide a useful framework for a 'how to' guide to writing reflective accounts of your own. Johns (1994) added a fourth stage, i.e. learning.

Stage 1: Return to experience

- Describe the experience, recollecting what happened in chronological order. The description should be fairly detailed but without judgement.
- *Notice* what happened/how you felt/what you did.

Remember that you need to reflect on what happened, not on what you *wished* had happened. The purpose of this stage is to help you stand back from the experience, clarify your perceptions and look at it again with the benefit of time and concentration.

Stage 2: Attend to feelings

- Note any positive or negative feelings, e.g. pleasure, annoyance, elation, anxiety, frustration, sense of achievement.
- Acknowledge negative feelings but don't let them form a barrier.
- Work with positive emotions.

Stage 3: Re-evaluate the experience

- Connect the ideas and feelings of the experience to those you had on reflection.
- Consider options and choices.

Stage 4: Learning

- How do I now feel about this experience?
- Could I have dealt better with this situation?
- What have I learnt from this experience?

Study problem

The outcomes of reflection on your experience may be that

- you would do something differently next time
- an issue has been clarified
- you become aware of new ideas
- you consider options and choices.

Comment on whether these outcomes apply to you and in what way. Remember that change/learning may be small/large, visible/non-visible to others, cognitive/affective.

Going back to stage 3 to explore it in more depth gives us a greater understanding of the process.

The following example suggests a structure for a professional journal and focus questions for you to consider when making your entries. The structure of the journal and many of the focus questions draw on ideas outlined in Calderhead and Gates (1993) and Furlong and Maynard (1995).

THE PROFESSIONAL JOURNAL

Entry 1: 'My personal theory'

- What qualities do you think are important in a teacher/trainer, and why? What do you feel are the sources of your ideas about these qualities?

Entry 2: 'In at the deep end' – initial encounters

- When you first started teaching/training, what were your expectations?
- To what extent were these realised?
- What were your 'reality shocks' or 'critical incidents'? (Draw on those experiences that were fundamental in shaping your approach to teaching/training.)

Entry 3: Planning for effective learning

- Over a 2–3-week period focus on the planning process you undertake for one group of learners/trainees, or one trainee.
- What were the intended/stated outcomes of the session(s)? Why were these outcomes selected?
- What prior understanding, skills or knowledge were you drawing on?
- What role(s) have you adopted in the process?

Entry 4: Strategies and approaches for effective learning

- Think about the strategies/methods you have planned to use in your teaching/training.
- How do you think your learners/trainees learn best?
- How successful do you think you have been in sustaining levels of motivation?
- What range of strategies/approaches and learning aids have you used and why?

Entry 5: The 'learning environment'

- What, for you, are the characteristics of a 'good session'?
- Why do you think that these qualities are important?
- What features promote and inhibit learning among those you work with? Why?

Entry 6: Assessment and feedback

- Over a 2–3 week period focus on the assessment procedures you undertake for one group of learners/trainees, or one trainee.
- What range of assessment tools and approaches have you used, and what reasons can you give for selecting these?
- How do you offer feedback to your learners on their levels of performance and areas for development?

Entry 7: Evaluating my teaching/training

- What approaches do you take to evaluate sessions *and* courses/programmes?
- What concrete steps have you taken to improve your effectiveness as a teacher/trainer?

Entry 8: Professional development

- As you work towards the end of this course, what do you think your immediate professional development needs are? Why do you think this?

Entry 9: Looking back

- To what extent have your earlier ideas about what it means to be a teacher/trainer been modified or challenged as a result of engaging with the ideas encountered on this course?

Study problem

Reflection exercise 1

1   Drawing on your own recent professional experience, identify an incident/issue/problem. It may have been positive (something you did/coped with well/something that pleased you/an event which was satisfying) or negative (an unexpected outcome/a situation that made you feel uncomfortable/an event that angered/frustrated or upset you).

- Write down everything that you can remember about this event. (Take your mind back and try to relive and purely describe events as they unfold. Don't try to analyse/justify yet.)
- Use the Boud *et al.*/Johns model of structured reflection to help you focus on your description of the experience and reflect upon it. Write your thoughts down as you re-evaluate the experience.

2   Work with a partner and take turns to share your reflective accounts. The person hearing the reflective account should use the 'focus questions' in Johns' model of structured reflection and the skills of reflective listening to give their partner the opportunity to share their experience and reflect more deeply on it.

Note: This exercise is designed to help you practise the skills of reflection-on-action. There may be some incidents/issues/problems that you prefer to reflect on privately at this point in time and in this context. Therefore, choose a partner that you feel you can confide in in confidence, *or* identify an issue/incident/event that you are comfortable sharing with others.

Reflection exercise 2

1   What are the advantages and difficulties of using reflection as a teaching/

learning strategy? Consider this from your own viewpoint as a 'learner' as well as in your professional capacity as a mentor/assessor.

2   As a mentor/assessor, what difficulties/dilemmas might you face in facilitating reflection-on-action in your learners/trainees/supervisors?
3   How helpful do you find reflection-on-action?
4   How can the concept of the reflective practitioner be incorporated into the curriculum?

Study problem

Many of you work in 'practice professions' (e.g. nursing, teaching, law, medicine).

- Plan an outline of a curriculum which will incorporate the concepts of reflection in action and theory of practice.
- Formulate your own conceptual framework based on the information gained from your reading on reflection.

MENTORING

The learner needs support and guidance in becoming a competent reflective professional. One way of providing this support and guidance is mentoring, which has been developed as part of the learner support systems in many organisations and professions (Neary 2000).

What is a mentor?

Over the past 20 years mentoring has developed as a 'learner support' system and should now be viewed as an important element within the curriculum.

In the study by Davies *et al.* (1994) 'mentor' was the preferred term used by practitioners in practice placements. For the purposes of this book a mentor is someone who assists and supports an adult learner taking a post-compulsory education course. In this case, it means that someone will be guiding learners through many hours of teaching practice. A mentor also keeps in touch with the course tutor or personal tutor in order to report on the learner's progress.

A mentor can be described as someone who accepts the role of facilitating an individual's learning. Many open learning schemes strongly encourage the learner to select a mentor, and often provide briefing materials for both the mentor and the mentee (the learner). Mentoring is described by Clutterbuck (1985) as 'intimate personal relationships frequently developed between the master and the apprentice' (p.1).

Curriculum developers will need to identify a model of mentoring to suit the needs of their learners and the type of course learners are about to enter (e.g. professional, vocational, academic, skills based, etc.).

The role of the mentor

The exact nature of the role of a mentor will depend on a number of factors. These include:

- the amount of time one can spend with the learner
- the atmosphere and organisation at one's place of work/college
- the skills and experience of the mentor
- the needs and interests of the learner
- the mentoring model in use at one's place of work/college.

The role will probably include functions which might be categorised as teacher, advocate, friend and facilitator. As a *teacher* one might need to:

- answer questions about the course material
- discuss ways of applying what is learned to the work situation
- give feedback on the learner's achievements
- assist with planning how objectives and learning outcomes might be achieved
- coach in or demonstrate practical skills
- help the learner review performance.

Being an *advocate* means acting on behalf of the learner to preserve or increase confidence and self-esteem. In this role one might:

- arrange for practical experience
- manage access to libraries
- delegate functions which give the learner extra responsibility.

As a *friend* one might:

- give the learner a lift when morale is low
- be available to listen and advise
- point out where the learner is going wrong
- point out ways to improve.

For the role of a *facilitator* (look again at chapter 3, p.63).

The relationship is frequently a new one for both mentor and learner, so both will need to agree the degree and the nature of the involvement that each is willing to undertake. An important part of the role of the mentor is to build an effective working relationship and to establish a partnership based on mutual trust, honesty and respect.

Here is what four learners have said about how their mentors help them.

I test my ideas out by talking them through with her; it helps to get another person's views and perspectives. They're usually a bit different from mine.

He points out things in the course that I might have skimmed over too quickly.

We discuss the assignments together before I begin work myself.

Our regular meetings help me to keep up my momentum.

The need for a mentor

There is a strong workplace tradition of mentoring in many industries and professions, whereby new recruits are assigned to a more experienced worker who initiates them into the workings of the organisation and helps them to develop their skills, understanding and attitudes.

Gains for the employing institution

- Improved communication between individuals at different levels
- Increased motivation of staff as interest is shown in their professional input
- Skills of staff are recognised more quickly
- Higher calibre staff are attracted
- A contribution to staff development across the whole institution
- Another mechanism by which the aims of staff appraisal and individual performance review (IPR) can be achieved
- The establishment of a body of mentors for general use with new learners

Gains for the mentee

- Improved self-confidence and motivation
- Fuller understanding of the mission and purpose of the institution
- Becoming more familiar with the ways of working of the establishment in areas such as health and safety, staff development and equal opportunities
- Fuller and better use of existing resources; development of new resources
- More creative response to environmental and administration pressures
- Personal and career development
- Specific help with meeting the outcomes of the institution/company
- Help in ensuring that the support of education is relevant to their work

Gains for the mentor

- Improved job satisfaction – the role of mentor boosts self-esteem
- Increased recognition within the establishment
- New perspectives are gained as one looks at procedures in a fresh light
- Improved communications between all levels of staff
- Opportunity for accredited training
- Mentoring offers a new and wider network for other mentors and trainers
- Introduction to lifelong learning

The upward spiral of development for the mentor and mentee

Learning is a process that allows us to move on an upward spiral of growth, change and continuous improvement. Through learning we increase our mental capacity with the aid of reading, writing, thinking and reflecting. We mature socially and emotionally by making consistent commitments to the mentor/mentee relationship and in helping the mentee (the learner) to develop also in an upward spiral. (The concept of the spiral curriculum is discussed in chapter 5.)

Defining the mentor/mentee standards

Standards and criteria should maintain 'mentee focus'. Within each topic a number of subtopics can be identified. Throughout the formulation of standards the mentor and mentee must attempt to ensure that all outcome criteria are measurable and/or observable. Precise mechanisms for assessment should be included and the practising mentor should be able to design measurement tools which meet the mentee's needs. Inherent in setting standards must be the fact that they require continued evaluation and refinement to meet the needs of a constantly developing professional (teacher, lawyer, etc.).

Before becoming a mentor one needs to be able to:

- interpret the curriculum
- manage the educational environment for the learner
- manage resources for self and learner
- manage the assessment and learning strategies
- manage change
- write standards and methods of evaluation
- gain helpful knowledge about the learner.

Study problem

Before going on to read about standards try writing two standards you would want your learner to be exposed to. These standards can also form the basis of a course, a module and lesson plans. You will find that these standards can also be used for quality assurance (see chapter 8).

The standards: a model

Are you a competent mentor? How do you know? The *standards* provide the answer. They indicate a range of activities (the elements of competence) a competent mentor can do or should be capable of doing. They also provide the indicators (the performance criteria) by which you can tell whether you are doing things competently or not.

So are you a competent mentor? Look at the standards carefully and assess your performance against them. The possible answers are:

- Yes. I am now competent (*halo supplied*). I do all the activities and I meet all the performance criteria.
- No. I am not yet fully competent. But I know what I need to work on and I will be competent by .... (*target date*).

CHECKLIST OF STANDARDS

ROLE DEFINITION
A mentor's role is:

To contribute to the learning, development and integration of the learners into the profession to the mutual benefit of all involved in health care.

ELEMENTS OF COMPETENCE
The overall function of the mentor is achieved by fulfilling the elements of competence listed below.

The mentor is able to

- Contribute to the initial development of the learner's learning and development programme
- Establish contact/relationship with learner
- Create (as far as practical) a physical environment appropriate to meetings/contact with learner
- Provide support to learner's progress on learning and development programme
- Contribute to modifications to learner's learning and development programme
- Review and report progress to motivate and encourage learner
- Provide guidance on possible future career development to learner (when required)
- Assist in the assessment of learner's performance
- Assist in minimising/avoiding conflict in learner's learning and development programme
- Liaise with other members of teaching staff and significant others on learner progress
- Terminate formal mentor relationship with learner.

THE PERFORMANCE CRITERIA

These indicate whether the elements of competence are being done properly or not. Three examples are given below, attached to their respective elements of competence.

Element 1: Contribute to the initial development of the learner's learning and development programme
Performance criteria

- Makes constructive suggestions to university staff about the learning experiences appropriate to learner's workplace learning and development programme
- Gives advice on practicable timescale for the agreed learning and development programme
- Assists in identifying learning experiences appropriate to learner's learning and development programme
- Identifies possible problem areas and indicates suggested arrangements for overcoming them
- Obtains copies of the learner's learning outcomes and development programme.

Element 2: Establish contact/relationship with learner
Performance criteria

- The learner is formally greeted on arrival to the practice placement
- A date and venue for the first meeting is agreed
- The necessary information is exchanged on mutual roles in the relationship

- The appropriate outlines of the relationship are identified and mutual expectations are agreed
- A timetable and venue(s) for future meetings are established and agreed
- A brief report/summary of the meeting is produced and a set of guidelines is agreed
- The learner is treated in a manner which is supportive but not imposing.

Element 3: Provide support to learner's progress on learning and development programme
Performance criteria
- Affords opportunities for the learner to reflect on and evaluate learning experiences
- Elicits the learner's perception of own strengths and weaknesses
- Examines the relationship between the learner's approach and the design of learning and development programme
- Ensures that any additional work is agreed with the learner
- The learner is treated in a manner which is supportive
- Constructively offers guidance and support between formal meetings.

Study problem

Using the Donabedian (1986) model of structure, process and outcome (Figure 4.9), formalise a working document which each mentor and learner can complete together. (See the example in Figure 4.10.)

Figure 4.9

The Donabedian model for setting standards (cited in RCN 1989)

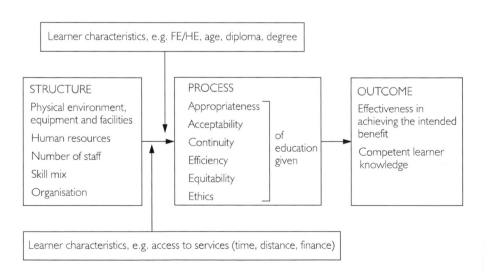

Figure 4.10 Example of a standard-setting statement

The learner will receive support and guidance from a named mentor, in order to facilitate their development as a practitioner.

Structure	Process	Outcome	Monitor/evaluate	Comments
Mentor must be willing to undertake this role and have a minimum of one year's experience since qualifying as a professional	The mentor should be identified prior to the learner starting work in the practice placement	The mentor is able to identify areas in which his/her professional development is occurring		
A mentor is defined as an experienced professional who demonstrates interpersonal and negotiation skills in an advisory capacity	A contract will be negotiated within one week of commencement	Both parties are able to express that the relationship is mutually beneficial		
The senior manager will arrange for a mentor to work with the learner	The mentor and mentee will have regular meetings at intervals acceptable to both parties	The relationship will be terminated at a mutually agreeable time		
The relationship will be agreed by the mentor and mentee	Areas of non-development will be identified and appropriate action taken			

NB: The word 'professional' can be exchanged for 'practitioner' i.e. teacher, lawyer, nurse, etc.

Anderson, G., Boud, D. and Sampson, J. (1996) *Learning Contracts: A Practical Guide*. London, Kogan Page.

Andrews, M. (1996) 'Using reflection to develop clinical expertise'. *British Journal of Nursing* 8(8): 508–13.

Bates, T. (1993) 'How external mentoring operates'. *Management Development Review* 6(4): 6–9.

Berte, N.R. (1975) *Individualising Education through Contract Learning*. University of Alabama Press.

Boud, D. Keogh, R. and Walker, D. (1985) *Reflection: Turning Experience into Learning*. London, Kogan Page.

Boud, D. (1981) *Developing Learner Autonomy in Learning*. Kogan Page, London.

Boyd, E.M. and Fales, A.W. (1983) 'Reflective learning: key to learning from experience'. *Journal of Humanistic Psychology* 23(2): 99–117.

Clarke, A. (1995) 'Professional development in practicum settings: reflective practice under scrutiny'. *Teacher and Teacher Education* 11(3): 243–62.

Copeland, U., Birmingham, C. and De La Cruz, E. (1993) 'The reflective practitioner in teaching: towards a research agenda'. *Teaching and Teacher Education* 9(4): 347–59.

Coutts-Jarman, J. (1993) 'Using reflection and experience in nurse education'. *British Journal of Nursing* 2(1): 77–80.

Cox, A. (1996) 'Teacher as mentor: opportunities for professional development'. In J. Robson (ed.) *The Professional FE Teacher*. Aldershot, Avebury.

Entwistle, N. and Ramsden, P. (1983) *Understanding Learner Learning*. Beckenham, Kent: Croom Helm.

Francis, D. (1995) 'The reflective journal: a window to pre-service teachers' practical knowledge'. *Teacher and Teacher Education* 11(3): 229–42.

Goldman, G. (1979) 'A contract for academic improvement'. In P.J. Hills (ed.), *Study Courses and Counselling*. London, Society for Research into Higher Education.

Hatton N. and Smith, D. (1995) 'Reflection in teacher education: towards definition and implementation'. *Teacher and Teacher Education* 11(1): 33–50.

Hoover, L. (1994) 'Reflective writing as a window on pre-service teachers' thought processes'. *Teacher and Teacher Education* 10(1): 83–93.

Johns, C. (1994) 'Nuances of reflection'. *Journal of Clinical Nursing* 3(2): 71–5.

Jowett V. (1995) 'Mentoring the "Working for a Degree" project'. Leeds Metropolitan University.

Kember, D., Jones, A., Yuenloke, A. *et al.* (2001) *Reflective Teaching and Learning in the Health Professions*. Blackwell Science UK.

Kolb, D.A. (1978) *Learning Style Inventory: Technical Manual*. Boston: McBeri.

Kolb, D.A. (1984) *Experiential Learning: Experience as the Source of Learning and Development*. Englewood Cliffs, New Jersey, Prentice-Hall.

Long, J. (1997) 'Mentoring for school-based teachers in education in Australia'. *Mentoring and Tutoring* 4(3): 11–17.

Murry M. and Owen, M. (1991) *Beyond the Myths and Magic of Mentoring*. San Francisco, Jossey-Bass.

Neary, M. (1992) 'Contract assignments: an integral part of adult learning and continuous assessment'. *Senior Nurse* 12(4): 14–17.

Neary, M. (1997a) 'Defining the role of assessors, mentors and supervisors', Part 1. *Nursing Standard* 11(42): 34–9.

Neary, M. (1997b) 'Defining the role of assessors, mentors and supervisors', Part 2. *Nursing Standard* 11(43): 34–8.

Neary, M. (1998) 'Contract assignments: change in teaching, learning and assessment strategies'. *Educational Practice and Theory* 20(1): 43–58.

Neary, M. (2000) *Teaching, Assessing and Evaluation for Clinical Competence: A Practical Guide for Teachers and Practitioners*. Cheltenham, Stanley Thornes.

Philips R, Neary, M. and Davies, B. (1996) 'The practitioner-teacher: a study in the introduction of mentors in the pre-registration nurse education programme in Wales'. *Journal of Advanced Nursing* 23. Part 1: 1037–44; Part 2: 1080–8.

Quicke, J. (1996) 'The reflective practitioner and teacher education: an answer to critics'. *Teaching and Teaching: Theory and Practice* 2(1): 11–12.

Richardson, S. (1987) 'Implementing contract learning in a senior nursing practicum'. *Journal of Advanced Nursing* 12: 201–6.

Schön, D. (1987) *Educating the Reflective Practitioner*. San Francisco, Jossey-Bass.

Schön, D. (1991) *The Reflective Practitioner: How Professionals Think in Action* (2nd edition). San Francisco, Jossey-Bass.

Searight, M.W. (1976) *Preceptorship Study: Contracting for Learning*. Philadelphia, F.A. Davies.

Smith, A. and Russell, J. (1991) 'Using critical learning incidents in nurse education'. *Nurse Education Today* 11: 284–91.

Spooner, A. (1993) 'Mentoring and flexible training'. *Management Development Review* 6(2): 21–5. Bradford, MCB University Press.

Stephenson, J. and Laycock, M. (1993) *Using Learning Contracts in Higher Education*. London, Kogan Page, pp.57–62.

Veale, D.J. and Wachtel, J.M. (1996) 'Mentoring and coaching as part of a human resource development strategy'. *Management Development Review* 9(6): 19–24. Bradford, MCB University Press.

Weil, S.W. and McGill, I. (eds) (1989) *Making Sense of Experiential Learning: Diversity in Theory and Practice*. Society for Research into Higher Education and Open University Press.

CURRICULUM DESIGN AND ORGANISATION OF SUBJECT CONTENT

5

Learning outcomes

To be achieved through the process of self-directed study, teacher/mentor support and sharing learning with fellow students
  By the end of this chapter you will be able to:

- explore the various curriculum designs and their appropriateness to adult learning
- discuss the importance of organising subject matter in a logical and notional sequence
- explore and analyse the content of a curriculum from your college
- design a scheme of work and plan a lesson for one hour based on your curriculum/ course/programme/module.

COURSE AND CURRICULUM DESIGN

Many teachers and lecturers do not realise their role in curriculum planning, design and development until they are suddenly faced with the request from heads of departments to 'create' new courses within their institutions (Neary 1996a), or directives from professional bodies responsible for maintaining standards for the interest and safety of the public, such as those for nurses, midwives, police and prison officers. Even the most prescribed courses allow teachers and lecturers the freedom to interpret and design these courses. The main emphasis is to develop these courses in such a way that will maximise learning opportunities for all learners, which is based on professional judgement. Curriculum design involves many aspects of college life, as depicted in the ABC of the curriculum in chapter 7 (Figure 7.1, p.170).

  Most of the examples given in this chapter are based on my experience as a nurse educator, teacher educator and mentor trainer for many organisations and institutions, including the prison service (see Appendices 1, 2, 3 and 4 for details). Other examples are taken from A-level courses in physical education, biology, animal science, psychology and science and technology, and are to be found at the end of this chapter.

Guidelines for curriculum development and design

The following broad principles should inform curriculum development and design:

1   Promote learning and professionalism.
2   Ensure other subject areas are applied to the chosen profession or vocation.
3   Integrate theory with practice by providing regular tutorials and set study periods for discussion on site.
4   Provide a person-centred approach to teaching and learning.

5   Enable learners to develop professional competence and to capitalise on their proven academic ability.

Designing a curriculum is like making a cake through following a recipe. There is an immense amount of choice of recipes. Individual cooks can add a raisin here or an almond there to put their own individual stamp on the product. However, the basic principle is to follow the details of the recipe through from collecting the resources and the means of production to making the final cake. This analogy suggests that both the structure and the action are to be designed, but it is sufficiently flexible to allow some to argue that the recipes must be followed in detail (National Curriculum) whilst others stress the cook's individual tastes (degree module). So the designs that we use, the form the designer follows, will be much influenced by the underlying view of education and the underlying conception of a curriculum. Let us examine a few of the well-known designs.

The spiral curriculum

In a linear approach to the presentation of curriculum content (Figure 5.1), different topics are presented sequentially according to psychological or logical requirements. An alternative approach is that which is sometimes described as a spiral curriculum (Figure 5.2). Using this approach an overview of the

Figure 5.1

The linear curriculum

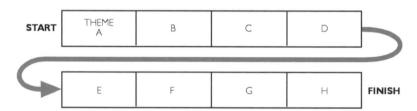

Figure 5.2

The spiral curriculum

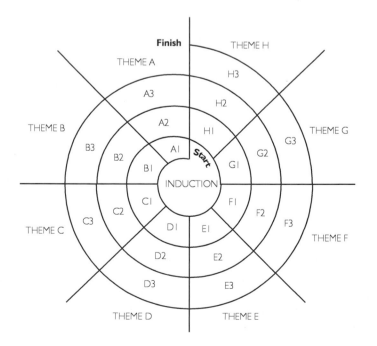

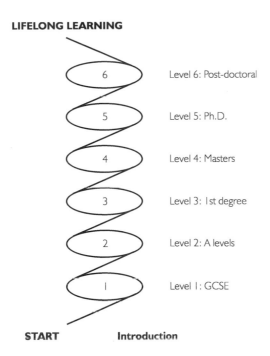

LIFELONG LEARNING

Level 6: Post-doctoral

Level 5: Ph.D.

Level 4: Masters

Level 3: 1st degree

Level 2: A levels

Level 1: GCSE

START   **Introduction**

Figure 5.3

The spiral curriculum in chemistry

subject may be given but the main feature is that various topics within the subject are studied at a relatively easy level and then the same topics are studied again but at a deeper level. The process may then be repeated. To a considerable extent this is the approach which learners of science experience (Figure 5.3). (There is a 'coverage' of chemistry at GCSE level and then many of the same topics are repeated at A level and degree level, but in much more detail.)

One advantage of this approach is that, fairly early on in their study of a subject, learners are able to gain an overview and so relate their more detailed studies of different topics. A disadvantage is that interest in particular topics may be lacking because those topics have already been encountered, be it at a lower level.

The best known proponent of the spiral curriculum is Jerome Bruner (1971a). But for a work which has been so widely quoted it says very little about the topic. It does, however, propose an educational principle that can usefully be extended from the school level, where it was originally applied, to other levels of education and training. The Bruner principle is roughly transcribed as: 'Any topic can be taught to any learner provided that it is presented at a conceptual level appropriate to the learner's present stage of intellectual development.'

The implication of this principle is that topics and themes will recur throughout a period of education, not by simple repetition but by review and representation in successively more complex treatments as the ability of the learner to absorb the instruction develops. This depends both on intellectual maturation and on the learning accumulated from experience.

To illustrate this in terms of a three-year course of vocational education and training we can consider two contrasting ways of organising and sequencing the learning in a course. In both cases we identify a number of themes/topics/content items which are to be learned during the course.

The first mode of organisation is what we can term the *linear sequence*. Here we compose a number of units or modules which are then treated in sequence, assessed, recorded and regarded as completed. The assumptions are that the units are free-standing, that there is no need for integration with other elements of the course and that what is learned at the start of the course will be retained by the end. Few schemes would be intended to operate quite in this way, but some unit-based schemes are prone to work out like this in practice.

On the other hand the *spiral curriculum* applied to the same example would require the themes or topics to be arranged in layers or levels within the scheme. Learning starts with a general induction which is followed by Unit A1, then B1 and so on until the first loop of the spiral is completed. The second circuit covers the same themes and topics, but at a more advanced conceptual level. Each theme or topic can be cross-related to or coordinated with the earlier learning of other units. Basic skills can be developed to a more advanced level, whilst regular reference to prior learning ensures that it is internalised.

Figures 5.1 and 5.2 are diagrams of the linear and spiral expressions of a unit-based course. Perhaps a better organic analogy is that of the onion – which grows in layers around a central core! Figure 5.4 is a specific example of a spiral curriculum model for one nurse education programme, which can be applied to any subject. Here the structure consists of the recurring theme of the Nursing Process. The curriculum has three parts or 'levels'. In Level 1 the learners learn about patient needs through the medium of the nursing process. in Level 2, they learn about patient problems, again through the nursing process; and in Level 3, about holistic nursing care, also through the nursing process. At each level, the nursing process is used and developed with increasing complexity and sophistication.

It is therefore recommended that a spiral curriculum design be adopted. Figure 5.5 (NNEB course) attempts to represent a spiral curriculum in which relevant and selected parts from each and every one of the Elements of Learning are input into each part of the programme. This will mean that during the Introduction of the Foundation of Theory and Practice the learner will receive a very 'broad but shallow' introduction, and as the learner progresses through the course all the themes will be picked up and related across the total care spectrum to the point of professional development. In this way it is firmly anticipated that learning opportunities will be greatly enhanced and that:

1   the knowledge will be tested in formative and/or summative assessment of each part and/or
2   the degree of competence will be achieved as part of the continuous assessment of theory and/or practice.

It is acknowledged that different stages of an NNEB course will receive a greater or lesser amount of some of the Elements of Learning shown in Figure 5.5; for example, Child Health will be given greater emphasis in Part B. However, some aspects of the care of children will be related to other concepts of curriculum.

The spiral

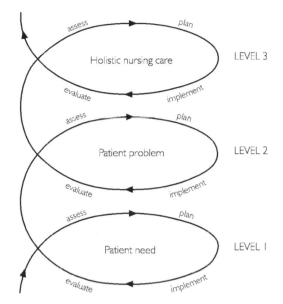

LEVEL 3

LEVEL 2

LEVEL 1

Figure 5.4

The spiral curriculum applied to nurse education

Subject details of levels

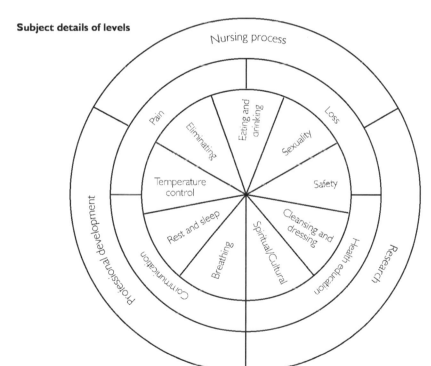

NNEB programme

ELEMENTS OF LEARNING	Introduction Foundation	Part A Normal Growth	Part B Child health	Part C Related studies	Professional development
Concepts of healthy child	→ (1)	→ (2)	→ (3)	→ (4)	→ (5)
Theories and models	→ (1)	→ (2)	→ (3)	→ (4)	→ (5)
Psychology/development	→ (1)	→ (2)	→ (3)	→ (4)	→ (5)
Sociology	→ (1)	→ (2)	→ (3)	→ (4)	→ (5)
Normal growth	→ (1)	→ (2)	→ (3)	→ (4)	→ (5)
Physiology	→ (1)	→ (2)	→ (3)	→ (4)	→ (5)
Anatomy	→ (1)	→ (2)	→ (3)	→ (4)	→ (5)
Care of children	→ (1)	→ (2)	→ (3)	→ (4)	→ (5)
Care of family	→ (1)	→ (2)	→ (3)	→ (4)	→ (5)
Care of acutely ill child	→ (1)	→ (2)	→ (3)	→ (4)	→ (5)
Practicum	→ (1)	→ (2)	→ (3)	→ (4)	→ (5)
Related studies	→ (1)	→ (2)	→ (3)	→ (4)	→ (5)
Research studies	→ (1)	→ (2)	→ (3)	→ (4)	→ (5)
Etc. (All units)	→ (1)	→ (2)	→ (3)	→ (4)	→ (5)

Numbers 1 → 5 represent the level or degree of difficulty to which the learner will study

Figure 5.5 The spiral curriculum in a Nursery Nursing Examinations Board (NNEB) course

Study problem

As a future professional (choose your own field) can you and a fellow learner adapt the spiral design to your curriculum planning and development? Consider the following questions:

● What are its constraints?
● What are its strengths?
● What age learner group might it be more suited to?

A curriculum based on the spiral design allows true professional/vocational theory to be formulated. It is acknowledged that most professions 'borrow' from other sciences. Left in isolation or as core subjects, those sciences remain 'pure'. When they are developed alongside the professional/vocational component, deductive theory formulation is facilitated; that is, the learner takes the science subject, applies it to the whole range of concepts being studied, and as a result learns about all aspects of their chosen profession. Any attempt on the teacher's part to be solely responsible for making those links (as would be the case in a linear curriculum) runs the risk of being ineffective, and probably unacceptable in an adult education environment. However, a linear curriculum must not be discarded as it has its place, for example in short courses which emphasise 'facts and figures', such as Research Methods.

Theme	Part A	Part B	Part C	Part D
Personalised approach to learning	➤ ➤ ➤ ➤ ➤ ➤ ➤ ➤ ➤ ➤ ➤ ➤ ➤ ➤ ➤ ➤ ➤ ➤ ➤			
Foundations of theory and practice in teaching and learning	➤ ➤ ➤			
Learner-centred learning		➤ ➤ ➤		
Advanced study skills and management of learning			➤ ➤ ➤	
The development of professionalism	➤ ➤ ➤ ➤ ➤ ➤ ➤ ➤ ➤ ➤ ➤ ➤ ➤ ➤ ➤ ➤ ➤ ➤ ➤			

Figure 5.6

A thematic approach to the curriculum

A thematic approach to the curriculum

The main disadvantage of a spiral curriculum developed in the manner postulated is that it is open to the charge of lacking structure. In order to create structure, a thematic approach is suggested, for example a course for a degree in education (Figure 5.6).

As can be seen from Figure 5.6, two themes would run throughout the whole of the course, namely Personalised Approach to Learning and Development of Professionalism. There would be a third theme in each part of the course, but this would vary according to the part. Thus in Part A the central theme would be the Foundations of Theory and Practice; in Part B the central theme would be Learner-centred Learning and in Part C it would be Advanced Study Skills and Management of Learning.

The spiral and competency-based curriculum

The spiral curriculum can be consistent with both the competency-based and process-based approaches, but the curriculum designer needs to have a clear idea of the eventual outcomes of the course and the intended learning processes which will bring these about.

Competency-based vocational education and training involves the acquisition of skills, associated knowledge and understanding, and the ability to apply these to relevant duties and tasks through appropriate processes. Design of a competency-based spiral curriculum at the professional level requires an ability to analyse the professional role in some detail. Duties and tasks associated with the role have to be taken into account, as does the unique body of knowledge of practice which is associated with the profession. 'Soft skills' or attitudes and values which affect human interactions must also be added to the store of curriculum content.

The curriculum planner's task is to ensure that the necessary content is covered but also to devise processes of learning which ensure that the wider aims of the scheme are addressed. If the spiral form of sequencing is adopted it is necessary to synthesise and sequence the elements in a way which offers a stimulating challenge to the learner at each stage. Whilst each theme or topic is revisited several times it is not a case of simple repetition. Existing knowledge and process skills are reviewed but are then used as a springboard for the attainment of clearly specified outcomes at successively more complex levels.

Assessment in the spiral and competency-based curriculum is necessarily progressive and cumulative. It offers both short-term and longer-term targets and provides feedback and reinforcement to the learner. It can, where the circumstances permit, employ mastery learning principles, which, in simple terms, mean that progress is based on attainment of outcomes rather than time. Some learners take less time than the norm. Others may need to take longer.

Defining competence

Competence can be defined as the possession and development of sufficient skills, knowledge, appropriate attitudes and experience for successful performance in life roles (Neary 1996a). Such a definition includes employment and other forms of work; it implies maturity and responsibility in a variety of roles; it includes experience as an essential element of competence. (Competencies will be considered again in Chapter 6.)

In recent years, increased attention has been drawn to the definition and assessment of competence in vocational education and training. Competence in the broadest sense has always been the goal of education, but the coordination of education, training and practical experience to ensure the personal development of competence in learners/trainees both as practitioners and individuals is often neglected (Neary 1992b).

Competence is a complex concept, involving knowledge, experience, transferable and specific skills and attitudes. It is often taken in an industrial context to mean simply fitness to perform a specific task. The FEU (1989a) takes the wider view that while training in specific competencies is a vital and necessary aspect of the formation of personnel, competence for life (including work) should be the ultimate goal of the formation process. In a work context, competence therefore implies the ability to deal with new as well as established tasks.

To define the curriculum in competence-based terms requires a description of the processes (modes of activity) involved in a given occupation. In generalised terms, it is suggested that the primary processes of an occupation are communication, planning, implementation and appraisal. Similar, if not identical, processes may be identified in other vocational areas and indeed in life roles generally. The four processes are seldom identifiable as discrete activities; in any given task they are usually to be found in combination. A brief description follows.

1 Communication

Communication includes finding and interpreting information and technical data; defining problems; 'reading' drawings and diagrams; interacting effectively with other people and with quasi-intelligent devices; and providing information in an appropriate form by oral and written methods, by drawings or sketches, and by demonstration.

2 Planning

Planning involves designing products, services and workplace layouts; selecting tools and materials; task analysis; organising time and work; testing and evaluation. It enables the optimal use of resources within given constraints. It requires computational and estimating skills, an understanding of the principles of appropriate science and technology, and the ability to order ideas and criteria logically and to set them out in diagrammatic form. It includes the review of plans in response to progress monitoring and appraisal is included. Planning activities extend the capacity of the participants in problem-solving, creativity, discrimination and decision-making.

3 Implementation

Implementation is the process of 'doing' or carrying through a task, translating a plan (and its revisions) into an outcome which may be (for example) a product, report or presentation, or some personal accomplishment. An understanding of and practical skills in the use of appropriate tools, instruments and other equipment are needed, together with a knowledge of the requisite materials, science and systems. Implementation involves preparation, carrying out the task and checking for completion, including clearing up. Implementation develops participants' ingenuity, persistence, reliability and teamwork skills.

4 Appraisal

Acquiring competence requires the ability to assess the adequacy with which objectives have been achieved. Self-appraisal should not be confused with external judgements required for accreditation purposes, although it may be associated with such assessments. Skills of measurement and testing and an understanding of monitoring processes and quality control may be required. In broader terms, a regard for the social, economic, political and environmental consequences of the profession is needed. The participants' capacity for judgement, self-awareness, self-criticism, discrimination and generalisation are reinforced.

It is suggested that the processes outlined above form the basis of competence in all occupations and therefore underlie the competence-based curriculum.

Study problem

Examine the comparisons between competency-based education and traditional education offered by Johnson (1974) (Figure 5.7) and compare these with the curriculum you are involved with.

The negotiated curriculum

The concept of a negotiated curriculum is a development of the idea that there should be greater learner involvement in the learning process. Design of the curriculum is based on theories which are attractive and workable. The design does not however guarantee delivery. This is still dependent on the quality of all those, on the-job and in the college, who form the tutorial team. Their collective skills and understanding of the curriculum process remain the

COMPETENCY BASED EDUCATION	TRADITIONAL EDUCATION
1. The main indicator of learner achievement is ability to do the job effectively.	1. The main indicators of learner achievement are knowledge of the subject and ability to do the job effectively and efficiently.
2. Once a learner has demonstrated ability to do the job, his or her preparation is complete. Time is not a factor. Some learners finish early, others late.	2. Learners operate within specified time limits, such as academic years, semesters, or quarters (or terms). Class hour requirements are generally adhered to.
3. The criterion of success is demonstration of ability to do the job. Mastery criteria are used to determine how well learners perform. These criteria must be met for learners to be considered competent.	3. The criteria of success are letter grades which indicate the extent to which the learner knows the required subject matter.
4. Entrance requirements are not of paramount concern. Learners start where they are. If they are not ready, they are helped to become ready.	4. Entrance requirements are important concerns. Learners who are not ready cannot be admitted.
5. Flexible scheduling of learning activities is essential to provide for individual differences among learners. This allows for year-round educational opportunities and numerous possible times for enrolment.	5. Learners are schedules for instructions into fairly rigid blocks of time. The academic year and infrequent mass registration are standard practices.
6. There are no fixed rules as to how, when, or where learning is to be accomplished.	6. On-campus classroom teaching is the most common approach to instruction. Required lengthy on-campus attendance is standard practice.
7. Opportunities are provided to acquire competencies in practical field or on-the-job experiences.	7. Practical field experiences are limited.
8. Learning (competencies) are presented in small learning units or modules, combinations of which are designed to help learners acquire full competence.	8. Learnings (subject matter) are organised into courses representing academic time units.
9. Provision is made for differences among learners in their styles of learning by providing them with various alternate paths for acquiring competence.	9. Lecture-discussion is the most common mode of presentation, supplemented by seminars, laboratory activities and limited field experiences. Little attention is given to study style of learning.
10. The criterion for a 'good' instructor is the extent to which he or she is effective and efficient in helping learners acquire the competencies they are seeking.	10. The criterion for a 'good' instructor is how much he or she knows about the subject and how well it is presented.

(Source: Johnson 1974)

Figure 5.7   Comparison of competency-based and traditional education (Johnson 1974)

dominant influence on quality. There are differing views about what can and should be negotiable as well as about the teacher's role in negotiation. Topics which might be negotiated include:

1 general organisation of a course
2 teaching/learning strategies
3 methods of assessment (perhaps including the actual marking) (see section on learning contracts in chapter 4)
4 content
5 duration.

The idea of a 'negotiated curriculum' is becoming more acceptable in adult education and lifelong learning, and as Huddleston and Unwin (1997) argue, there are valuable opportunities for teachers and learners to work together to determine what each wants in the way of learning outcomes and so negotiate a 'micro' curriculum.

Arguments for a negotiated curriculum include:

1 Adult learners are the best people to decide their own educational needs.
2 Adult learners can bring considerable experience of their own to the educational situation.
3 It can motivate learners.
4 Learners should have the 'freedom' not be told what they should study.

There are of course strong arguments against a negotiated curriculum. These include:

1 Genuine negotiation is not really possible because the learner has insufficient knowledge of the learning processes and the content associated with the subject.
2 Education is a social activity involving the sharing of ideas (a totally negotiated curriculum might lead to each learner doing something different and studying in isolation).
3 There is an external body of knowledge and skills to which learners should be introduced.

In one sense the idea of a negotiated curriculum stands in direct opposition to the idea of a 'compulsory core curriculum' for all. Although mainly concerned with school education, J.P. White in *Towards a Compulsory Curriculum* (1973) makes some interesting points about choice and experience. Greater choice and experience can be achieved through the reflective process, yet there are too few curricula that embody this process of teaching and learning.

Study problem

As a professional (choose your own field) can you and a fellow learner adapt the curriculum designs discussed above for your curriculum planning and development? Consider the following questions in relation to a particular design (e.g. spiral or negotiated curriculum):

1 What are its constraints?
2 Where are its strengths?

3   What age learner group might it be more suited to?
4   What should the curriculum express?

Advantages of a negotiated curriculum

1   Curricula can be expressed in ways which reflect the realities of a profession's practice.
2   Learning experiences can readily be structured to include or simulate actual industrial activities.
3   Assessment and the maintenance of standards can be related to clearly stated criteria for satisfactory performance.
4   Attention can be given to the development of transferable skills which tend to be neglected or treated in isolation by traditional curricula.
5   Learners can more readily see the relevance of their studies to their intended occupation, with a corresponding improvement in motivation, since they are engaged in tasks which apply theory to practice.
6   The integration of education and training (between which traditional curricula tend to impose a false dichotomy) becomes a real possibility and is indeed encouraged.

A model for curriculum design planning

Problems in the definition or analysis of the term 'curriculum' often (rightly or wrongly) merge into 'models' or accounts of the 'elements' of the curriculum. Useful background reading can be found in Lawton (1973). Lawton presents a number of 'models': the one given here (Figure 5.8) is Lawton's own. It is probably consistent with his suggestion that 'curriculum' needs to be defined 'in terms of the whole learning situation' and not just in terms of the content of a teacher programme (Lawton 1973, p.36).

Study problem

Lawton's model and comments are given below. The following points are for consideration and discussion with fellow learners.

1   Lawton does not seem to have made up his mind whether he sees his model as a representation of what happens anyway (contingently? necessarily?) or of what ought (but does not, at least normally) happen. What he says in the short extract given is consistent with both these (inconsistent) positions. What do you think it is – a representation of what is or what ought to be (or neither)
2   Do you agree with the content of his boxes – i.e. are these the elements on which decisions either are or should be (which is it?) made in the 'curriculum process'? Can you suggest alternatives or additions? Does it (or something similar) apply equally to schools, further education and higher education?
3   Can you suggest substantive content for all or some of the boxes (either Lawton's or proposed alternatives)? Again, be careful to distinguish whether you are suggesting content that reflects what is the case or what (in your judgement) ought to be.

Is this a possible task – even given plenty of time? Consider carefully the implications of your answer.

4   The last sentence of Lawton's comment is worth serious scrutiny as a bit of theorising about education and the curriculum. What is 'an historical accident'? What does the word 'accident' do here? Is the curriculum of our schools and colleges 'an historical accident', and what does it mean to say that it is? Does it, for example, mean there is on that account something wrong with it? What is an historical non-accident? What were, say the Second World War, the Russian Revolution, female suffrage and the 1944 Education Act?

Do you agree with the assumption Lawton makes about who has the right to decide on and plan the curriculum?

What do you think of the assumptions made in the (it seems to me) glib and easy contrast between the time and opportunity to plan a 'curriculum' and 'drift' and from year to year patching up a timetable? What assumptions are made here about a planned curriculum?

Dennis Lawton's curriculum model

All teachers have theories which they try to put into practice. Perhaps their theories are sometimes half-baked, and perhaps their practice is sometimes inconsistent, but if any theory is to become practical it must have the teacher at the center of the model. Bearing this in mind, I would suggest a very simple flow diagram as a basis for considering the curriculum process. All teachers have certain quasi-philosophical views on the aims of education, the structure of knowledge and what is worthwhile (Box 1). Similarly, all teachers have certain quasi-sociological notions about society, social change, the needs of the individual in society, and so on (Box 2). From the interaction of these two sets of ideas I suggest that, especially if these ideas were clarified and systematized, teachers would be able to make some kind of ideal selection from the culture (Box 3). Teachers also have psychological theories, even if these are out of date, or incomplete, which they might bring to bear at this stage (Box 4) and produce a curriculum organized in terms of stages, sequence and so on (Box 5). The ideal might have to be modified still further by the practical realities of limited staff and equipment (Box 6) before reaching the timetable stage (Box 7). I am not suggesting that this is what does happen at the moment, but it is what could happen in schools if teachers had the time and opportunity to plan a curriculum rather than drift on from year to year patching up a timetable which most realize is no more than an historical accident. (Lawton 1973, pp.20–1)

Study problem

Examine Lawton's boxes in more detail and discuss with fellow learners how these might or might not help you in designing and developing a new curriculum for your professional or subject area.

Figure 5.8

Dennis Lawton's curriculum model (Lawton 1973)

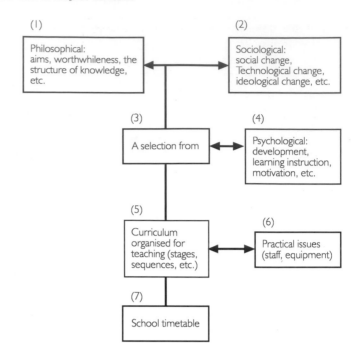

ORGANISATION OF SUBJECT CONTENT

The subjects constituting a course can be brought together and presented to the learner in different ways. Courses such as GCSE, B/TEC, NVQ, GNVQ, degrees, etc., are characterised not only by the subjects they include but also by the format and arrangement of these subjects.

1 The subject based curriculum

The subjects have a distinct and separate identity and are taught independently of each other.

2 The coordinated curriculum

Coordination is the process of linking different subjects or part subjects in a curriculum structure, so as to effect complementarity and interaction between subjects, but retaining the characteristics of each constituent subject or subject area.

A coordinated curriculum establishes a link between subjects on a collaborative or supportive basis; for example in animal behaviour (linking physics, chemistry and biology), or nurse education (linking psychology, sociology, biology and nursing practice) or teacher training (linking psychology, sociology, history of education and policies – see Appendix 1).

A coordinated curriculum involves choosing a common theme, which is considered from the perspectives of different subject areas; for example, the Open University's foundation course in social science in which the theme of 'population explosion' is approached through sociology, psychology, geography, economics and politics; or the PGCE post-compulsory course in

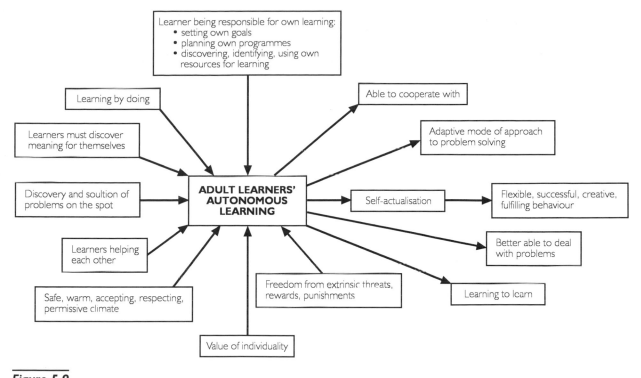

Figure 5.9

Treatment of a common theme in a negotiated curriculum (Neary 1998)

which 'adult learners' is the central theme and is approached through a variety of teaching and learning strategies (see Figure 5.9).

3 The integrated curriculum

Integration is the process of merging different subjects or part subjects through their coordinated use so that the individual components lose their original subject identity and a new curriculum study area emerges. (See Figures 5.10 and 5.11 for examples.) Integration can be intra-disciplinary or inter-disciplinary.

- *Intra-disciplinary integration:* the integration of subjects within a particular field of knowledge, for example integration of two or more of the sciences.
- *Inter-disciplinary integration:* the integration of subjects or part subjects from different fields of knowledge into a new curriculum study area; for example, technology brings together science, economics, aesthetics, etc. A common core for vocational preparation brings together number and its application, communication, problem-solving and planning, manual dexterity, and computer literacy/information technology.

CREDIT TRANSFER SYSTEMS AND MODULARISATION

The introduction of the modular system in most UK universities has led to what we call 'stand alone' modules with a currency of 20 university credits.

Figure 5.10

Example of an integrated curriculum: Revised BTEC First in Caring

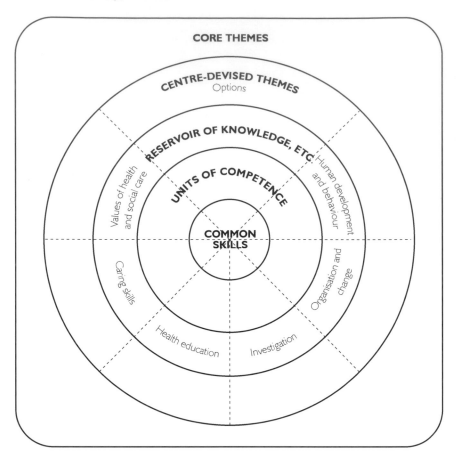

Integrated course structure

Students who successfully complete modules at one university can 'carry' these to another university (transfer of credits) and gain credits for them. It is now possible to collect credits from various universities and be awarded a degree; this is referred to as a credit transfer system.

Credit transfer systems

Accreditation of Prior Experiential Learning (APEL)

APEL is concerned with assessing and accrediting learning outcomes resulting from life and work experiences as a basis for creating new routes into higher education, employment and training opportunities and achieving professional status. The term 'experiential learning' in this context refers to learning which has not been validated previously within an educational or professional system of accreditation.

A frequently stated aim of APEL is to reduce inequalities in society and create new opportunities for so-called 'disadvantaged' groups. APEL is seen as an important means of widening access to higher and continuing education for people who, by virtue of their age, gender, race and socio-economic

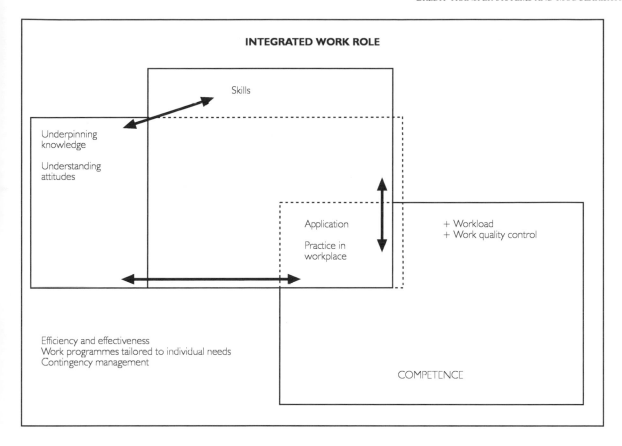

INTEGRATED WORK ROLE

Skills

Underpinning
knowledge

Understanding
attitudes

Application

Practice in
workplace

+ Workload
+ Work quality control

Efficiency and effectiveness
Work programmes tailored to individual needs
Contingency management

COMPETENCE

Figure 5.11

Suggested model for the development of competence in an integrated curriculum

background and/or prior educational qualifications, have traditionally been under-represented.

More recently APEL has come to be seen as not just providing alternative routes of entry to, and exemption from, certain courses in higher education, but also as a means of gaining entry to professions, to jobs and employment progression, and to training and development opportunities sponsored by employers.

The focus of APEL is on the outcomes of learning that has taken place prior to the point of assessment and accreditation; learning experiences are regarded merely as the means through which specific knowledge and skills were acquired. The Council for National Academic Awards (now disbanded) stated that it is not important where, why or how learning is achieved but rather to identify what has been learnt and can be assessed (CNAA 1988).

Hinman (1987) and the UKCC *Fitness for Practice* (1999) for the nursing profession suggest the use of some kind of portfolio as a means of documenting learning outcomes. Processes associated with good practice in APEL are summarised by Mansell (1987) (essential reading). Keeton (1981) suggests that APEL processes and procedures are relevant at a number of points in the educational experience of the learner, and that therefore they should not be restricted to one-off exercises at entry, but rather applied right across the curriculum and at all points of assessment.

Credit Accumulation and Transfer Scheme (CATS)

For some time there has been an awareness of the need for practitioners from a variety of professions (e.g. teachers, nurses, doctors, engineers) to develop skills and knowledge which will allow them to maintain professional competence throughout their working lives. This has given rise to the need to find ways of giving formal recognition to what practitioners already know and can do, regardless of whether this knowledge has been gained as a result of formal courses of study or informally through life experiences. These processes, if recorded, can be used as evidence towards gaining formal academic recognition for work already undertaken through such methods as CATS. CATS goes a long way towards placing the emphasis on what has been learnt rather than where or how that learning has been acquired.

CATS is based on the principle that appropriate learning, wherever it occurs and provided that it can be assessed, should be given academic credit. This means that practitioners could gain credit for learning through work, through short courses they have attended, and through experiences such as voluntary work. It has provided a system for APEL. CATS works by allowing participants to accumulate credit for assessed learning. CATS points can provide a flexible route towards a higher academic award, as shown below.

CATS points	Award
120 at Level 4	Master level
120 at Level 3	First Degree level
120 at Level 2	Diploma level
120 at Level 1	Certificate level

Remember that each academic institution designs and operates its own CATS scheme.

Study problem

With a fellow learner discuss what a participant in CATS would need to do in order to progress through the scheme. The box below may help you in your discussion.

The *Nursing Times* (6 April 1994) has this to say: 'To start with, none of our learning can be accredited until it has been assessed and it cannot be assessed until it has been identified' (Unit 3, p.3), and offers four interrelated stages in the profile and portfolio construction. These are:

- systematic reflection on experience
- identification of significant learning
- identification of evidence to support claims
- submission of portfolio or profile for formal assessment.

Study problem

As a practitioner in your chosen profession, how would you go about collecting the evidence you need to be credited? Use the box to help you map out your own experience.

---

1   Reflection on experience

2   Identification of significant learning

3   Evident to support claims
    a   Direct evidence

    b   Indirect evidence

4   Construction and submission

Adapted from Unit 3, *Nursing Times*, 6 April 1994

Modularisation

A module can be defined as a part or unit of an educational programme. Modular systems can help in the application of credit transfer systems.

Jarvis (1995) suggests that a 'course' may be the course of study followed by an individual within the institution or it may be a single course offered to a specific group of students (e.g. teacher training, nurse education, etc.) As modularisation has developed so the term 'course' has tended to refer to students' individual programme of study. He argues that modules are individual courses, and are designated by the number of hours of learning that a student is expected to undertake; for example, a 50-hour module may involve 15 hours of teaching, 15 hours of private study and 20 hours of assignments.

According to Tuxtworth (1985), locally devised modular schemes may have limited purposes, but where a system-wide modularisation is proposed there has to be a comprehensive rationale for the reform. It is likely that the aims for such an exercise will include changes to establish or improve the system in terms of the following concepts:

- clarity and simplicity of structure
- rationalisation of provision
- equality of access and opportunity
- credit transfer
- multi-agency provision, i.e. education, off-the-job training and work-based learning
- clear routes for progression
- cumulative assessments and credits
- flexible learning opportunities

- economy of operation
- operability in resource terms
- credibility with users of the scheme
- comprehensiveness in terms of the range of opportunities available.

Many of these concepts are not dependent on modularisation for their achievement but there are some which cannot be delivered by the range of monolithic schemes currently used. When embarking on modular reform it is sensible to have a set of criteria from which submissions can be developed and against which they can be evaluated.

Defining a module

As stated above, a module can be defined as a part or unit of an educational programme. It can be further defined in terms of one or more of the following (see also the working definition at the end of this section, p.126).

- study time or course hours
- a list of content (subject knowledge, skills)
- a set of process skills
- a range of prescribed or described learning activities
- a schedule of learning outcomes in the form of competence statements
- a set of outcomes contributing to certification.

Time base

Defining modules as a time period, even if this is qualified as being notional, always seems to give problems. Many would like to avoid making any reference to time in order to focus attention on processes and outcomes and to follow 'mastery learning' principles. But because time is linked to costs and the use of resources, this issue cannot be avoided for long. Educational planners have to allocate resources and thus must be able to estimate how many and what variety of modules can be offered within a given operating period.

Content

Where the purpose of a module is to achieve mastery of a particular subject content or skills it may be justifiable to limit the module by providing a list of items of knowledge to be covered, or a number of product skills to be acquired. It has to be said, however, that this is against the trend of curriculum design, which tends to emphasise 'process' skills rather than the learning of specific product skills. The assumptions are that process skills are more transferable than product skills and that, if processes and intended learning strategies are indicated, teachers can select content which will serve as a vehicle for the development of process skills.

Process skills

Examples of curriculum specification by process skills now abound, including the NVQ, the GNVQ, the Youth Training Scheme Core and the GCSE grade-related criteria. Some of these specifications need much interpretation by teachers to turn them into operational form. Statements such as 'can structure and recall knowledge by use of appropriate classifications and patterns of thought' only become intelligible when they are given a context, a content range and examples of what is to be structured.

Prescribed or described learning activities

Learner-centred techniques such as problem-solving, case studies, assignment work and work experience are often seen as crucial to the educational process and may form a substantial element in module specification. Experiential learning in art or drama, for example, may be critical to the attainment of educational aims and may justifiably be put forward without specification of learning objectives. The assumption is that the completion of the activities constitutes achievement of the educational goals without the need for assessment of outcomes.

Module types

Within a comprehensive modular scheme there will be a range of modules designed to service particular purposes. The range will usually include modules for:

- general education in core subjects or areas
- general education in optional or additional areas
- exploratory and preparatory pre-vocational education, e.g. pre-nursing courses
- core areas related to vocational education and training, such as maths, science, communications, information technology, enterprise skills
- developing technical/vocational competencies common to a number of occupations
- specific occupational training and related education
- meeting the specific needs of individuals' employing organisations
- giving structure, purpose and recognition to the skills developed through work experience or residential courses
- project-based work which serves specified aims and also acts as cross-modular activity to give some measure of coherence to a programme.

Levels

A major issue is whether or not modules can, or should, be free-standing in a hierarchy of levels according to perceived academic difficulty or other criteria. Curriculum module designers will need to consider the extent to which prior knowledge and skills are needed, and to indicate prerequisites where appropriate. There are some areas of study which permit a 'pick and mix' approach. There are other subjects where a sequence of modules in ascending order of difficulty would be preferable.

The suggested levels are keyed to ranges of skills, to the complexity of their application and to the extent of responsibility involved in deploying them. This is an approach which has particular reference to professional education and training.

Modules may represent 'sets of outcomes contributing to certification'. In such a case, examining/awarding bodies will find it necessary to specify or accredit approved programmes or combinations of modules needed for a certificate of award. There may also be stipulations about:

- content and standards within modules
- assessment arrangements
- the length of time which may be taken to complete a programme

- whether individual modules will be certificated separately or only in combinations.

Rigid programme requirements would negate some of the aims of modularisation, but most colleges are now asserting their responsibilities in relation to 'assessment standards' and may be expected to have more real influence over vocational education and training programmes than some have exercised previously.

From an educational viewpoint, there are attractions in the notion of modular programmes based on core modules plus options to form alternative 'pathways' within a given scheme. The need or desire to promote coherence and coordination of learning would lead to preferred combinations being indicated with some inclusion of cross-modular work. Excessive concern with integration on the part of educators may lead to differences of perception between parties to the process; the learner, the employer and the educator may seek different goals. Such differences demand time and mechanisms for negotiation and counselling at points where decisions are taken about enrolment and progression.

Assessment

It is almost inevitable in a modular scheme not tied to a set timetable, that assessment must be carried out locally to approved arrangements. Local assessment with external modification seems the most obvious, if not the only way. But modularisation does not resolve assessment problems on its own; there are perennial issues to be addressed here, arising in a different form:

- A module is an aggregation of elements of learning. What proportion of these elements must be successfully completed for the module as a whole to be passed?
- Is it possible to 'fail' a module or will partial completion be credited?
- How will the marks or grades within a module be combined to produce a result for a module?
- How will process outcomes be assessed and graded?
- Where competence-based outcomes are assessed is there the need also to apply tests of cognition and understanding?
- How will individual learner records (showing modules taken and completed) be maintained – bearing in mind the possibility of different sequences, different combinations within programmes, etc?
- Should standards be centrally set or locally derived?
- How can the costs of moderation and administration be kept within reasonable bounds when modular programmes in different institutions are not 'in phase', as they are when everyone works to the same calendar?
- What particular assessment problems arise when we seek to assess process-based outcomes?

In a modular system the providing institution is likely to have to assume most of the responsibility for assessment, but with moderators and external examiners acting more in relation to programmes and accredited institutions than to modules. There is a great need for teachers/tutors to improve their assessment skills through INSET and ILT programmes for university lectures or some kind of staff development programme. It cannot be assumed that the problem of reliability is simply solved by more detailed specification of outcomes and the creation of very detailed regulations for assessment. More bureaucracy will not replace the necessity for improved skills and shared understandings between local assessors and external examiners.

Profiles and records of achievement

The relationship between performance in individual modules and overall records of achievement in a programme will need some consideration. In a 'pick and mix' system there may be no perceived need for any overall record. The list of modules achieved and their individual performance profiles may be seen as sufficient. But where core competencies are being delivered through a range of subject-based or vocationally orientated modules there is an assumption that the programme outcomes are more than the sum of the parts, as represented by individual module records. In this case some kind of summarising record will be needed.

The elaboration of assessment records to provide both module and programme information for individuals who may be following different combinations of modules will increase the volume and complexity of administration within providing institutions. The need to keep the system simple is obvious – particularly where several different agencies are involved in delivering the total programme. Curriculum management systems within institutions may need to change to accommodate the higher levels of coordination needed with multi-agency provision. Programmes cannot be 'owned' by single departments but have to be managed across institutions and consortia.

A prime aim of modularisation is to increase the range of options open to all adult learners, and to provide programmes which can be tailored to the needs of individual learners. What these needs are, and who determines them, will not always be clear – but what is certain is that the professional responsibilities of teachers and others who advise young people will be increased when real choices are open to the clients.

Modularisation in one institution may improve the organisation of learning in the school, but because of limitations on resources and learner numbers, may not generate new options. Modularisation at system level is needed to increase and open up access to a wider range of resources. The implication here is that large organisational units are needed, and that cooperation, rather than competition, between providers has to be generated. The key role of local education authority officers in fostering consortia and other forms of system coordination is already emerging in pre-vocational education, and even in general education in some areas. The review of vocational qualifications ought to promote extension of the process, but it is difficult to see how this will happen unless the curriculum planners and developers for vocational qualification and similar programmes take a radical stance and positive view of the potential role of modularisation in effecting necessary change. Many universities now offer free-standing Masters modules at 20 credits at M (Masters) level, whilst at the same time incorporating many of the teaching and learning strategies identified in chapter 4 (learning contracts, etc.).

Working definition of modularisation

Modularisation needs to be understood at three levels:

1 Modules
- independent units of credit
- competence based
- notional time base

2 Modular programme
- modules assigned for structural purposes
- strong overall design framework, including arrangements for:
    a. information, guidance and support
    b. assessment, review and adjustment
    c. certification and credit-worthiness
    d. arrangements for access and progression

3 Modular system
- giving credit transfer for each unit and combination of units articulating with preceding education and with any subsequent education and training
- covering the range of attainments
- enabling feasible delivery with a consistent and simple format promoting equality of opportunity and esteem with a support training and research programme

CURRICULUM DESIGN IN PRACTICE

Many newly qualified teachers are asked to become members of a curriculum planning team, which causes them some anxiety because they have no experience or knowledge of curriculum design and development. Many of the PGCE courses for post-compulsory education only cover the 'theory' and not the 'practicum', i.e. the application of curriculum studies to the real world of colleges. The following study problem will help to prepare you for the future planning of your own curriculum.

Study problem

Chapter 3 introduced you to curriculum models. On your own, or with a fellow learner, design a curriculum using one of the models to suit the professional area in which you hope to teach.

- Discuss with a fellow learner the rationale for your choice of design and model.
- What theoretical framework have you used to design your curriculum model?
- Discuss the rationale for your choice.
- Have you considered the function of CATS and APEL in your curriculum?
- Have you considered the use of self-directed learning approaches in your design? (See the box above and Figure 5.12 guidance.) If not, why not?

Study problem

Having completed your curriculum design, examine the examples of curricula set out on pp. 128–38:

GCE AS/A level Physical Education
GCE AS/A level Biology
BTEC Animal Breeding and Behaviour
GCE AS/A level Psychology
BTEC Science and Technology.

Now design a scheme of work and a one-hour lesson plan from any of these examples. Your tutor and/or your teaching practice mentor will help you here. Follow the outline in the diagram below.

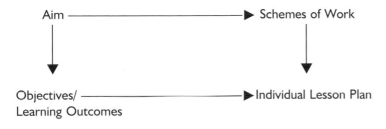

Figure 5.12 is an adaptation to suit our modern courses of a diagrammatic approach to the curriculum for adult learners.

Programme planning	Programme administration	Managing the teaching and learning processes and experiences
Identification of needs	Promotion and probability	
Identification of education goals	Finance facilities	Selection of: • methods • strategies • techniques • devices • resources
Arrangement of learning tests	Instruction, teacher training and selection	
Measurement of achievement	Scheduling	
	Counselling	

EVALUATION
AND
QUALITY AUDIT

Figure 5.12

A diagrammatical approach to the curriculum for adult learners

1 PHYSICAL EDUCATION (GCE AS/A Level)

The focal points of this Physical Education specification are 'participation' and 'performance'. By integrating experiences gained in participation and performance in physical activity with learning about participation and performance, the specification aims to encourage Advanced Subsidiary and Advanced Level candidates to:

- develop knowledge, understanding and skills in a range of physical activities
- understand factors that impinge on their participation and performance in physical activity
- observe, analyse, and evaluate performance as thoughtful participants and intelligent performers
- improve their own and other people's performance
- develop critical appreciation of historical, social, cultural and moral contexts that give meaning to participation and performance in physical activity.

In addition to these aims, the specification encourage Advanced Level candidates to:

- further develop a capacity to think critically about the constituent components of performance in physical activity
- understand local, regional and national provision for participation in physical activity in the context of global trends.

SUMMARY OF ASSESSMENT

Advanced Subsidiary

PE1 Introduction to Performance in Physical Activity

Written examination paper
Short-answer questions – 1½ hours, 30% AS (15% AL)

PE2 Developing Performance in Physical Activity
Coursework Portfolio (Internal Assessment) 40% AS (20% AL)

PE3 Participation and Performance in Physical Activity: Historical, Social, Cultural and Moral Issues

Written examination paper
One compulsory essay and one essay from a choice of four – 1½ hours, 30% AS (15% AL)

Advanced (the above plus the following A2 units)

PE4 Exercise, Health and Fitness

Written examination paper
Short-answer questions and one compulsory essay – 1 hours, 15% AL

PE5   Optimal Performance
        Research Report (Internal Assessment) 20% AL

PE6   Participation in Physical Activity: Thinking Globally Acting Locally
        Written examination paper
        Two essays from a choice of three – 2 hours, 15% AL

Advanced Level

PE4: Exercise, Health and Fitness

Module outline

1. Defining 'exercise', 'health' and 'fitness'
2. Developing health-related exercise programmes
3. Exercise adherence
4. Testing and measuring fitness: laboratory and field tests
5. Monitoring, modifying and developing fitness training programmes
6. Mobility and flexibility: countering the ageing process
7. Diet
8. Drugs
9. Body images
10. Personal choices and investments: lifestyle commitments and intelligent consumption

In this module candidates can nominate **two activities** to provide the focus for learning about exercise, health and fitness issues. **One of the choices must be an exercise activity**.

The module will be assessed by short-answer questions and one compulsory essay.
Time: 1 hour 45 minutes.

Module content
This module is a direct attempt to deal in a critical manner with the concepts of 'exercise', 'health' and 'fitness'. Candidates can nominate **two** activities **to provide the focus for learning about exercise, health and fitness issues**. One of the choices must be an exercise activity. The proposed content includes:

1. **Defining 'exercise', 'health' and 'fitness'**
   An opportunity to provide conceptual clarity and operational definitions of 'exercise', 'health' and 'fitness'. Development of an appropriate vocabulary to unpick debates. What measures can be used? Are there any determinants of people's health status? What do we know about life chances and quality of life?

2. **Developing health-related exercise programmes**
   How are health-related exercise programmes developed? Is there any

consensus about essential components? How to monitor effects? Lifestyle issues.

3. **Exercise adherence**
    What factors encourage or limit adherence to an exercise programme? Examples of research into adherence.

2 BIOLOGY (GCE AS/A level)

Introduction

Criteria for GCE Advanced Subsidiary and Advanced GCE

This specification meets the General Criteria for GCE Advanced Subsidiary (AS) and Advanced (A) and the Subject Criteria for AS/A Biology issued by ACCAC/QCA (June 1999).

Both the Advanced Subsidiary and Advanced GCE qualifications will be reported on a five-grade scale of A, B, C, D and E. Candidates who fail to reach the minimum standard for grade E are recorded as U (unclassified), and do not receive a certificate. The level of demand of the Advanced Subsidiary examination is that expected of candidates half way through a full Advanced course.

The AS assessment units will have equal weighting with the second half of the qualification (A2) when these are aggregated to produce the Advanced award. AS and A2 will each consist of three assessment units, referred to in this specification as BI 1–3 and BI 4–6 respectively. This will allow candidates the opportunity to be assessed either in stages throughout the course, or for all assessments to be taken at the end of the course.

Recommended Prior Learning

Some prior knowledge of biological concepts is recommended. Prior learning from courses other than GCSE or from work based experience may provide a suitable foundation for this course of study.

Mathematical requirements are specified in the subject criteria and repeated in appendix 1 of this specification. It is recommended that, in addition, an understanding of some basic chemical concepts would be advantageous at the start of the course, although knowledge could be acquired during the teaching of the course.

It is recommended, therefore, that an understanding of the following terms is acquired before the end of the course: ion, electron, atom, molecule, element, covalent bond, electrovalent bond, hydrogen bond, condensation reaction, hydrolysis, oxidation, reduction, pH, buffer, diffusion, solubility, partial pressure, along with an understanding of the electromagnetic spectrum and meaning of chemical formulae and the manipulation of chemical equations.

Candidates with Particular Requirements

Requests for consideration of special assessment requirements and special consideration should be submitted to the WJEC. The procedures operated by the WJEC comply with the Joint Forum regulations and guidance entitled 'Candidates with Special Assessment Needs'.

Rationale

Biology provides a wide breadth of knowledge which touches on many varied aspects of a range of topics. These range from the internal workings of organisms in physiology and the interdependence of living things in ecology, to social issues including man's influence on the environment and the ethical considerations of genetics.

The study of biology therefore encourages an appreciation of these issues and their implications as well as providing an insight into the living world.

The WJEC specification is intended to define a body of knowledge and skills which is considered essential to the study of biology at this level. It provides a broad view of all the major aspects of the subject and an appreciation of their interdependence. The breadth of study and updated content will enable the implications of modern biology to be appreciated and the importance of the role of these studies in understanding environmental, ethical and social issues and their implications. An understanding of scientific method as the means by which the body of scientific knowledge is increased and an enquiring and critical approach is to be fostered, including an awareness that different perceptions, predictions and interpretations may be applied according to context.

The practical work serves to illustrate and to promote an investigatory approach. The use of computer technology such as CD-Roms, the Internet and computer simulations is encouraged.

It is intended that the use of a variety of approaches will stimulate interest, promote understanding and engender an overall appreciation and sense of wonder at the living world.

The broad objectives therefore are:

- to provide a broad factual base and skills
- to stimulate an interest in the subject
- to facilitate a critical appreciation of issues arising from the subject.

Aims

The aims of the specification at AS and Advanced are, as cited in the subject criteria, as follows:
(a) To enable candidates to develop essential knowledge and understanding of concepts of biology, and the skills needed for the use of these in new and changing situations.
(b) To enable candidates to develop an understanding of scientific methods.
(c) To encourage candidates to be aware of advances in technology, including information technology, relevant to biology.
(d) To enable candidates to recognise the value and responsible use of biology in society.

(e) To encourage candidates to sustain and develop their enjoyment of, and interest in, biology and provide a stimulus for further reading.

In addition a further aim at Advanced is:

(f) To enable candidates to show knowledge and understanding of facts, principles and concepts from different areas of biology and to make and use connections between them.

Additional aims of the specification are also:

(g) To provide a suitable foundation for the study of biology or related courses in further and higher education.

(h) To encourage candidates to develop the skills of collecting and analysing information and providing a suitable concise and coherent explanation or description.

(i) To stimulate candidates' interest in, and awareness of, the social, technological, environmental and economic impact of biology in present day society.

(j) To provide candidates not intending to study biology at a higher level with a useful and worthwhile course.

GCE AS/A LEVEL BIOLOGY 2

Key Skills

The Key Skills qualification requires that candidates demonstrate achievement in communication, application of number and information technology. Further guidance and details of the exact requirements may be obtained from WJEC support and guidance material.

The assessment units provide a range of possible opportunities both to develop Key Skills and generate evidence of attainment at level 3. The following table indicates the location within the assessment units of these opportunities. However, it does not preclude the presence of other opportunities within the assessment units which are dependent on individual teaching programs and strategies.

Opportunities include: class discussions and presentations, the use of graphs and diagrams along with written descriptions to present and explain topics, data collection both through practical or laboratory work and through secondary sources such as the Internet and computerised information and retrieval systems.

What you must do	Content area reference within section 3									
Communication (level 3)										
C3.1a Discussion	1.4	1.6	1.5	2.4	2.5	2.6	4.6	4.8	5.2	5.5
C3.1b Presentation	1.4	1.6	1.5	2.4	2.5	2.6	4.6	4.8	5.2	5.5
C3.2 Read and Synthesise	1.4	1.6	1.5	2.4	2.5	2.6	4.6	4.8	5.2	5.5
C3.3 Write	1.4	1.6	1.5	2.4	2.5	2.6	4.6	4.8	5.2	5.5

Application of number (level 3)

N3.1 Plan and interpret						5.2	
N3.2 Multi-stage calculation	1.2					5.2	
N3.3 Interpret results	1.2			4.5		5.2	
N3.3 Present findings	1.2			4.5		5.2	

Information technology (level 3)

IT3.1 Plan and use sources	1.6	1.5	2.5	2.6	4.6	4.8	5.2	5.5
IT3.2 Develop and exchange	1.6	1.5	2.5	2.6	4.6	4.8	5.2	5.5
IT3.3 Present information	1.6	1.5	2.5	2.6	4.6	4.8	5.2	5.5

The wider Key Skills of problem solving and working with others may be addressed, more particularly through practical work, although the amassing of evidence for a group discussion, for instance on ethics, could also involve group working. Improving own learning and performance permeates all subject areas and assessment objectives, although it may be related to the acquiring of specific skills, as in competence in IT or laboratory procedures and equipment, or through the understanding of particularly complex areas of subject matter.

3 ANIMAL BREEDING AND BEHAVIOUR (BTEC)

Description of unit

This unit provides an introduction to the breeding of animals and the study and understanding of their behaviour. It develops students' knowledge of the management of breeding stock and the care of youngstock. It also enables students to consider learning, behaviour and training of animals, and the relationship between these aspects.

Summary of outcomes

To achieve this unit a student must:

1 Evaluate the selection and management of breeding stock
2 Review modern advances in reproductive technology
3 Identify learning methods and behaviour patterns
4 Investigate the practical application of animal psychology.

Content

1 Selection and management of breeding stock

Selection of breeding stock: suitable breeding females and stud males, genotypes, phenotypes, health, temperament and performance
Management of breeding stock: stud males, breeding females throughout oestrus, mating, pregnancy, parturition and rearing
Breeding problems: infertility, dystocia, post-partum problems

Care of youngstock: rearing, hand rearing and fostering, weaning, socialisation, early training, homing

Breeders' responsibilities: ethics, legislation, identification of stock, registration and breed societies

2 Reproductive technology

Biotechnology: infertility treatments, superovulation and synchronisation, ovulation indicators, artificial insemination, embryo transplant, pregnancy diagnosis, cloning, birth control, genetic analysis and engineering, transgenics

Scientific advances and ethics: research justification, commercial sponsorship and utilisation, ethical viewpoints, techniques – advantages and disadvantages

3 Learning methods and behaviour patterns

Learning methods: fixed action patterns, imprinting, spatial learning, habituation, latent learning, imitation, associative learning

Communication: visual, auditory, olfactory, tactile

Animal behaviour: socio-biology, relationships – inter- and intra-specific, predator/prey, social hierarchy, territoriality, reproductive behaviour – courtship, mating, post-mating, parturition, nursing and parenting, bonding and imprinting, photoperiodism and orientation behaviour, behavioural comparisons between domesticated and wild species

Neural control of behaviour: homeostasis, chemoregulation, thermoregulation

4 Animal psychology

Domestication: history, species suitability, utilisation

Conditioning and behaviour modification: classical and operant conditioning, conflict behaviour, displacement behaviour

Animal intelligence: sentience, self awareness, culture

Training methodology: utilisation of natural behaviour in training objectives, training programmes, welfare considerations

Outcomes and assessment criteria

Outcomes	Assessment criteria To achieve each outcome a student must demonstrate the ability to:
1 Evaluate the **selection and management of breeding stock**	• Review the selection of suitable breeding stock • Describe appropriate management of breeding and youngstock • Identify common breeding problems • Describe responsible breeding practice
2 Review modern advances in **reproductive technology**	• Analyse the role of biotechnology in practical animal breeding • Evaluate merits, disadvantages and conflicting viewpoints about scientific reproductive techniques
3 Identify **learning methods and behaviour patterns**	• Describe the different methods of learning in animals • Identify and describe communication in animals

4	Investigate the practical application of **animal psychology**	• Evaluate animal behaviour patterns and strategies • Explain the role of neural control in behaviour • Describe the process of domestication of animal species • Explain conditioning and behaviour modifications • Review the meaning of and evidence for animal intelligence • Evaluate training methodology.

4 PSYCHOLOGY (GCE AS/A Level, 2001/2002)

Prior level of attainment and recommended prior learning

This specification is suitable for the diverse range of candidates who wish to develop their interest and enjoyment in Psychology, fostering its value in lifelong learning.

It is not necessary for candidates to have studied GCSE Psychology before commencing work on this specification and no prior knowledge of Psychology is necessary. It is desirable for candidates to have achieved Grades A–C in GCSE, or the equivalent, in English and Mathematics before commencing this specification, though no formal qualification is required.

AIMS

At AS and A Level

This specification in Psychology encourages candidates to:

(a) Study psychological theories, research, terminology, concepts, studies and methods.
(b) Develop skills of analysis, interpretation and evaluation.
(c) Develop an understanding of different areas of Psychology, including the core areas of Cognitive, Social, Developmental, Physiological Psychology and Individual Differences and Research Methods.
(d) Design and report psychological investigations, and analyse and interpret data.
(e) Develop an understanding of ethical issues in Psychology, including the ethical implications of psychological research.

At A Level

In addition, this A level specification in Psychology:

(a) Includes the study of psychological principles, perspectives and applications.
(b) Enables candidates to explore and understand the relationship between psychological knowledge, theories and methodology and their relationship to social, cultural, scientific and contemporary issues.
(c) Enables the development of critical and evaluative skills in relation to theory, empirical studies and methods of research in Psychology.

(d) Enables candidates to have an understanding and critical appreciation of the breadth of theoretical and methodological approaches in Psychology.

Assessment Objectives

All candidates are required to meet the following assessment objectives. The assessment objectives are to be weighted as indicated in Sections 7.2 and 8.4.

At A level candidates are required to demonstrate both their knowledge and understanding and their ability to analyse in greater depth and to a wider range of content than at AS.

Scheme of Assessment

Advanced Subsidiary (AS)
The Scheme of Assessment has a modular structure. The Advanced Subsidiary (AS) award comprises three compulsory assessment units which assess the teaching and learning modules described in the subject content as shown below.

Unit 1	Written Unit	1 hour
33⅓ % of the total AS marks	62 marks	

This unit will be divided into two, equally weighted sections.

Section A Cognitive Psychology: Memory

Section B Developmental Psychology: Attachments in development

There will be **two** structured questions in each section, of which candidates must answer **one from each section.**

Unit 2	Written Unit	1 hour
33⅓ % of the total AS marks	62 marks	

Section A Physiological Psychology: Stress

Section B Individual Differences: Definitions and models of abnormality

There will be **two** structured questions in each section, of which candidates must answer **one from each section.**

Unit 3	Written Unit	1 hour
33⅓ % of the total AS marks	62 marks	

Section A Social Psychology: Social influence
There will be **two** structured questions, of which candidates must answer **one.**

Section B Research Methods
This section will comprise **two** compulsory, short answer questions. Stimulus material may be included in these questions. The questions will focus upon issues related to designing, conducting and reporting psychological investigations.

5 SCIENCE AND TECHNOLOGY (BTEC)

Main Aims

To develop a critical approach and an ability to apply scientific and technological principles, reasoning and skills to problems and issues of everyday life.

To develop an appreciation of and interest in science and technology and their interrelation with society and the environment.

To develop a responsible attitude to the moral and legal implications of science and technology.

Sub-Aim 1

To develop a critical approach and an ability to apply scientific and technological principles, reasoning and skills to problems and issues of everyday life.

Course Objectives	Suggested Teaching/Learning Activities
The course should provide opportunities for the young person to	
1.1. Demonstrate a knowledge and understanding of a range of scientific phenomena, facts, laws, principles, and concepts, using appropriate vocabulary	It is suggested that young people should carry out projects/assignments which cover as wide a variety of objectives as possible, where appropriate integrating objectives from other core areas with those in Science and Technology. Projects should cover a variety of themes from science and technology, and where possible, should have some relevance to young people's occupational preferences (see vocational groupings).
1.2. Identify and describe the nature of simple scientific and technical problems (ref: Industrial, Social and Environmental Studies 5.3)	
1.3. Suggest and select alternative explanations, causes or solutions (e.g. by forming hypotheses, using models, using analogies)	
1.4. Plan investigations and design experiments in order to test explanations.	
1.5. Follow technical instructions, work to a plan	
1.6. Select, assemble and use scientific and technical apparatus and instrumentation appropriately and safely (ref: Practical Skills 1.6)	
1.7. Observe and record data and procedures systematically and accurately in a suitable form (ref: Communication 1.2, Numeracy 1.9)	

Continued overleaf

1.8. Interpret and evaluate data and results of experimental work in order to make deductions and draw conclusions

1.9. Evaluate an investigation/experiment/ procedure (e.g. identify sources of error and explain their significance, devise and use simple tests to check the validity of measurements and experimental work)

1.10. Generalise as and when appropriate from experimental results

Sub-Aim 2 (example)
To develop an appreciation of and interest in science and technology and their interrelation with society and the environment.

LESSON PLANNING

Lesson planning involves a consideration of the following:

- aims and objectives
- content and subject matter
- evaluation and assessment
- methods and learning experiences
- structure and organisation
- rationale.

Main points to remember when planning a lesson

Before planning your lesson you should reflect on the points listed below. The less experienced teacher should make lesson notes.

1 The students

- Who are they?
- What is their academic standard/level?
- Knowledge, understanding and attitude towards subject matter
- Any problems (known from previous experience)

2 Subject matter

- Relates to curriculum, syllabus or scheme of work
- Approach to delivery
- Learning objectives
- Teaching method: how appropriate and why?
- Audio-visual aid (AVA): how helpful?
- General heading of lesson
- Any test/assessment
- How to evaluate

3 Resources

- Time available

- How quickly should progress be made?
- Time of day
- Where is lesson to be taught: classroom, laboratory?
- Special apparatus
- AVA

Lesson structure

There are four main parts to a well-planned lesson:

- introduction
- central section (development)
- conclusion (recapitulation)
- evaluation

All parts should be carefully planned. The conclusion is as important as the introduction. A conclusion provides a final opportunity of ensuring consolidation, assimilation and retention and ought to include a revision which may be in the form of a question and answer session. (See Figure 5.13.)

Date:	Title of course:
Class:	Duration of lesson: 1 hour

Subject of lesson:

Aim of lesson:

Learning objectives:

Rationale:

TEST or ASSESSMENT of Student learning

Approx. time	Lesson content and development	Method	AVA
10 mins	Introduction Recapitulation of last session	Exposition QPA	
5 mins	Statement and explanation of lesson objectives		
15 mins	DEVELOPMENT 1 Concept I: Contents of lesson	Exposition QPA	OH projector
15 mins	Concept II: Content of lesson	Exposition and discussion	Flip chart
5 mins	DEVELOPMENT 2: Consolidation Recapitulation via discussion	QPNA	OH projector
2 mins	Announcement of title and intention of next lesson	Exposition	

AVA: audio-visual aid; QPA: question, pause and answer; QPNA: question, pause, nominate and answer

Figure 5.13

Structure for a lesson plan and sequence of lesson content

Teacher's aim in planning a lesson

A teacher's aim in planning a lesson must be to motivate, stimulate, communicate, hold attention, achieve defined objectives, control the lesson and give feedback. A lesson should:

- be pitched correctly
- be related to what the students already know
- have realistic and clear goals/objectives
- be orderly, logical and consequential
- have an ordered, simple and clear exposition
- be presented to ensure student/teacher activity and involve a variety of media
- proceed from the known to the unknown
- proceed from the simple to the complex
- proceed from the concrete to the abstract
- proceed from the particular to the general
- proceed from observation to reasoning
- proceed from the whole to the parts and back to the whole.

Questions used by the teacher during a lesson should be:

- clear, precise, unambiguous and relevant
- carefully prepared and timed.

The best-laid plans can go astray, however, and it may be necessary to modify your lesson.

Consider the following section on aims and objectives when planning your lesson.

Aims and objectives

These constitute the basic elements in educational planning. Although they exist at different levels of generality, collectively they make up the building blocks of the total programme. The most general aims are broad and often abstract in their expression, and will offer guidance as to the general direction of educational information. At another level they will be less broad and general, and as such will form the basis of curricula; unlike the more general aims they will suggest tangible achievements and imply rather more specified time limits.

Aims

An aim is defined as a general expression of intent, and the degree of generality contained in the statement may vary from the very general in the case of long-term aims to the much less general in the case of short-term aims.

Objective/learning outcomes

By contrast, objectives are characterised by greater precision and specificity; again, at one extreme will be objectives that are fairly specific and at the other objectives that are extremely so.

Long-term aims and short-term aims

Long-term aims form the basis of a college's *raison d'être*, thus defining the nature and character of its overall educational programme in relation to social and individual needs. Short-term aims will constitute the logical starting point for curricular construction and the devising of schemes of work.

Objectives expressing varying degrees of specificity will be derived from such aims, especially the short-term ones, and will represent their translation into specific and tangible terms necessary for planning a course of lessons (referred to as a scheme of work), individual lessons or units of learning on which the ultimate realisation of the aims depends.

The following example of an aim and a learning objective will help the reader to see the distinction between them more clearly.

Aim

To provide the student with the opportunity to explore and acquire a knowledge and understanding of the society in which they live.

Learning objective

At the end of the lesson the student will be able to describe in detail the principle characteristics of the society in which they live.

CONCEPTUAL FRAMEWORKS

Curriculum design is often developed from conceptual frameworks. Teacher training schemes are increasingly becoming skills based, with associated supportive theory. This has required curriculum planners to examine alternative models for curriculum design. When courses were heavily knowledge based and theory preceded practical experience, a curriculum based upon a taxonomy as described by Bloom (1965) was and still is useful (though Bloom's taxonomy is not the only conceptual framework and indeed, it could be argued, it should not be). The students follow a series of levels, commencing with a basic knowledge, and then progress through increasingly complex intellectual stages until the higher level of understanding has been reached. An experience-based course does not deny intellectual skills; indeed, the reverse is the case, for it seeks to integrate them with both attitudinal and psychomotor skills to produce a student who can recognise the relationship between thinking, feeling and doing. When a student teacher learns from a particular experience in a classroom, they do not just learn a piece of knowledge or a physical skill or undergo a feeling in isolation each from the other. Any experience in which the student participates has a degree of knowing, feeling and doing, and we refer to these as domains; hence there is a cognitive domain for knowing, an effective domain for feeling and attitudes and a psychomotor domain for physical action or doing. In devising a course using these separate domains of behaviour so that each subject is planned for, the knowledge part of it is designed to be taught first, then the practical aspects, and finally the attitudes or feeling about it. There is a risk that this might seem artificial and inappropriate, but most teacher educators do their best to design a course that ensures the integration of all three domains through the teaching, learning and assessment processes.

Steinaker and Bell (1979) describe an approach to teaching, learning and assessing that claims not to break down human behaviour artificially into knowing, feeling and doing but to see human experience as a whole, bigger than the sum total of its parts. Curriculum planners need reminding that human behaviour is a holistic process and that all three domains of behaviour need to be integrated in a compatible and complementary manner for relevant learning to occur. Where the main approach to learning consists of deliberate exposure of the student to situations or experiences, it is becoming increasingly referred to as experiential learning (see chapter 4). If an entire curriculum is based upon a sequence or series of levels of experience for which there are appropriate learning outcomes and competences to be achieved, learning principles and learning strategies, then it is reasonable to call this an 'experiential taxonomy'. There are five levels of experience, from exposure to the situation to the final level of dissemination (Neary 2000, p.140). These are described briefly as follows:

Experiential taxonomy model

1 **Exposure:** Consciousness of an experience. This involves two kinds of exposure and a readiness for further experience.

    1.1 *Sensory:* Through various sensory stimuli one becomes exposed to the possibility of an experience.

    1.2 *Response:* Peripheral mental reaction to sensory stimuli. At this point one rejects or accepts further interaction with the experience.

    1.3 *Readiness:* At this level one accepts the experience and anticipates participation.

2 **Participation:** The decision to become physically a part of an experience. There are two levels of interaction within this category.

    2.1 *Representation:* Reproducing an existing mental image of the experience, mentally or physically or both, i.e. visualising, verbalising, role playing, dramatic play. This can be done in two ways.

    2.1.1 *Covertly:* as a private, personal 'walk through' rehearsal.

    2.1.2 *Overtly:* in a small/large group, interaction, i.e. the classroom or playground.

    2.2 *Modification:* The experience develops with the input of past personal activities and the experience grows. As there is a personal input into the participation one moves from role-player to active participant.

3 **Identification:** As the participant modifies the experience, the process of identification with the experience begins. There are four levels of activity within this category.

    3.1 *Reinforcement:* As the experience is modified and repeated there is a reinforcement of the experience involving a decision to identify with the experience.

    3.2 *Emotional:* The participant becomes emotionally identified with the experience. It becomes 'my experience'.

    3.3 *Personal:* The participant moves from an emotional identification to an intellectual commitment which involves a rational decision of identification.

    3.4 *Sharing:* Once the process of identification is accomplished the participant begins to share the experience with others as a positive factor in the participant's life. This kind of positive sharing continues through category 4 (internalisation).

4   **Internalisation::** The participant moves from identification to internalisation when the experience begins to affect the lifestyle of the participant. There are two levels in this category.

   4.1 *Expansion:* The experience enlarges into many aspects of the participant's life, changes attitudes and activities as a result of the experience. When these become more than temporary the participant moves to the next category.

   4.2 *Intrinsic:* The participant's lifestyle becomes characterised by the experience and that character remains more constant than at the expansion level.

5   **Dissemination:** The experience moves beyond internalisation to the dissemination of the experience. It goes beyond positive sharing which began at level 3 and involves two levels of activity:

   5.1 *Informational:* The participant seeks to stimulate others to have an equivalent experience through descriptive and personalised sharing (advertising).

   5.2 *Homiletic:* The participant sees the experience as an imperative for others to have.

It should be noted that the categories of this taxonomy are stated in positive terms, while an experience can bring forth either positive or negative reactions. For the purpose of teaching and learning a positive statement of categories is essential. A teacher seldom, if ever, purposefully plans experiences in which learners are expected to react negatively.

One notes that this Experiential Taxonomy relates closely to existing taxonomies of educational objectives. It is perhaps most closely related to the Affective Taxonomy, particularly in the Identification (3) and Internalisation (4) categories. Yet it augments the affective domain by specifying the exposure and motivational aspects of experience in its Exposure (1) category. Additionally, it adds a further dimension of human activity beyond category 3 of the Affective Taxonomy (Characterisation of a Value Complex) by including the process of disseminating an experience. This is not touched upon by the Affective Taxonomy. This Experiential Taxonomy provides, therefore, a more complete classification of human activity than does the Affective Taxonomy (Steinaker and Bell 1979).

Study problem

1   Examine each level of the Experiential Taxonomy carefully and place your learners at the level you perceive they are at.

2   Now take the opportunity to work with your learner and ask them to place themselves at the level they perceive to be at.

3   Compare the outcomes. If they differ, you both will need to discuss the reasons and rationales and a plan of action may need to be agreed to help bring the positions closer to each other.

4   You may need to create and agree a new learning contract to enhance further developments.

FURTHER READING

Bernstein, B. (1975) *Class, Codes and Control. Vol. 1: Theoretical Studies towards a Sociology of Language*. London, Routledge and Kegan Paul.

Bines, H. (1992) 'Issues in course design'. In H. Bines and D. Watson (eds), *Developing Professional Education*. Buckingham, Society for Research into Higher Education and Open University Press.

Boone, E. (1985) *Developing Programmes in Adult Education*. Englewood Cliffs, New Jersey, Prentice Hall.

Bourner, T., Martin, V. and Race, P. (eds) (1993) *Workshops that Work*. Maidenhead, McGraw-Hill.

Brundage, D.H. and Macheracher, D. (1980) *Adult Learning Principles and Their Application to Programme Planning*. Toronto, Ontario Institution for Studies in Education.

Chickering, A.W. (1983) *Education, Work and Human Development: Making Sponsored Experiential Learning Standard Practice*. New Directions for Experiential Learning, No. 20. San Francisco, Jossey-Bass and Cael.

Jessup, G. (1994) *GNVQ: An Alternative Curriculum Model*. London, NCVQ.

Lambert, P. (1987) 'The assessment of prior learning: curriculum duplication'. In C. Griffin (ed.), *Assessing Prior Learning: Progress and Practices*. Conference report, June. London, Learning from Experience Trust.

Mansell, E. (1987) 'The way ahead: priorities for the future'. In C. Griffin (ed.), *Assessing Prior Learning Progress and Practices*. Conference report, June. London, Learning from Experience Trust.

UNDERSTANDING COMPETENCIES AND LEARNING OUTCOMES

6

Learning outcomes

To be achieved through the process of self-directed study, teacher/mentor support and sharing learning with fellow students
By the end of this chapter you will be able to:

- define competencies and learning outcomes
- discuss the elements and principles of a competence-based learning programme
- design your own course, identifying the learning outcomes and competencies to be achieved
- explain how competencies can be assessed and the levels at which they can be achieved.

UNDERSTANDING COMPETENCIES

There has been much debate over the last 20 years on issues relating to objectives, learning outcomes, competencies and competence. Whilst much is written to help clarify meaning, much confusion still exists which does not enhance the quality assurance process, so let's start with understanding.

Runciman (1990) described 'competence' as over- rather than ill-defined. The growing concern to find ways of assessing it seems to have heightened such confusion. The critics of the competence-based movement (Ashworth and Saxton 1990; Fagan 1984; Hyland 1991, 1992 and 1993; Jessup 1990 and 1991; McAleavey and McAleer 1991; Marshall 1991) have claimed that competence-based education is essentially concerned with performance in employment. They castigate the attempt to specify what is to be achieved and measured as nothing more than reconstituted behaviourism, in which traditionalist origins are clearly to be found. While constructed out of a fusion of behavioural objectives and accountability (Fagan 1984, p.5), specific accounts of competence seek to remain true to the behaviourist enterprise by insisting that the assessment of competence is independent of any learning process and should ideally be undertaken in the workplace. This specific conception of competence, founded squarely on behaviourist learning principles, suffers from all the weakness traditionally identified with such programmes (Radford and Govier 1980). Nevertheless, it is our contention that comprehensive assessment only occurs when natural interactions are guided and not bound to behavioural objectives.

Defining competencies

The standard Training Agency (1989, p.1) definition of competence is as follows:

[Standards] will form the prime focus of training and the basis of vocational qualifications. Standards development should be based on the notion of competence which is defined as the ability to perform the activities within an occupation. Competence is a wide concept which embodies the ability to transfer skills and knowledge to new situations within the occupational area. It encompasses organisation and planning of work, innovation and coping with non-routine activities. It includes those qualities of personal effectiveness that are required in the workplace to deal with co-workers, managers and customers.

Brown and Knight (1995) argued that:

Competence probably replaces, albeit at a more sophisticated level, the concept of skills. That doesn't necessarily make it easier to understand what competencies are, let alone how they are to be recognised. (p.27)

Miller *et al.* (1988) suggested two senses in which competence can be defined. First, competence may be equated with performance, the ability to perform nursing tasks. Second, competence may be viewed as a 'psychological construct', requiring evaluation of learners' abilities to integrate cognitive, affective and psychomotor skills when delivering nursing care. While Runciman (1990) recognised the difficulty in observing this psychological construct, she suggested that it can be 'seen' through the individual's competent performance. It can be argued therefore the two senses are not mutually exclusive. Miller *et al.* (1988) suggested that the level of the learners' performance is dependent on the development of their psychological constructs.

Wolf (1989) argued that 'competence' was about the ability to perform at agreed standards, incorporated in a statement of competence which specified the nature of the particular, performable occupational role. Competence is a construct and not something that we can observe directly.

However, we may be able to find good, observable, measurable performance. Messick (1975 and 1982) agreed that the available definitions were not in fact very specific, but did tend to indicate what sort of measures definers accepted as a source of evidence. Most of the situations in which people were serious about measuring competence tended to be vocational, such as nursing, social work and teaching. 'Definers' usually meant the people who controlled licensing and qualifications. In nursing and teaching, competencies to be achieved were identified by the professional body. In developing competence-based vocational training and qualifications, most emphasis has been on 'output', on encouraging the direct assessment of 'performance', preferably in the workplace, as the preferred measure of competence. Contemporary psychological theory sees human beings as creators of mental models, general 'schemata' which they apply to particular circumstances and modify with experience (Jeeves and Greer 1983; Race and Brown 1995; Snow *et al.* 1980; Sternberg 1986). This approach emphasises that 'knowing' something involves knowing when to access it, and being able to do so when appropriate. Messick (1982) argued:

At issue is not merely the amount of knowledge accumulated, but its organisation or structure as a functional system for productive thinking, problem solving, and creative invention. The individual's structure of knowledge is a critical aspect of ... achievement ... A person's structure of knowledge in a subject area includes not only declarative knowledge about substances (or information about what), but also procedural knowledge about methods (or information about how), and strategic knowledge about alternatives for goal setting and planning (or information about which, when and possibly why) ... Knowledge structure basically refers to the structure of relationships among concepts. But as knowledge develops, these structures quickly go beyond classifications of concepts as well as first-order relations among concepts and classes to include organised systems of relationships or schemes. (pp.1–3)

Another way of putting this is to say that, whenever we learn something specific, we also learn something general.

Whatever the knowledge is which goes to make up an occupational or professional competence, it is unlikely to be just factual. All the research on critical reasoning (Forsythe *et al.* 1986) found information to be a necessary condition of competence. However, Eraut (1985) argued that tests that measure only factual recall are inadequate measures of knowledge and unlikely to provide much evidence of professional competence.

Elements and principles

An overall competence is made up of a number of 'elements' (see chapter 5). But the way in which complex activities are 'made up' of elements of competence is unspecified. In fact, the individual elements of a complex skill cannot even be defined independently of the rest. For example, let us consider the following competence: 'to advise on the promotion of health and the prevention of illness' (UKCC Rule 18 1989). What are the specific elements which make up this particular competence? Do these elements add up to the competence and this alone? Surely they are intermeshed aspects of a very broad and complex intention. Take the further example of 'asepsis'. A learner may learn what to do and what not to do by assimilating a long list of rules such as hand-washing, disposal of soiled dressings, bed spacing, and so on. But this does not ensure that the learner knows the principles of asepsis.

All of the elements need to be seen as together constituting a common whole if competent care is to be achieved. Some teachers may overcome this problem by emphasising the rationale for teaching the principles of asepsis, rather than demonstrating the step-by-step approach favoured by others.

McGagaghie *et al.* (1978) argued that the desirable attributes of a professional, whether lawyer, teacher, hairdresser, physician or basic medical scientist, are determined by many influences. Expert opinion, the practice setting, the types of clients and their problems to be encountered, the nature of a discipline or a specialism, the stage of socio-economic development of a community or nation (present as well as future) all need to be considered. In reaching a decision about the competence goals for a specific curriculum, planners may either examine all or select only a few of these essential determinants, depending upon the type of professional being educated and trained, the curriculum level, or simply the time and resources available. Whatever sources are employed, the primary consideration in planning must always be the nature of the professional role a learner must play, not merely the information that college staff or experts are most comfortable in teaching.

The critics of this model rarely get beyond the question: 'What is competence practice?' It would be pointless to suggest that there is a single definition. Competence includes a broad range of knowledge, attitudes and observable patterns of behaviour which together account for the ability to deliver a specified professional service. The competent individual can correctly perform numerous (but not necessarily all) tasks, many of which require knowledge, theories, principles of social sciences or comprehension of the social and cultural factors that influence the climate. Competence in this sense also involves adoption of a professional role that values human life. The competencies to be achieved are many and multifaceted. They may also be ambiguous and tied to local custom and constraints of time, finance and human resources. Nevertheless, a competence-based curriculum in any setting assumes that the many roles and functions involved in the learner adults' work can be defined and clearly expressed. It does not imply that what are defined are the only elements of competence, but rather that, that which can be defined represents the critical point of departure in curriculum development. Careful delineation of these components of, for example, teaching practice can be regarded as the first and most critical step in designing a competence-based curriculum. When learners master the functions that constitute an acceptable repertoire of professional practices they are judged to be ready to work as competent individuals.

Teaching for competence

According to Boss (1985) teaching for competence is the most challenging aspect of a teacher's role. With the vast increase in knowledge, technology and complexity in society, employers must respond to constant demands for educated competent professionals who not only need knowledge and skill but must also be able to make critical judgements and smart decisions, solve highly complex problems, think critically and be reflective practitioners.

During the past 20 years, various instructional strategies have been proposed and described in the literature. Each method was claimed to increase the effectiveness of learner learning. While evidence showed that organisation and presentation could induce a difference in learners' learning, each method also requires to be seen in relation to a greater goal: that of teaching for competence. The challenge for the lecturer and teacher is to select appropriate learning outcomes which will lead to achieving the competencies, specify evaluation indicators and develop a functional instructional delivery system.

Practitioners and teachers argue that competence is more than knowledge and skill. Values, critical thinking, professional judgement, formulation of attitudes, the integration of theory from the humanities and the sciences into the professional role are also competencies.

What should competence-based education aspire to do?

Boss (1985, pp. 8–12) suggests that competence-based education should aspire to include the following characteristics:

1   Competencies should guide educational planning, where each describes the

desired behavioural outcome, and this guides planning, implementation of learning experiences, and the prescription of methods of evaluation.

2 Competencies should derive from roles and emphasise performance rather than knowledge, emphasising how the learner will use their acquired knowledge, accepting that application of knowledge does not end with simple recall. The competency should always be stated in such a way as to answer the question: 'What will the learner be doing?'

3 Competencies should emphasise professional judgement, not just psycho-motor skill, for skills competence is not simply performing a skill. It includes making some judgement about the accuracy and appropriateness of the skill and it implies a standard of excellence. The competency should be oriented to directing and ensuring learning in the higher levels of cognitive, affective and psychomotor domains.

4 Competencies should state the conditions under which a learner performs actions or behaviours and the standard of such performance. Examples of a competency statement from specific curricula might be:

- *Counselling curriculum:* Given a client experiencing psychological stress (condition), the learner will be able to assess and intervene (action) so that the client can more effectively cope with the stress (standard of performance).

- *Health and Social Care curriculum:* Given a post-operative client (condition), the learner will assess (action) fluid and electrolyte status and implement (action) nursing interventions that will assist the client to maintain fluid and electrolyte balance (standard of performance).

- *Research Methods curriculum:* Based on the principles of design and analysis (condition), the learner will be able to analyse (action) critically (standard of performance) a research study and determine the applicability of the findings to practice.

Such a competence-based curriculum clearly calls for new skills on the part of teaching staff, practitioners who enact the roles of mentor and assessor and evaluator of learners' learning. Moreover, its existence presupposes the identi-fication of 'experts' from whom judgements are sought. An example of the machinery that might be used in such an exercise was developed by Neary (1992b). Here the Curriculum Planning Team (CPT) brought together a number of practitioners and other professionals with proven records of expertise in their specialist area of practice. These professionals became the Specialist Planning Group (SPG). Their remit was to respond to the seven activities set out in Figure 6.1.

A conceptual framework of professional competency

Instead of attempting to utilise every element in the professional role, Jarvis (1983, p. 35) has suggested that it is necessary to analyse the concept of competency and that this might help provide a basis upon which a curriculum could be constructed. It was suggested that this could be built upon the triple foundations of the practitioner's knowledge, skills and attitudes:

- *Knowledge and understanding of:* relevant academic discipline(s), psychomotor elements, interpersonal relations, moral values

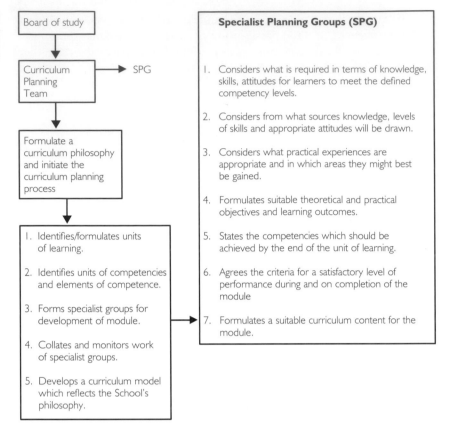

Figure 6.1

Using experts in specialist groups to define competencies

- *Skills to:* perform the psychomotor techniques, interact with members of the role set
- *Attitudes that result in:* a knowledge and commitment to professionalism, a willingness to play the role in a professional manner.

From such a basis it should be possible to devise the content of any curriculum but, at the same time, it allows for negotiation between all interested parties as to what is actually included. It might be objected that attitudes should not constitute part of the training, but, since adult education is a humanistic enterprise, it is maintained here that attitude education is an important element in the preparation of educators of adult learners.

Assessing competence

The belief that competence must be measured is not universally shared. Over 20 years ago Sheehan wrote of his concerns about a lack of valid measurement in education but concluded that 'those concerned with education should measure but should not confine themselves to measurement' (Sheehan 1979, p.56).

Benner also warned that it is premature to place too much faith in the assessment of certain competencies. There is a danger that we may be 'carried along by a technological, measurement-orientated age' (Benner 1982, p.303).

Similarly Andrusyszyn (1989) addressed the problems in trying to assess competencies in the affective domain and noted:

> the subjectivity associated with clinical evaluation of the affective domain renders it difficult to measure and grade. Although the mechanisms discussed are useful tools with which to provide insight into learners' attitudes and values, they may not provide hard data that can be measured for the purpose of assigning a grade. (p.77)

Since the 1960s there have been many attempts to reach the goal of a more objective approach. A number of techniques have been tested including simulation exercises and group video testing, critical incident technique and the use of the computer (Fivars and Gosnell 1966; Matthews and Viens 1988; Miller *et al.* 1988; Ross *et al.* 1988). Boreham (1978), however, pointed out the validity problems of not assessing the 'real life' situation, which presents its own problems according to the study by Long (1976). He identified that some assessors carrying out assessments found little time to complete the assessment forms and final interviews. They were open to influence by factors other than the learner's ability.

UNDERSTANDING LEARNING OUTCOMES

There is much activity in this area of teaching and the assessing of learning. Two recent documents, *Fitness for Practice* (UKCC 1999) and *Higher Education Credit Initiative Wales* (Interim Report of the Education Division of the Welsh Assembly, 1995) highlighted the need for clarity in this area.

According to UDACE (1991):

> Aims and objectives are primarily the language of course designers. They describe what the course sets out to do and can tend to preserve traditional course structures by discouraging comments and input from other professionals, employers, government learners and significant others. (p.1)

What is a learning outcome?

A learning outcome is a statement of what a learner is expected to know, understand or be able to do at the end of a period of learning. It will include an indication of the evidence required to show that the learning has been achieved. This may be contained in a separate assessment criterion statement or within the learning outcome statement.

Writing learning outcome statements

Differences in style

There are several styles of writing learning outcomes. It may be seen as appropriate to specify one style for adoption, but since some suggest that style may vary with subject matter, a broad policy that emphasises clarity may be preferable. It is possible to tighten up the regulations at a later date. Below are some styles for writing learning outcomes.

1 *Learning outcome incorporates assessment criteria*, providing an indication

of what the learner will be expected to do in order to demonstrate that the learning has been achieved.

2 *Learning outcome used with separate assessment criteria – more learning outcomes than assessment criteria:* The assessment criteria indicate what must be done to demonstrate achievement of the learning. Having fewer assessment criteria than learning outcomes means that assessment criteria are written in a more general manner and are less prescriptive of the form of assessment to be used (or are easier to apply when a single assessment, such as an essay, is used).

3 *Learning outcome used with separate assessment criteria – fewer learning outcomes than assessment criteria:* this is similar to (2), but the assessment criteria will tend to be more detailed.

There are other types of learning outcome statements that, for example, use performance criteria instead of or in addition to assessment criteria, or include range statements to define the scope of learning.

Specifications

Learning outcomes do not specify content for learning (though they may give an indication of it), nor do they specify what is taught or the strategy by which it is learned. They are written in language that is simple, non-technical and takes account of its audience. Since learning outcomes may be introducing the module to potential learners, they may be regarded as having a motivational role.

Most learning outcomes (with or without assessment criteria included – see above) are written in the format 'At the end of the period of learning, the learner will be able to . . .'.

The explicit and entailed nature of the learning outcomes makes it easier for educators to understand the nature of the adult education curriculum and to make realistic inputs to its development. Learning outcomes also make it easier for learners to understand what is expected of them and to take greater responsibility for their own learning. Learning outcomes can also help practitioners in the assessment of (for example) learners' teaching practice competence skills once they know what learners are expected to achieve. This can be a means of developing alternative approaches to teaching and learning, resulting in greater flexibility and wider participation in learner learning. However, if learning outcomes are too specific they can restrict learner learning. If too much emphasis is placed on a predetermined outcome it can result in a dangerously narrow approach to learning. But all practitioners do need to have a sense of what it is they want their learners to achieve by the end of a particular experience. The learning outcomes, when achieved, lead the learner towards becoming a competent practitioner.

General considerations

When planning the curriculum there are some issues of learning outcomes and assessment that may require to be considered on an institutional policy basis. For example, the failure to achieve even one learning outcome *should* mean that the module has not been achieved; only the non-achieved learning outcome should then need to be reassessed. Following on from this, compensation is difficult to justify in a system fully based on learning outcomes. On a more positive note, it can be the case that learning outcomes in some modules may match those already achieved elsewhere and will not need to be assessed a second time.

Learning outcomes need to be understood by everyone, not just subject experts. Every practitioner and learner should be able to understand any of the outcomes developed and comment in terms of clarity (see below). Issues concerning the perception of the task can usefully be raised in a mixed group. One of the ideas behind the establishment of learning outcomes is, after all, the generation of consistency and clarity across all subject areas.

Distinction from teaching intentions

Used in their more casual manner, aims and objectives have not always been required to distinguish between teaching intentions (e.g. 'to review methods of maintaining a positive learning environment') and those focused on learning (e.g. 'learners will be able to discuss simple methods of maintaining a positive learning environment'). A useful 'warming up' exercise is to present a list of aims and objectives written in both modes, requesting that they are separated.

Learning outcomes are usually of a better quality if written by several people before launching a new curriculum. It is useful if outcomes are reviewed by others. Apart from the quality issue, this can ensure that improvement in technique continue.

Specificity

While learning outcomes should be clear and precise, too much specificity, or too clear an identification of the performance required, restricts flexibility in learning and assessment strategies that will fulfil the outcome. The provision of exemplars will help to clarify this issue.

The number of learning outcomes

In most practice placements opportunistic learning can be described in less than 10 learning outcomes. The existence of more will probably mean that they are too specific.

Words used in learning outcomes

Learning outcomes should employ terms that indicate a recognisable standard. For example, a word such as 'good' tends to be personally referenced, and a word such as 'understand' raises the question 'when do you know a thing is understood?' Qualifying words or the inclusion of range statements can help.

Learning which is difficult to describe in terms of learning outcomes

In such cases a change of frame of reference usually helps. For example, negotiated learning can be written in terms of the activities of negotiation and implied self management (or why else use this strategy?) in the form of learning contracts (see chapter 4).

The structure of learning outcomes

A learning outcome is likely to contain the following components:

- a verb which indicates what the learner will be able to do, and which will indicate a means of demonstrating that the learning has been acquired
- word(s) that indicate what the learner is acting on/with, or word(s) that describe the verb (i.e. how the activity is done) when the outcome is a skill
- word(s) that indicate the nature (in context or standard expected) of the performance required as evidence that the learning has been achieved.

The components of *assessment criteria* will be much the same, but they will emphasise the demonstration of learning to a defined standard. For example:

The learner will list (= verb) correctly (= standard) 4 principles of adult learning by referring to M. Knowles (1990) and D. Boud (1981) (= condition).

Here the assessment criterion is built into the learning outcome.

Vocabulary for writing learning outcomes

Finding the right words for use in writing learning outcomes can be difficult, particularly when the learning outcome and/or assessment criterion must mesh with the generic level descriptors. The following list is provided as an aid in this process. The words are organised for convenience under headings that might be seen to accord with those from Bloom's taxonomy (Bloom 1965). However, no hierarchy is intended. Some words would fit several headings and a child of eight years can synthesise a word from a series of letters. The words are simply a vocabulary list gleaned from a variety of sources.

Activities giving evidence of knowing
Define, describe, extract, identify, know, label, list, match, measure, name, organise, outline, present, recall, recognise, recount, relate, repeat, reproduce, select, state, underline, write.

Activities giving evidence of comprehension
Interpret, clarify, classify, compare, comprehend, contrast, convert, defend, discuss, distinguish, estimate, exemplify, explain, express, extend, find, formulate, generalise, give examples of, identify, illustrate, indicate, infer, judge, justify, name, paraphrase, perform, predict, present, report, represent, restate, rewrite, select, summarise, translate.

Activities giving evidence of application of knowledge and understanding
Apply, assess, change, choose, compute, construct, demonstrate, demonstrate an understanding, discover, draw (up), exemplify, explain how, find, give examples, illustrate, manipulate, modify, operate, practise, predict, prepare, produce, relate, select, show, solve, use, verify.

Activities giving evidence of analysis
Demonstrate evidence of recognition, analyse, break down, categorise, compare, conclude, contrast, criticise, devote, diagnose, differentiate, distinguish between, divide/subdivide, elucidate, evaluate, examine, identify, illustrate how, infer, justify, outline, point out, question, relate, resolve, select, separate.

Activities giving evidence of synthesis

Propose, account for, alter, argue, build up, combine, compile, compose, conclude, create, derive, design, develop, devise, engender, enlarge, explain, formulate, generalise, generate, integrate, manage, modify, order, organise, plan, précis, present, put together, rearrange, reconstruct, relate, reorganise, report, restate, revise, select, structure, suggest, summarise, synthesise, teach, tell, write.

Activities giving evidence of evaluation

Judge, appraise, assess, choose, compare, conclude, contrast, criticise, defend, describe how, determine, discriminate, evaluate, justify, question, rate, value.

Study problem

Design one learning outcome from each of the six taxonomy levels above. Remember that words such as *comprehend*, *demonstrate*, *recognise* must identify the means in which this can be tested. For example:

- The learner will demonstrate a high level of awareness by participating in a class debate during the lesson, or
- The learner's contribution to the debate will demonstrate his/her level of understanding.

Format for writing course aims/objectives as learning outcomes

The following format may be useful in writing learning outcomes for courses which are currently described in terms of teaching intentions (in the form of

Teaching intentions (aims/objectives) (a)	Learning outcomes (b)
	Extra learning outcomes (c)
Assessment details (d)	

aims or objectives). It is based on the notion that many teaching intentions (box a) can be translated fairly into learning outcomes (box b).

There may, however, be some learning outcomes that are not expressed in teaching intentions. For example, teaching intentions may not specify expected learning or attainment resulting from private study time, while learning outcomes should express this. Provision is made for these extra learning outcomes in box c.

Box d, Assessment details, will contain a brief description of assessment tasks in order to demonstrate how the tasks are related to the assessment criteria within (or alongside) the outcome statements.

Within the higher education institution the learning outcomes will be written to reflect the different levels required by courses at certificate, degree and Masters level, for the purpose of academic accreditation. In practice placements, for example teaching skills, learning outcomes will also be written at different levels to reflect the competencies to be achieved at the various stages of the learning programme.

Structure and layout

Four levels of descriptors, developed by the Wales Access Unit and South East England Consortium (SEEC) 1995 (and currently in the process of revision), are described in Figures 6.2 and 6.3 (1, 2 and 3 at undergraduate stages and M for Master's stage). They are arranged under subheadings in three categories: operational context, cognitive descriptors and other transferable skills. These subheadings describe vocational and academic and, in some cases, social learning. The descriptors are classified in two formats, one in which the different descriptors are grouped under each level (e.g. all Level 1 descriptors on the same page) (Figure 6.2) and one in which all of the levels are described under each of the categories (Figure 6.3). It is thought that the former arrangement will be more convenient for practitioners and teachers.

Most descriptors will be relevant for most disciplines or areas of study, some will not be relevant to some disciplines or areas of study. For example, it is unlikely that psychomotor skills will have much relevance to the study of Classics.

Characteristics of the descriptors

The generic level descriptors are generalised learning outcomes for learning at four stages in higher education. These stages do not necessarily accord with year of study (but may do in, for example, the traditional three-year undergraduate degree). This means that a degree course of four or five years can still fit the structure of level descriptors.

The descriptors can be seen as a set of templates which can, among their range of uses, guide the writing of learning outcomes for modules or be used to identify the level of work presented for accreditation of prior learning. In order to use the generic level descriptors as templates it is helpful to read the descriptors in both their vertical and horizontal contexts.

The writing of learning outcomes for a module will be guided by the level descriptors. This means that a module with its learning outcomes will only be relevant to one level. It is primarily the assessment criterion part of a learning outcome that will characterise the level.

Figure 6.2 Generic level descriptors (arranged by stage of study) (Wales Access Unit and SEEC 1995)

LEVEL M

	CHARACTERISTICS OF CONTEXT	RESPONSIBILITY	ETHICAL UNDERSTANDING
	Characteristics of context are:	Requirements of responsibility are:	Requirements of ethical understanding are:
1. Operational contexts	Complex, unpredictable and normally specialized contexts demanding innovative work which may involve exploring the current limits of knowledge.	Autonomy within bounds of professional practice. High level of responsibility for self, possibly others.	Awareness of ethical dilemmas likely to arise in research and professional practice. An ability to formulate solutions in dialogue with peers, clients, mentors and others.

	KNOWLEDGE AND UNDERSTANDING	ANALYSIS	SYNTHESIS/CREATIVITY	EVALUATION
	The learner:			
2. Cognitive descriptors	Has great depth of knowledge in a complex and specialized area and/or across specialized or applied areas. S/he may be working at the current limits of theoretical and/or research understanding.	Can deal with complexity, lacunae and/or contradictions in the knowledge base and make confident selection of tools for the job.	Can autonomously synthesize information/ideas and create responses to problems that expand or redefine existing knowledge and/or develop new approaches in new situations.	Can independently evaluate/argue alternative approaches and accurately assess/report on own/others' work with justification.

	PSYCHOMOTOR	SELF-APPRAISAL, REFLECTION ON PRACTICE	PLANNING AND MANAGEMENT OF LEARNING	PROBLEM SOLVING	COMMUNICATION AND PRESENTATION	INTERACTIVE AND GROUP SKILLS
3. Other transferable skills descriptors	Has technical mastery of a skill, performing smoothly, precisely and efficiently. Able to plan strategies and tactics and adapt effectively to unusual and unexpected situations.	Engages with a critical community; reflecting habitually on own and others' practice in order to improve own/others' action.	Is autonomous in study/ use of resources; makes professional use of others in support of self-directed learning.	Can isolate, assess and resolve problems of all degrees of predictability in an autonomous manner.	Can engage in a full professional and academic communication with others in their field.	Can work with and within a group towards defined outcomes and can take role as recognized leader or consultant. Has ability to negotiate and handle conflict. Can effectively motivate others.

Figure 6.2 Continued

LEVEL 1

	CHARACTERISTICS OF CONTEXT	RESPONSIBILITY	ETHICAL UNDERSTANDING
	Characteristics of context are:	**Requirements of responsibility are:**	**Requirements of ethical understanding are:**
1. Operational contexts	Defined contexts demanding use of a specified range of standard techniques.	Work is directed, with limited autonomy within defined guidelines.	Awareness of ethical issues in current area(s) of study. Ability to discuss these in relation to personal beliefs and values.

	KNOWLEDGE AND UNDERSTANDING	ANALYSIS	SYNTHESIS/CREATIVITY	EVALUATION
	The learner:			
2. Cognitive descriptors	Has a given factual and/or conceptual knowledge base with emphasis on the nature of the field of study and appropriate terminology.	Can analyse with guidance using given classifications/ principles.	Can collect/collate and categorize ideas and information in a predictable and standard format.	Can evaluate the reliability of data using defined techniques and/or tutor guidance.

	PSYCHOMOTOR	SELF-APPRAISAL, REFLECTION ON PRACTICE	PLANNING AND MANAGEMENT OF LEARNING	PROBLEM SOLVING	COMMUNICATION AND PRESENTATION	INTERACTIVE AND GROUP SKILLS
3. Other transferable skills descriptors	Able to perform basic skills with awareness of the necessary tools and materials and their potential uses and hazards. Needs external evaluation.	Is largely dependent on criteria set by others but begins to recognize own strengths and weaknesses.	Can work within a relevant ethos and can access and use a range of learning resources.	Can apply given tools/ methods accurately and carefully to a well-defined problem and begins to appreciate the complexity of the issues.	Can communicate effectively in a format appropriate to the discipline and report practical procedures in a clear and concise manner with all relevant information.	Meets obligations to others (tutors and/or peers); can offer and/or support initiatives; can recognize and assess alternative options.

Figure 6.2 Continued

LEVEL 2

	CHARACTERISTICS OF CONTEXT	RESPONSIBILITY	ETHICAL UNDERSTANDING
	Characteristics of context are:	**Requirements of responsibility are:**	**Requirements of ethical understanding are:**
1. Operational contexts	Simple but unpredictable or complex but predicable contexts demanding application of a wide range of techniques.	Management of processes within broad guidelines for defined activities.	Awareness of the wider social and environmental implications of area(s) of study. Ability to debate issues in relation to more general ethical perspectives.

	KNOWLEDGE AND UNDERSTANDING	ANALYSIS	SYNTHESIS/CREATIVITY	EVALUATION
	The learner:			
2. Cognitive descriptors	Has a detailed knowledge of (a) major discipline(s) and an awareness of a variety of ideas/contexts/frameworks which may be applied to this.	Can analyse a range of information within minimum guidance, can apply major theories of discipline and can compare alternative methods/techniques for obtaining data.	Can reformat a range of ideas/information towards a given purpose.	Can select appropriate techniques of evaluation and can evaluate the relevance and significance of data collected.

	PSYCHOMOTOR	SELF-APPRAISAL, REFLECTION ON PRACTICE	PLANNING AND MANAGEMENT OF LEARNING	PROBLEM SOLVING	COMMUNICATION AND PRESENTATION	INTERACTIVE AND GROUP SKILLS
3. Other transferable skills descriptors	When given a complex task, can choose and perform an appropriate set of actions in sequence to complete it adequately. Can evaluate own performance.	Is able to evaluate own strengths and weaknesses; can challenge received opinion and begins to develop own criteria and judgement.	Accepts a broad-ranging and flexible approach to study; identifies strengths of learning needs and follows activities to improve performance; is autonomous in straight-forward study tasks	Can identify key elements of problems and choose appropriate methods for their resolution in a considered manner.	Can communicate effectively in a format appropriate to the discipline and report practical procedures in a clear and concise manner with all relevant information in a variety of formats.	Can interact effectively within a learning group, giving and receiving information and ideas and modifying response where appropriate. Is ready to develop professional working relationships within discipline.

159

Figure 6.2 Continued

LEVEL 3

	CHARACTERISTICS OF CONTEXT	RESPONSIBILITY	ETHICAL UNDERSTANDING
	Characteristics of context are:	**Requirements of responsibility are:**	**Requirements of ethical understanding are:**
1. Operational contexts	Complex and unpredictable contexts demanding selection and application from a wide range of innovative or standard techniques.	Autonomy in planning and managing resources and processes within broad guidelines.	Awareness of personal responsibility and professional codes of conduct. Ability to incorporate a critical ethical dimension into a major piece of work.

	KNOWLEDGE AND UNDERSTANDING	ANALYSIS	SYNTHESIS/CREATIVITY	EVALUATION
	The learner:			
2. Cognitive descriptors	Has comprehensive/detailed knowledge of (a) major discipline(s) with areas of specialization in depth and an awareness of the provisional nature of the state of knowledge.	Can analyse new and/or abstract data and situations without guidance, using a wide range of techniques appropriate to the subject.	With minimum guidance can transform abstract data and concepts towards a given purpose and can design novel solutions.	Can critically review evidence supporting conclusions/recommendations including their reliability, validity and significance and can investigate contradictory information/identify reasons for contradictions.

	PSYCHOMOTOR	SELF-APPRAISAL, REFLECTION ON PRACTICE	PLANNING AND MANAGEMENT OF LEARNING	PROBLEM SOLVING	COMMUNICATION AND PRESENTATION	INTERACTIVE AND GROUP SKILLS
3. Other transferable skills descriptors	Can perform complex skills consistently, with confidence and a degree of coordination and fluidity. Able to choose an appropriate response from a repertoire of actions, and can evaluate own and others' performance.	Is confident in application of own criteria of judgement and in challenging received opinion in action and can reflect on action.	With minimum guidance, can manage own learning using full range of resources for discipline; can seek and make use of feedback.	Is confident and flexible in identifying and defining complex problems and the application of appropriate knowledge and skills to their solution.	Can engage effectively in debate in a professional manner and produce detailed and coherent project reports.	Can interact effectively within a learning or professional group. Can recognize or support leadership or be proactive in leadership. Can negotiate in a learning/professional context and manage conflict.

Figure 6.3 Individual level descriptors

Cognitive descriptors

LEVEL	KNOWLEDGE AND UNDERSTANDING The learner:	ANALYSIS	SYNTHESIS/CREATIVITY	EVALUATION
M	Has great depth of knowledge in a complex and specialized area and/or across specialized or applied areas. S/he may be working at the current limits of theoretical and/or research understanding.	Can deal with complexity, lacunae and/or contradictions in the knowledge base and make confident selection of tools for the job.	Can autonomously synthesize information/ideas and create responses to problems that expand or redefine existing knowledge and/or develop new approaches in new situations.	Can independently evaluate/argue alternative approaches and accurately assess/report on own/others' work with justification.
3	Has a comprehensive/detailed knowledge of (a) major discipline(s) with areas of specialization in depth and an awareness of the provisional nature of the state of knowledge.	Can analyse new and/or abstract data and situations without guidance, using a wide range of techniques appropriate to the subject.	With minimum guidance can transform abstract data and concepts towards a given purpose and can design novel solutions.	Can critically review evidence supporting conclusions/ recommendations including their reliability, validity and significance and can investigate contradictory information/identify reasons for contradictions.
2	Has a detailed knowledge of (a) major discipline(s) and an awareness of a variety of ideas/contexts/frameworks which may be applied to this.	Can analyse a range of information within minimum guidance, can apply major theories of discipline and can compare alternative methods/ techniques for obtaining data.	Can reformat a range of ideas/ information towards a given purpose.	Can select appropriate techniques of evaluation and can evaluate the relevance and significance of data collected.
1	Has a given factual and/or conceptual knowledge base with emphasis on the nature of the field of study and appropriate terminology.	Can analyse with guidance using given classifications/principles.	Can collect/collate and categorize ideas and information in a predictable standard format.	Can evaluate the reliability of data using defined techniques and/or tutor guidance.

Figure 6.3 Continued

Other transferable skills descriptors

LEVEL	PSYCHOMOTOR The learner:	SELF-APPRAISAL, REFLECTION ON PRACTICE	PLANNING AND MANAGEMENT OF LEARNING	PROBLEM SOLVING	COMMUNICATION AND PRESENTATION	INTERACTIVE GROUP SKILLS
M	Has technical mastery of a skill, performing smoothly, precisely and efficiently. Able to plan strategies and tactics and adapt effectively to unusual and unexpected situations.	Engages with a critical community reflecting habitually on own and others' practice in order to improve own/others' action.	Is autonomous in study/ use of resources; makes professional use of others in support of self-directed learning.	Can isolate, assess and resolve problems of all degrees of predictability in an autonomous manner.	Can engage in full professional and academic communication with others in their field.	Can work with and within a group towards defined outcomes and can take role as recognized leader or consultant. Has ability to negotiate and handle conflict. Can effectively motivate others.
3	Can perform complex skills consistently, with confidence and a degree of coordination and fluidity. Able to choose an appropriate response of actions and can evaluate own and others' performance.	Is confident in application of own criteria of judgement and in challenging of received opinion in action and can reflect on action.	With minimum guidance, can manage own learning using full range of resources for discipline; can seek and make use of feedback.	Is confident and flexible in identifying and defining complex problems and the application of appropriate knowledge and skills to their solution.	Can engage effectively in debate in a professional manner and produce detailed and coherent project reports.	Can interact effectively within a learning or professional group. Can recognize or support leadership or be proactive in leadership. Can negotiate in a learning/professional context and manage conflict.
2	When given a complex task, can choose and perform an appropriate set of actions in sequence to complete it adequately. Can evaluate own performance.	Is able to evaluate own strengths and weaknesses; can challenge received opinion and begins to develop own criteria and judgement.	Adopts a broad-ranging and flexible approach to study; identifies strengths of learning needs and follows activities to improve performance; is autonomous in straight-forward study tasks.	Can identify key elements of problems and choose appropriate methods for their resolution in a considered manner.	Can communicate effectively in a format appropriate to the discipline and report practical procedures in a clear and concise manner with all relevant information in a variety of formats.	Can interact effectively within a learning group, giving and receiving information and ideas and modifying response where appropriate. Is ready to develop professional working relationships within discipline.
1	Able to perform basic skills with awareness of the necessary tools and materials and their potential uses and hazards. Needs external evaluation.	Is largely dependent on criteria set by others but begins to recognize own strengths and weaknesses.	Can work within a relevant ethos and can access and use a range of learning resources.	Can apply given tools/ methods accurately and carefully to a well-defined problem and begins to appreciate the complexity of the issues.	Can communicate effectively in a format appropriate to the discipline and report practical procedures in a clear and concise manner with all relevant information.	Meets obligations to others (tutors and/or peers); can offer and/or support initiatives; can recognize and assess alternative options.

Figure 6.3   Continued

Operational contexts

LEVEL	CHARACTERISTICS OF CONTEXT Characteristics of context are:	RESPONSIBILITY Requirements of responsibility are:	ETHICAL UNDERSTANDING Requirements of ethical understanding are:
M	Complex, unpredictable and normally specialized contexts demanding innovative work which may involve exploring the current limits of knowledge.	Autonomy within bounds of professional practice. High level of responsibility for self, possibly others.	Awareness of ethical dilemmas likely to arise in research and professional practice. An ability to formulate solutions in dialogue with peers, clients, mentors and others.
3	Complex and unpredictable contexts demanding selection and application from a wide range of innovative or standard techniques.	Autonomy in planning and managing resources and processes within broad guidelines.	Awareness of personal responsibility and professional codes of conduct. Ability to incorporate a critical ethical dimension into a major piece of work.
2	Simple but unpredictable or complex but predictable contexts demanding application of a wide range of techniques.	Management of processes within broad guidelines for defined activities.	Awareness of the wider social and environmental implications of area(s) of study. Ability to debate issues in relation to more general ethical perspectives.
1	Defined contexts demanding use of a specified range of standard techniques.	Work is directed, with limited autonomy within defined guidelines.	Awareness of ethical issues in current area(s) of study. Ability to discuss these in relation to personal beliefs and values.

The writing of learning outcomes with reference to explicit level descriptors can help to ensure consistency of outcome statements across subject/discipline areas. Learning outcomes facilitate consistency in providing a common format for the description of disparate forms of learning. Academic, vocational, experiential learning, on or off campus, work-based or community-based learning can all be described in learning outcomes and thus more easily compared.

Modules described in a similar style that use learning outcomes are more comprehensible. This clarity benefits learners and those who guide learners in their choices of learning course, and staff from the same and different subject areas. For example, the planning of related and possibly overlapping modules is facilitated by clear statements of learning outcomes for each. Similarly, the use of learning outcomes that are related to level descriptors can facilitate discussions between course leaders and external examiners.

Centralised or departmental record-keeping is aided by clarity and consistency in the description of modules. This can be related to the development of learner transcripts, and there are similar advantages where learners transfer from one institution to another or where they apply for accreditation of their prior learning.

There are educational implications for staff in explicitly anticipating the learning that can result from their professional activities. The design of teaching activities can be more focused, and when learners are clearer about what is expected of them the teaching/learning processes can be made mutually more effective. Because it is desirable to write learning outcomes in collaboration with others, there is an opportunity to develop more coherency within and between modules (Neary 1996a).

The transparency created by the writing of learning outcomes in relation to generic level descriptors can be a threat in demonstrating various inconsistencies across an institution or institutions. However, in the solution of these inconsistencies lies one means of upholding standards in adult and higher education.

Study problem

Study the generic level descriptors in Figures 6.2 and 6.3 and structure your own learning outcomes to reflect the learning opportunities you have to offer to:

1   Year 1 learner: Access course
2   Year 3: Masters course

You should include both theory and practice learning outcomes.

Look again at chapter 5 and consider the alternative models, e.g. the Experiential Taxonomy.

FURTHER READING   Bates, L. and Riseborough, C. (1995) Special issues on Competence and the National Vocational Qualification Framework. *British Journal of Education* 8(1) and 8(2).

Beaumont, G. (1995) *Review of 100 NVQs and SVQs*. A report submitted to the Department for Education and Employment. London, DFEE.

Brookfield, S. (1986) *Understanding and Facilitating Adult Learning*. Milton Keynes, Open University Press.

Brown, S. (1994) 'Assessment: a changing practice'. In B. Moon and A. Shelton Hayes (eds), *Teaching in the Secondary School*. London, Open University/Routledge.

Capey, J. (1995) *GNVQ Assessment Review: Final Report of the Review Group*. London, NCVQ.

Eraut, M. (1994) *Developing Professional Knowledge and Competence*. London, Falmer Press.

Hodkinson, P. and Issitt, M. (1995) *The Challenge of Competence*, London, Cassell Education.

Hyland, T. (1992) 'The vicissitudes of adult education: competence, epistemology and reflective practice'. *Education Today* 42(2): 7–12.

Hyland, T. (1993) 'Competence, knowledge and education'. *Journal of Philosophy of Education* 27(1): 55–66.

Jarvis, P. (1995) *Adult and Continuing Education: Theory and Practice* (2nd edition) London, Routledge.

Jessup, G. (1990) 'The evidence required to demonstrate competencies'. In H. Black and A. Wolf (eds), *Knowledge and Competency: Current Issues in Training and Education*. Sheffield, COIC.

Smith, G. (1993) *BTEC GNVQs and Development in Vocational Education*. Adults Learning (5). Leicester NIACE.

7 CURRICULUM AND COURSE EVALUATION

Learning outcome

To be achieved through the process of self-directed study, teacher/mentor support and sharing learning with fellow students
   By the end of this chapter you will be able to:

- define evaluation
- explain why the curriculum must be open to scrutiny
- examine and analyse the various modes of evaluation identified in this chapter
- design an appropriate evaluation tool which will meet the needs of your subject area to be taught.

EVALUATION: A HOLISTIC APPROACH

Trevor Welland, of Cardiff University, informs us that evaluation is arguably the least understood and most neglected element of curriculum design and development. Teachers and lecturers often spend many hours carefully considering course aims, learning objectives, learning outcomes, competencies to be achieved, teaching, learning and assessment strategies. At curriculum planning team meetings, detailed accounts of content, methods of presentation and analysis of resources will be examined. All too often education can be identified as the afterthought attached to the rest of the curriculum. Course evaluation and the assessment of learner learning outcomes tend to be dealt with as separate items from the other elements of the curriculum. This is often done for the purposes of clarity and discreteness. It does tend to isolate them from what should be a holistic approach to the description of curriculum design and development.

A curriculum open to scrutiny

The curriculum must be open to scrutiny, given that we might have spent many hours in developing a new curriculum. There is a danger that, being so involved and committed to it, we may fail to see the flaws in our work.

   Allowing our work to be scrutinised by others will help us avoid mistakes and also help us to learn from others about the processes in curriculum development. These processes help us to examine and assess our courses, make changes and even identify areas for research. Scrutiny helps us to identify the areas of course strengths and weaknesses and ensures that the course is meeting the relevant criteria agreed by the institution or organisation and other relevant professional and examining bodies.

   Scrutiny is a set of procedures designed to support staff in the development and revision of courses. Armitage *et al.* (1999) suggest five stages to this process:

1   Course development/revision
2   Internal scrutiny
3   Revisions to original proposal
4   External scrutiny
5   Course approved to operate.

The contents of the course which should be scrutinised include:

1   The rationale for the proposed course and its philosophy and charter (see the example in Appendix 4).
2   Statement of course aims
3   Course content in terms of objectives and outcomes
4   Course structure and organisation, such as scheme of work, learner experiences and mode of attendance
5   Teaching, assessing and learning strategies, including new innovative methods and justification for these
6   Criteria for entry and policies
7   Evaluation process
8   Costs, to include staffing, resources, accommodation, overheads, etc.
9   Evidence of and research to support the rationale and justification for the course and its strategies and policies.

Neary (2000) argued for the need to evaluate the curriculum, and one area that we need to examine in more detail is that of evaluation itself.

INTRODUCTION TO EVALUATION

Do not sit in appraisal of others, or your own work will be measured. For in the same way as you apply assessment criteria to others, performance indicators will be defined for you and against them you shall be appraised. (Professor Phil Race, ACETT, University of Glamorgan, Pontypridd, at an International Conference in York, 6 April 1992)

Reflection and evaluation are inherent in the job. It is impossible to meet the demands of teaching without planning, organising, monitoring and evaluating the activities you carry out. (Kyriacou 1991, p.124)

Evaluation is one of the most important tools available to you in the development of your teaching, and your ability to facilitate your learners' learning.
  Good quality evaluation requires that you develop and practice a range of techniques.
  Evaluation is a dynamic process, by which you exercise and develop skills and qualities of reflective teaching ... (Ashcroft and Foreman-Peck 1994, p.166)

What is evaluation?

[The] process that relates to the identification, description and appraisal of the effects and effectiveness of all aspects of teaching. (Heathcote et al. 1982, p.132)

The evaluation process should focus on:

- all educational strategies and content
- learners and their learning
- the wider context of education: teachers and teaching methods
- the learning environment: the institutional setting, resources, the local community, the political climate.

Key questions

- What can we evaluate?
- What techniques are available in order to carry this out?

The philosophy of evaluation

Downie (1967) suggested that:

- Each individual should receive the education that most fully allows them to develop their potential.
- Each individual should be so placed that they contribute to society and receive personal satisfaction in so doing.
- Fullest development of the individual requires recognition of their essential individuality along with some rational appraisal by themselves and others.
- The judgements required in assessing an individual's potential are complex in their composition, difficult to make and filled with error.
- Such error can be reduced but never eliminated. Hence any evaluation can never be considered final.
- Composite evaluation by a group of individuals is much less likely to be in error than evaluation made by a single person.
- The efforts of a conscientious group of individuals to develop more reliable and valid appraisal methods lead to the clarification of the criteria for judgement and reduce the error and resulting wrongs.
- Every form of appraisal will have critics, which is a spur to change and improvement.

CURRICULUM EVALUATION

In recent years there have been many curriculum developments affecting schools, further and higher education and education for the professions. Naturally, people have wished to ask questions about these developments and to compare them with each other and with previous curricula. To do this is to be involved in curriculum evaluation. In such a dynamic field of study it is hard to find a useful, precise definition of curriculum evaluation. One definition offered by Hamilton (1976) suggests that it is the process or processes used to weigh the relative merits of those educational alternatives which, at any given time, are deemed to fall within the domain of curriculum practice. More recently Armitage *et al.* (1999) have described it as

> *all about finding out if our new course is working properly. It involves generating data through a process of enquiry and then, on the basis of this, making judgements about the strengths and weaknesses and the overall*

effectiveness of the course, and making decisions about how to improve it further. (p.194)

Very many people are involved in curriculum evaluation. Many of them have always been so involved, usually on an informal and subjective basis. In recent years we have seen attempts to make evaluation more precise and formal. In part, this reflects a concern with accountability.

Study problem

What would you include in the evaluation process of your curriculum? Here are some suggestions:

- purpose of the curriculum
- organisational context of the curriculum
- organisation of the curriculum
- aims and objectives and mission statements
- content, assessment strategies and teaching strategies
- effectiveness in terms of learners' learning outcomes
- effect on learners' employment prospects
- cost-effectiveness
- quality of resources and college buildings
- quality of teaching, feedback and support systems.

Figure 7.1 will also help you to decide.

Types of evaluation

There are many types of curriculum evaluation. At one time there was emphasis on checking 'quality' in terms of measuring the fit between stated intentions and observed outcomes. However, the concept of curriculum evaluation has been gradually broadened with time so that, while this aspect is not neglected, there is more emphasis on evaluating the intentions, analysing unintended outcomes and seeing the curriculum in as broad a context as possible.

The earlier process was usually a form of 'summative evaluation', in which the final scheme was evaluated after it had been prepared and put into use. There has been a move towards 'formative evaluation', which is concerned with the evaluation and improvement of a course as it is being prepared.

Practical difficulties in evaluation

Whatever strategy is adopted, and however the role of the evaluation is viewed, many difficulties are encountered.

Among these are problems in:

- obtaining and treating data (dispersion, small sample sizes, etc.)
- obtaining replies to questionnaires etc.
- being objective (particularly if the evaluator is closely associated with the development team)

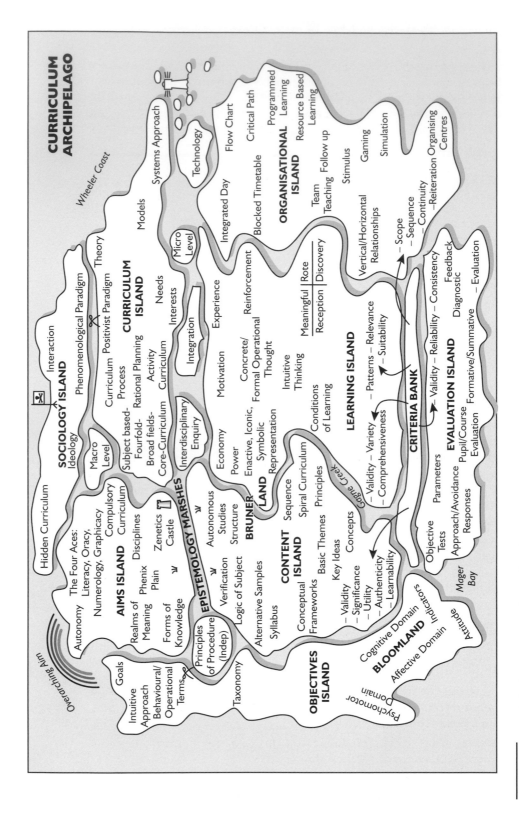

Figure 7.1 An ABC of the curriculum (James Eaton)

- dealing with differences in basic value positions (concerning education, society, etc.)
- 'keeping up' with curriculum developments.

Contrasting strategies of curriculum evaluation

Evaluation strategies reflect shifting paradigms. The two mentioned below are perhaps best regarded as showing a particular emphasis; they are not completely exclusive.

1 'Agricultural botany' paradigm

This emphasises the importance of logical deductions from experimental (usually quantitative) data. It leads to a hypothetico-deductive methodology which owes much to the mental testing tradition in educational psychology.

Parlett and Hamilton (1972) (and many others) claim that such studies are artificial and restricted in scope. Other objections to the methodology include:

- Very large samples are needed.
- It assumes that schemes are not modified during study.
- It restricts the scope of a study.
- It is insensitive to local effects.
- It cannot cope with the diversity of questions posed by different interest groups.

2 'Anthropological research' paradigm

To deal with the above objections, Parlett and Hamilton (1972) suggested that we should move towards 'illuminative evaluation', which is based on an anthropological research paradigm associated with the social sciences. In this the attempted measurement of 'educational products' is abandoned for intensive study of the whole curriculum development. The innovation is not studied in isolation but in the broader context of the educational institution and society.

Methods used in illuminative evaluation might include:

- observation
- interviews with participants
- questionnaires
- analysis of documents and background information.

A framework for curriculum evaluation

There are many models for curriculum evaluation. They overlap considerably in their approaches; no single model can be regarded as appropriate for all evaluations.

One useful model is Daniel Stufflebeam's Context, Input, Process, Product (CIPP) model (1971). The key emphasis is on decision-making. Indeed, Stufflebeam defined evaluation in the following terms: 'Educational evaluation is the process of delineating, obtaining and providing useful information for judging decision alternatives.'

The four elements of evaluation in this model are:

Context evaluation, which deals with whether or not to offer a curriculum and, if so, what its parameters will be including focus, goals and objectives – learning outcomes.

Input evaluation, which relates to deciding what resources and strategies will be used to achieve curriculum goals and objectives.

Process evaluation, which focuses on determining what effect the curriculum has on learners in school.

Product evaluation, which deals with examining the curriculum's effects on former learners.

Perhaps it is a strength of Stufflebeam's model that it draws upon and overlaps with others. For example, it is related to Parlett and Hamilton's illuminative evaluation, but it also has points in common with Tyler's (1949) objectives model.

Evaluation of recent curriculum developments

The large-scale curriculum development which is now taking place in further, higher and adult education obviously needs evaluation, including evaluation of various aspects of college life as shown in Figure 7.2. This needs to be formative as well as summative evaluation. Such evaluation is not easy. It is important that it is not just left to official bodies, but that teachers, learners and significant others become involved in evaluation themselves, now that teachers are much more involved in curriculum development. This will involve showing something of the different strategies that can be adopted so that teachers can evaluate curricula themselves and interpret other evaluation data.

Figure 7.2

Evaluation needs

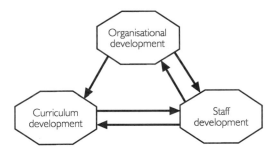

Data-gathering strategies
These strategies relate to the CIPP model discussed above.

Context
This includes a needs assessment. Task analysis, context evaluation is often speculative since 'hard' data may not always be available; there is a need to investigate the changing nature of social needs, the state of the economy, rapid advances in technology, etc.

Input
This may include group consensus, expert judgement, literature and materials examination, pilot experimental and quasi-experimental efforts.

Process
This includes teacher behaviour measures, teacher rating measures, standardised achievement measures, expert-referenced measures and teacher-constructed knowledge and performance instruments (standard setting).

Product
Among those measures most frequently utilised in product evaluation are the skills survey, job satisfaction and job satisfactoriness. Information that may be gathered through questionnaires includes worker mobility, salary, unemployment and additional training taken by the worker.

The value of evaluation

Curriculum or course evaluation is concerned with 'the collection and analysis of evidence about a course, the discussion of that evidence, the sharing of findings and suggestions among the interested parties' (Eraut 1982). Thus, the aim is to understand the course, so as to sustain it, develop and where possible improve it. But what are the drawbacks and benefits of undertaking the evaluation?

The most obvious cost/drawback is that of staff time. Time must be found to plan, carry out, analyse, interpret, implement and review the curriculum. Is enough time allowed for staff to draft questionnaires, carry out interviews and analyse the results in addition to dealing with the agenda of course team meetings?

Evaluation can be a slow and rather threatening process: 'In evaluating the course you're evaluating yourself and colleagues' (FEU 1983, p.53). What was private may become public. But surely this could be considered a benefit? Similarly, the findings and the processes of evaluation can appear to threaten the stability of an organisation: 'Findings may suggest that course decision-makers in the past had been wrong, that future decisions could usefully be taken by other groups, or that the allocation of course responsibilities and resources should be appraised' (FEU 1983, p.53). But although a college structure may be disrupted, the benefits would outweigh any drawbacks of evaluation.

According to Rowntree (1981, p.284), several dangers became apparent in responding to evaluation data One of the big dangers is being 'bowled over by the sheer volume of diverse information'. Just as one sometimes only hears what one wants to hear, so it is that confronted with a large amount of diverse information one sees 'only those items that confirm what one wants to do in the course anyway'. Another danger is of responding too fast or too drastically to evaluation data: 'Major changes are best made slowly over a cycle of several courses'.

In addition to the 'benefits' already mentioned, evaluation – both formal and informal – can identify areas of the course which are functioning well and those which are in need of improvement. Evaluation provides sufficient authority (or proof) for improvements to be considered or carried out. If we are to continue getting the funds and resources and manpower we need for courses, we must prove that they can be used to good effect. The actual process of evaluation itself can stimulate curriculum development. An evaluation can improve colleague–employer relations. It can also improve learner–staff relations: 'Talking and listening to learners can strengthen the staff's understanding of the learner's experience of the course and perhaps the learner's understanding of staff aims and problems' (FEU, 1983, p.54).

The status of a course can be increased, but perhaps the most important outcome of evaluation is an awareness about staff development:

> *It can develop the skills and knowledge needed for designing, developing and administering courses; for collaborating with other staff, for negotiating access to sensitive areas of activity; for acting effectively within an organisation; and for introducing deliberate self-appraisal. (FEU 1983, p.54)*

From my own experience of running short and long courses (teacher training and nurse education), I believe that evaluation, and the 'value' that can be gained from it, is probably the most neglected aspect of training. In-depth evaluation is costly and time consuming, but this should not prevent evaluation at a more immediate level from taking place. In addition to the standardised evaluation form which is completed half way through a course, a more comprehensive form devised for that particular course should be filled in by all learners, both half way through the course and at the end of it. The results would give an idea not only of teacher performance but of how useful the course had been and improvements that could be made for future courses. As Broadbent (1977) wrote: 'The function of evaluation is not so much to chalk up marks for the learner or tutor, as to give them both the chance to set the past in a realistic light and so release themselves into the future' (pp.421–57).

Other still-relevant writers on evaluation include Cronbach (1963) and Stufflebeam (1971), who have described evaluation as a collection of information for making decisions about the curriculum and a scientific attack on the problem of curriculum renewal.

Lindblom (1964) states that evaluation is a science of muddling through and puts forward two models of decision making 'root' and 'branch'. The latter is 'complex judgmental' and the former 'rational comprehensive'. Is the evaluator qualified to pass judgements, or do they pass on the information to those who can?

Eisner (1966, pp.67, 72) states that certain learning outcomes are unpredictable and complex in that they surprise both the teacher and the learner. Scriven (1973) launched a concept of goal-free evaluation, actual effects against a profile of demonstrated needs. The evaluator needs to be unhampered by contact with the intentions of the programme builder.

Parlett and Hamilton (1972) polarise evaluation into two camps, 'psychometric' and 'illuminative', the latter orientated towards processes rather than products.

MacDonald (cited in Tawney 1976) argues that evaluation is a political activity and offers three models: democratic, autocratic and bureaucratic. The last is an unconditional service to government agencies who have control over educational resources. The evaluator accepts the values of those who hold office and offers information which will help them accomplish their political objectives. The viewpoints of many commentators of curriculum evaluation are put forward by the authors to allow the curriculum designers to view their own perceptions of evaluation from an objective judgemental perspective.

COURSE EVALUATION

Course evaluation is at a micro level and should be carried out by course tutors and other teachers. It consists of three components:

1   Evaluation by learners of practical experience. This takes place as soon as possible after completion of each experience.
2   Evaluation by learners of theoretical input offered by the college. This can take place at the end of each study week (preparation and consolidation).
3   Course tutor's evaluation of the module as a whole, taking into account the comments of learners, the tutor's self-appraisal and perceptions of the value of the module.

Armitage *et al.* (1999) remind us of three models of evaluation: classical evaluation, evaluation by behavioural objectives and qualitative evaluation.

1   *Classical evaluation* is scientific and views the course as an experiment or treatment to be administered to the learners. Its overall aim is to collect data and reports which will help to judge the course effectiveness.
2   *Evaluation by behavioural objectives* is also scientific and also views the course as something of an experiment but draws on behavioural notions of learning and curriculum design.
3   *Qualitative evaluation* views the course as a scientific experiment, but is concerned with a host of content and process issues, such as the course intentions and organisation, its intended outcomes as well as its unpredictable outcomes.

An overview of course evaluation may be helpful at this stage: see below and Figures 7.3, 7.4 and 7.5.

Course evaluation is:
●   a continuous process
●   based upon criteria
●   cooperatively developed
●   concerned with measurement of the quality and effectiveness of the course and the learning programme, and of the effectiveness of teachers.

Use of evaluation tools

Cycles of review
Four 'cycles of review' can be established at different levels of course organisation. These come into play at different times and at different intervals as courses progress.

1   The immediate use of the evaluation is to enable the tutor to make future adjustments to those aspects of teaching and an organisation which fall within his or her sphere of control. This could include items such as lesson content and teaching method plus the reorganisation of teaching/learning time within the specific module under review.
2   The teaching team can also discuss the evaluation after each module of experience with particular reference to items such as educational visits,

Figure 7.3

An overview of evaluation

EVALUATION
- Planning process by which the course was produced
- Proposes aims, objectives, content of course
- Proposed teaching strategy
- Materials and facilities
- Institutional setting

PRELIMINARY EVALUATION
Before learners start the course

CRITICAL COMMENTS
By people whose views we know we can respect

EXAMPLE
- Subject experts
- Teachers
- Learners

CONTENT ANALYSIS
- Evaluation of academic credibility
- Likely educational effectiveness

CONTINUOUS MONITORING
Keeping on EYE on things

CASUAL EVALUATION
Part of the everyday business of teaching
So-called 'eyes in the back of their heads'
Awareness, 'a classroom sense'

END-OF-COURSE EVALUATION

DELIBERATE
- Discussion
- Interviews
- Questionnaires

practical placements, etc. There may be a need to monitor more closely the learning experience of learners during future modules, and decisions on any future action will be made at this time.

3 Where major changes in the curriculum seem necessary, these can be referred to the curriculum monitoring team for action. These could include major changes in the allocation of learners where, for example, an existing service area is no longer appropriate and alternative placements may need to be found.

Additionally, new resources may be identified by the curriculum monitoring team which may improve the course, and action will be initiated by the team in such cases. Examination results can also be

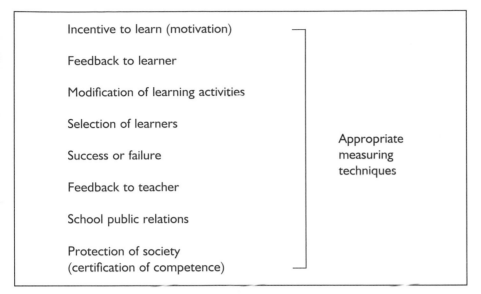

Figure 7.4

What learner evaluation is for

monitored by the curriculum monitoring team and can be considered in conjunction with the evaluation experience previously elicited.

4   The college board responsible for overseeing curriculum and examinations should consider the efficiency of the course both educationally and economically within the context of other courses, including post-basic courses being organised by the college.

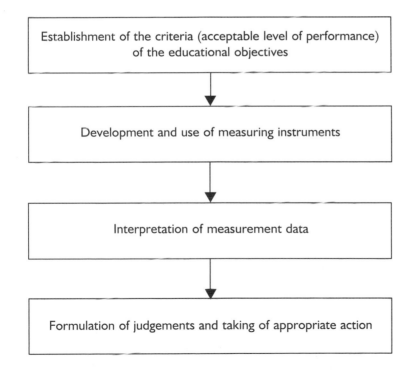

Figure 7.5

Four steps in learner evaluation: one model

Figure 7.6

A framework for curriculum
evaluation (Neary 1996a)

COURSE REVIEW PROCEDURES

Steps

Rolling programme of quinquennial review
↓
Annual programme (presented to Faculty Board)
↓
Course Directors and Course Committee initiate process by identifying
current and future changes in the course (since last reviewed) based on
annual course reports, etc.
↓
Draft submission scrutinised by Dean, Associate Dean for Quality Assurance
and other relevant persons
↓
Faculty **Pre-review exercise** (established by Faculty Board) including internal
and external panel members (at least one month before)
↓
Final **Amendments to document**
↓
Pre-review meeting
↓
Review
↓
Recommendations/conditions for continued approval

Figures 7.6 and 7.7 give an outline of two curriculum evaluation processes.

Broadbent (1977) suggested that the function of evaluation is not so much
to chalk up marks for either learners or teachers, as to give them both the
chance to see the past in a realistic light and so release themselves into the
future. Rowntree (1981) advised that an evaluation may address such
questions as:

- Did the course attract enough learners?
- Were they sufficiently qualified?
- Did enough of them last the course?
- Were the standards high enough?
- Was the course cost-effective?
- Were the learners satisfied?
- Were the teachers satisfied?
- Were other (significant other) interested parties satisfied?
- What needs to be changed?

Case study model of evaluation

Kenworthy and Nicklin (1989) have this to say about the case study model of
evaluation:

*A wide range of evaluation techniques are used in this model in order to
obtain as complete an account as possible of the whole course, or course
unit. It will therefore employ both quantitative and qualitative methods,
which will include measurement, interviews, observations and the use of*

Figure 7.7 External and internal course evaluation: a summary

A. Organisational Level	B. Personnel involved	C. Information sources	D. Items evaluated	E. Further action
1. Course	Course tutor, learners	Learners' oral and written critiques	Relevance of objectives/outcomes, teaching/learning experiences, balance of programme	Report to curriculum planning sub-committee, Board of Study, curriculum monitoring team
2. Curriculum planning development team	Course tutor, learners, main lecturers, principal advisory tutor, vice-principal, librarian	Learners' oral and written critiques, curriculum documents, teaching staff reports, assessment results, examination results	Relevance of objectives/outcomes, teaching/learning experiences, balance of programme, relevance of content, curriculum policies	Develop as required within agreed parameters, recommendation for policy change, report to national bodies
3. Academic and administrative	Director, assistant director, all teaching staff, librarian, registrar, administrative assistant	Learners' oral and written critiques, curriculum documents, teaching staff reports, assessment results, examination results/reports	Relevance of objectives/outcomes, teaching/learning experiences, balance of programme, relevance of content, curriculum policies	Recommendations for change to curriculum monitoring team, recommendation for change to Board of Study, report to national bodies.
4. Board of Education Board of Study Outside agencies	Chairman and members	Board of examiners' reports, director's report, curriculum documents	Any or all aspects of courses	As terms of reference allow

ACTIVITY: Examine each item under identified group headings and reflect on the rationale and relevance of each item in relation to teaching and assessing students.

questionnaires. Because of its very nature, it would normally be carried out by an external agency and therefore will have significant cost consequences. An example of case study evaluation is that of employing an independent research body or organisation to evaluate a course or a component of a course. This may be appropriate when implementing a new scheme or modifying an existing scheme of training. The difference between this evaluation model and that concerned with others resides not in its process but in its functional outcome. Although the outcomes are presented to decision-makers, the purpose of the case study is not necessarily commissioned in order for a decision to be made. It is more likely to be employed to confirm or support a decision that has already been taken and implemented. (p.127)

EVALUATION OF ASSESSMENT TOOLS

One area we fail to evaluate adequately is that of assessment tools.

Some definitions: a reminder

It should be remembered that *education* is defined as a process developed for bringing about changes in the learner's behaviour. At the end of a given learning period there should be a greater probability that types of behaviour regarded as *desirable* will appear; other types of behaviour regarded as undesirable should disappear. The *educational objectives/learning outcomes* define the desired types of behaviour taken as a whole; the teacher should provide a suitable environment for the learner's acquisition of them.

Evaluation in education is a *systematic process* which enables the teacher to 'measure' to what extent the curriculum is successful. *Assessment* measures how well learners have attained the *educational objective*. Evaluation always includes *measurements* (quantitative or qualitative) plus a value judgement.

To make measurements, *measuring instruments* must be available which satisfy certain requirements so that the results mean something to the teacher, the school, the learner and society which, in the last analysis, has set up the educational structure.

In education, measuring instruments are generally referred to as *tests* or *exams* and must not be confused with evaluation, which measures the success of a course, programme and curriculum as a whole.

Among the qualities of a test, whatever its nature, four are essential, namely *validity, reliability, objectivity and practicability*. Others are also important, but they contribute in some degree to the qualities of validity and reliability.

Main qualities of a measuring instrument

The four main qualities of any measuring instrument (test or examination) are validity, reliability, objectivity and practicability.

Validity

Validity is the extent which the test used really measures what it is intended to measure. No outside factors should be allowed to interfere with the manner in which the evaluation is carried out. For instance, in measuring the ability to synthesise, other factors such as style should not compete with the element to be measured in such a way that what is finally measured is style rather than the ability to synthesise. Validity is a concept which relates to the results obtained with a test and not to the test itself. It relates more specifically to the interpretation of the results obtained by means of the test. The notion of validity is a very relative one. It implies a concept of degree, i.e. one may speak of *very valid, moderately valid or not very valid* results.

Content validity is determined by the following question: Will this test measure, or has it measured, the matter and the behaviour that it is intended to measure?

Predictive validity is determined by questions such as the following when the results of a test are to be used for predicting the performance of a learner in another domain or in another situation: To what extent do the results obtained during the teaching practice predict the learners' potential success – the likely outcome of their achievements?

Reliability

Reliability is the consistency with which an instrument measures a given variable. Reliability is always connected with a particular type of consistency: consistency of the results in time; consistency of the results according to the questions; consistency of the results according to the examiners. Reliability is a necessary but not a sufficient condition for validity. In other words, valid results are necessarily reliable, but reliable results are not necessarily valid. Consequently, results which are not very reliable affect the degree of validity. Unlike validity, reliability is a *strictly statistical concept* and is expressed by means of a reliability coefficient or through the *standard error* of the measurements made.

Reliability can therefore be defined as the degree of confidence which can be placed in the results of an examination. It is the *consistency* with which a test gives the results expected.

Objectivity

Objectivity is the extent to which independent and competent examiners agree on what constitutes a 'good' answer for each of the items of a measuring instrument.

Practicability

Practicability depends on the time required to construct an examination, to administer and score it and to interpret the results, and on its overall simplicity of use. It should never take precedence over the *validity* of the test.

Other qualities of a measuring instrument

- *Relevance:* the degree to which the criteria established for selecting questions (items) so that they conform to the aims of the measuring instrument are respected. This notion is almost identical to the one of content validity, and the two qualities are established in a similar manner.
- *Equilibrium:* the achievement of the correct proportion among questions allocated to each of the objectives.

- *Equity:* the extent to which the questions set in the examination correspond to the teaching content.
- *Specificity:* the quality of a measuring instrument whereby an intelligent learner who has not followed the teaching on the basis of which the instrument has been constructed will obtain a result equivalent to that expected by pure chance.
- *Discrimination:* the quality of *each element* of a measuring instrument which makes it possible to distinguish between good and poor learners in relation to a given variable.
- *Efficiency:* the quality of a measuring instrument which ensures the greatest possible number of independent answers per unit of time.
- *Time:* it is well known that a measuring instrument will be less reliable if it leads to the introduction of non-relevant factors (guessing, taking risks or chances, etc.) because the time allowed is too short.
- *Length:* the reliability of a measuring instrument can be increased almost indefinitely by the addition of new questions *equivalent* to those constituting the original instrument.

TECHNIQUES OF EDUCATIONAL MEASUREMENT AND EVALUATION

Human behaviour is so complex that it cannot be described or summarised in a single score.

The manner in which an individual organises their behaviour patterns is an important aspect to be appraised. Information gathered as a result of measurement or evaluation activities must be interpreted as a part of the whole. Interpretation of small bits of behaviour as they stand alone is of little real meaning.

The techniques of measurement and evaluation are not limited to the usual paper-and-pencil tests. Any piece of valid evidence that helps a curriculum planner and learners in better understanding the curriculum and that leads to helping the learners to understand themselves better should be considered worthwhile. Attempts should be made to obtain all such evidence by any means that seem to work.

The nature of the measurement, appraisal and evaluation techniques used influences the type of learning that goes on in a classroom. If learners are continually assessed on knowledge of subject content, and if the mode of delivery is continually evaluated, they will tend to study better and teachers will also concentrate their teaching efforts more effectively. A wide range of evaluation activities covering various objectives of a course will lead to varied learning and teaching experiences within a course (see Figure 7.8). The development of any evaluation programme is the responsibility of all the staff involved in curriculum development, the learners and the teachers. Maximum value can be derived from the participation of all concerned.

The importance of teamwork

The planning of an evaluation system is obviously not simple. It is a serious matter, for the quality of education will partly depend on it. It has been stressed many times, moreover, that it should be a group activity. As stated above, evaluation must be planned jointly; that implementation of any

Figure 7.8 A framework for curriculum evaluation (Neary 1993)

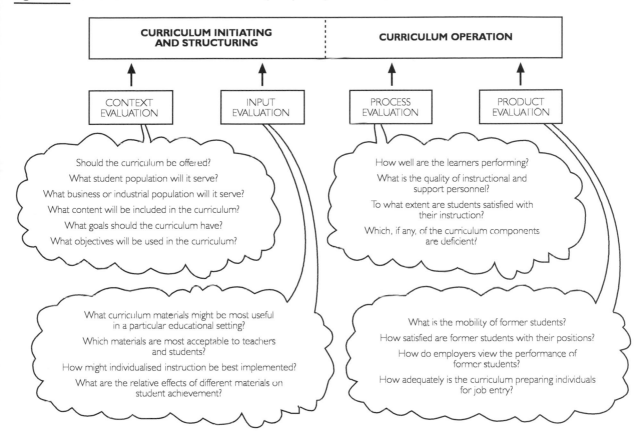

evaluation programme is the responsibility of the teachers, in collaboration with learners and the administration; that evaluation carried out jointly by a group of teachers is less likely to be erroneous than when carried out by one person; and finally that critical analysis of a test by colleagues is essential to its sound construction.

This work performed jointly by a group of teachers calls for a coordinating mechanism. The terms of reference of each group and group member must be defined explicitly and known to all. The institution's higher authorities must provide the working groups and their members with the powers corresponding to the task to be accomplished.

Figure 7.8 shows one type of organisation which can meet the needs of a given institution. Other types of organisation can be envisaged, according to existing structures and local traditions. As Downie (1967) has pointed out, we should not change anything that works satisfactorily, but what is satisfactory for some is not necessarily good enough for others. Evaluation and teaching are a matter for teamwork.

Providing evaluation data for the public

Educational institutions are beginning to adopt a holistic approach, with the aim of describing the work of a project in a form that would make it accessible to public and professional judgement. Therefore all the data will initially be accepted because in view of the potential significance of so many aspects of the curriculum a complete description of its experience is needed, as is the awareness of a full range of relevant phenomena. As a result a more sophisticated model of curriculum evaluation – a process model – needs to be completed. This does not set out to measure the results of a project in simple terms, but to provide continuous feedback to all involved with planning and implementation and curriculum development. It is also concerned with the meaning of the curriculum as much as with an evaluation of its worth.

The same general approach can be adopted to the form of evaluation as suggested by Stake's (1973) 'portrayal' evaluation and Parlett and Hamilton's (1972) 'illuminative' evaluation. 'Portrayal' is seen as an attempt not to analyse the results of a curriculum in terms of its pre-specified aims and objectives but to offer a comprehensive portrayal of the programme which views it as a 'whole' and to endeavour to reveal its total substance (Kelly 1986).

'Illuminative' evaluation is concerned with description and interpretation rather than measurement and prediction (Parlett and Hamilton 1972, p.88). Kelly (1986) goes on to explain that such an approach has three stages:

1   Investigators observe.
2   They enquire further.
3   They seek to explain.

As a result an 'information profile' is put together. This information profile can be published in the form of a report made available to the public and to professionals. Parlett and Hamilton (1972, p.99) remind us that the purpose of illuminative evaluation is to illuminate and to help the curriculum planners to sharpen discussion, disentangle complexities, isolate the significant from the trivial and raise the level of sophistication of debate.

According to White (1971) the questions to be asked in any process of evaluation are of two logically discrete kinds. Some of them are empirical questions which explore the relative merits of a curriculum in terms of its costs and its effectiveness. Other questions raise those difficult issues of value that we can never get far from in any discussion of education. These are about ends rather than means; they ask whether the purposes of the activity are the right purposes, whether the experience being offered to learners is of educational value. Here the concern is to evaluate the goals and the underlying principles of the curriculum itself and not merely the effectiveness of its procedures. Hamilton (1976, p.11) wrote that 'evaluation is a multi-faceted phenomenon encompassing a range of diverse properties and that we should avoid too tight a definition of the kind that is likely to inhibit further understanding of evaluation'.

Many curriculum innovations have been developed over the past century; the attempts to measure the effectiveness and the desirability of such innovations have led to the emergence of a further, involved and complex area of curriculum studies, i.e. evaluation. Evaluation should be undertaken not only of major innovations but also of individual projects and of single lessons. Both the 'macro' and the 'micro' aspects of this issue must be borne in mind. The best example of recent evaluation at both of these levels has been in nurse education, at national level through the *Fitness for Practice Report* (UKCC 1999) and at college level in readiness for the Quality Teaching Audit (QTA) and Research and Development exercise carried out by individual universities. Curriculum planners are now realising that evaluation has to be an integral part of any curriculum development and that we need to assess very carefully the results of any changes that have been introduced.

DIFFERENT PURPOSES OF EVALUATION AND ASSESSMENT

There exists some confusion between evaluation and assessment. Both involve similar procedures such as gathering data and issues concerning changes in learners' behaviour. However, the purposes for which these data are collected are quite different in the two cases. The data collected for curriculum evaluation are to provide a basis upon which decisions can be made about the curriculum and not as diagnostic evidence for the making of decisions about aspects of learners learning outcomes (see p.186).

According to Taba (1962), curriculum evaluation becomes part of curriculum research. All evaluation procedures treat all curriculum planning and approaches as hypotheses to be tested. We must remind ourselves that the curriculum is a dynamic and continuously evolving entity.

Evaluation is arguably the least understood and most neglected element of curriculum design and development. All too frequently, evaluation has been identified as an afterthought attached to the rest of the curriculum strategy. Lawton (1973) suggested that such an attitude is not unreasonable because it is

Evaluation model	Mode of evaluation	Function of the evaluation	Comments
Classic/experimental	Quantitative	Measurement of behaviour using precise behavioural objectives	An eclectic approach – does not consider broader course values
Illuminative (anthropological)	Qualitative	Description and interpretation based upon observation and interview	Danger of being subjective – role conflict
1. Briefing decision makers	Both quantitative and qualitative	Bureaucratic: consultant	May be seen as providing decision makers with the information they require
2. Briefing decision makers	Both quantitative and qualitative	Autocratic: expert adviser	It is expected that the evaluation results will be acted upon
3. Briefing decision makers	Both quantitative and qualitative	Democratic: information service	Provides a detailed report without recommendations
Teacher as researcher	Both quantitative and qualitative	Dual role of both curriculum developer and evaluator	Use of triangulation? Subjectivity? Role conflict
Case study	Both quantitative and qualitative	Factual reporting	Expensive if using an external agency; may be used to confirm beliefs

Figure 7.9

Summary of evaluation models (Kenworthy and Nicklin 1989)

a fact that issues of evaluation present some of the most difficult problems for curriculum planners.

Examining a number of different evaluation models (James 1983; Lawton 1973; Rowntree 1981; Stenhouse 1975), Kenworthy and Nicklin (1989, p.128) argued that the issues involved in evaluating an educational course as complex as one for adult education cannot be effectively encompassed by one model, and offered a summary of models as shown in Figure 7.9.

Study problem

It is widely held that all personnel involved both at a planning stage and during implementation ought to contribute to the evaluation of an educational activity. Should there be an opportunity to involve all of these 'principal participants' in evaluation, or should advice be sought from 'expert evaluators' not directly involved with the course, such as researchers, consultants or advisers? What do you think?

QUANTITATIVE AND QUALITATIVE APPROACHES

Quantitative approaches are employed in many questionnaires, attitude scales, observation schedules, interaction analyses and other forms of rating scale. Criticisms of the quantitative approach are that it is restrictive and a possible denial of exposure of important evaluation issues. These problems are sometimes claimed to be lessened by using qualitative methods which 'illuminate' educational experiences and may yield 'richer' information. However, it may be hard to collect and not easily summated for reference, as was evident in Neary's study (1996a). While qualitative evaluation frequently employs a range of appropriate methods, such as interviews, discussion, participant and non-participant observation, diaries, self-reporting and critical incident techniques, Gale and O'Priory (1981) have made the point that it need not be entirely open-ended or unstructured. Many evaluation strategies combine both quantitative and qualitative instruments, and evaluation tools which encompass both quantitative and qualitative modes may well constitute a necessary definition of adequacy if results are to be relied upon as an adequate basis for improving the schemes. One such improvement, it is argued by Schön (1991), can be developed through the concept and practices of reflection (see chapter 4).

Evaluation: a summary

- Evaluation is not assessment.
- Evaluation is central to good practice.
- Honest evaluation will challenge practice.
- It may serve a variety of purposes.
- It may be undertaken by 'insiders' or 'outsiders'.
- All aspects of education should be subject to evaluation.
- A range of methods are available for this diversity of purpose.
- Evaluation is important to reflective practice and professional development.

- 'Ad hoc' (formative) evaluation can be done at any time during the programme.
- Summative evaluation is done at the end of the course.
- Evaluation involves the systematic collection of evidence:
  learner needs
  available resources
  application of a range of teaching/learning methods
- It can be a 'painful' process.
- It challenges assumptions.
- It redefines problems as opportunities.

What can we evaluate?

'Macro' level

- Reviews teaching as a whole
- Takes place at the end of the course
- Is an aspect of whole institution exercise

'Micro' level

- Aims and objectives
- Teaching strategies
- Assessment
- Course organisation
- Resources

What techniques are available for the purposes of evaluation?
(Quantitative and qualitative)

- Questionnaire
- Structured interview
- Group discussion
- Personal reflective diary
- Observation by a colleague
- Paper/Post-It note comment sheets

Other forms of 'evidence'

- Learner assessment performance
- Moderator's report
- Minutes of course team meetings
- Consultation with industry
- Consultation with colleagues

Policy context

- Learner as 'consumer'/quality of learner experience
- Shift in responsibility of quality assurance from national boards to the institutions themselves

Study problem

1 On your own, or with a fellow learner, design an evaluation form for your course using the same headings (A–E) as in Figure 7.7.
2 Examine one curriculum you are involved in, and apply the questions in each section in Figure 7.8.
3 Using the examples evaluation forms in Figures 7.10 to 7.13, design your own form for your course.

Evaluation seeks to achieve quality by examining a number of different models. It is apparent that an educational course cannot be effectively evaluated by using just one model. Whilst educational factors are of prime concern in any course, the political issues of service provision and staffing establishments cannot be ignored. Performance indicators that reflect both quantitative and qualitative measures in input and output terms are increasingly required by education authorities and their managers as part of quality assurance programmes.

Whilst the expressed need to obtain value for money and accountability in all aspects of public service has to be fully supported, it is essential that managers should recognise that quality can cost money. A more efficient use of that money is always possible, but there comes a point at which efficiency cannot be increased and consequently any reduction of resources at that point will result in lowered quality.

Both assessment of learner attainment and course evaluation must be seen as integral features of any course and not mere adjuncts to the content and teaching/learning strategies. At each stage of course design and planning conscious effort must be given to build in appropriate assessment procedures and devise mechanisms for evaluating the outcomes in relation to the course unit goals and objectives. Childs (1985) goes so far as to suggest that an evaluation strategy ought to be outlined before the course content and its application are formalised. This becomes imperative where assessment and evaluation are more than just a summative appraisal of the learner's overall attainment and the terminal conclusion of the course's worth.

It cannot be denied that carefully structured assessment and evaluation strategies are very time-consuming for all concerned, from the learner to the curriculum development team, but they should be viewed as an economical investment that enables a course to be dynamic and responsive to the need for change where necessary. What appears to be irrefutable is that it will be extremely difficult for courses in the future to survive if they do not have as an integral feature assessment and evaluation strategies that are consistent with the goals and competences which the course seeks to achieve (Kenworthy and Nicklin 1989).

STUDENT EVALUATION SHEET

NAME OF TUTOR:
COURSE:

**WITH EACH OF THE COMMENTS BELOW, PLEASE TICK THE BOX THAT
CORRESPONDS TO YOUR EXPERIENCE**

	Totally agree	Mostly agree	Mostly disagree	Totally disagree
The lecturer captured interest at the beginning of the lesson	☐	☐	☐	☐
The aims and objectives of the lesson were clearly stated	☐	☐	☐	☐
The lesson was well structured, with a clear introduction, development of ideas and conclusion	☐	☐	☐	☐
The lesson was well delivered and interesting	☐	☐	☐	☐
The learners were encouraged to participate actively	☐	☐	☐	☐
The lecturer spoke clearly and audibly	☐	☐	☐	☐
The lecturer used good-quality aids, e.g. overheads, handouts	☐	☐	☐	☐
The lecturer used a variety of delivery methods, e.g. input, discussion, group work	☐	☐	☐	☐
The lesson went at the right pace for me	☐	☐	☐	☐
The lecturer explained the subject matter clearly	☐	☐	☐	☐
The lecturer periodically reviewed what we had covered in the lesson	☐	☐	☐	☐
The lecturer checked that learners had understood the subject of the lesson	☐	☐	☐	☐
The lecturer gave the opportunity for learners to ask questions	☐	☐	☐	☐
The lecturer had a good relationship with the learners, e.g. used names, encouragement	☐	☐	☐	☐
The lecturer was enthusiastic about the subject of the lesson	☐	☐	☐	☐
The lecturer was approachable	☐	☐	☐	☐
The lecturer made it clear what work had to be done after the lesson	☐	☐	☐	☐

FURTHER COMMENTS:

Figure 7.10   Example of a learner evaluation sheet (1)

Figure 7.11

Example of a learner
evaluation sheet (2)

EVALUATION OF TEACHING, ASSESSING AND EVALUATION COURSE

(Please feel free to comment on the following)

1 How clear were the aims of this course?

....

....

....

2 Did you understand the terminology used?

....

....

....

3 What did we leave out?

....

....

....

4 How useful was it having an experienced assessor to practise with in the clinical area?

....

....

....

5 How can we improve the course/book/guidelines/etc.?

....

....

....

PARTICIPANT EVALUATION QUESTIONNAIRE

As a participant in a 'training event', your reflections can provide important information. Your views will be valuable in helping to shape future policy and practice.

To complete the questionnaire, please award a score by marking one box alongside each question. You are invited to add comments at the end.

Low   High

1. How clear were you about what you wanted from the event?

   | 1 | 2 | 3 | 4 | 5 |

2. Did you achieve your objectives?

   | 1 | 2 | 3 | 4 | 5 |

3. Did the content of the event match its publicity?

   | 1 | 2 | 3 | 4 | 5 |

4. How relevant did you find the content of the event to your anticipated future work/career?

   | 1 | 2 | 3 | 4 | 5 |

5. Was the content pitched at a level appropriate to your needs/interest?

   | 1 | 2 | 3 | 4 | 5 |

6. How appropriate were the teaching/facilitating strategies used?

   | 1 | 2 | 3 | 4 | 5 |

7. Were any materials (including AVA) appropriate and of a satisfactory quality?

   | 1 | 2 | 3 | 4 | 5 |

8. Was the nature and range of activities sufficient to sustain your interest?

   | 1 | 2 | 3 | 4 | 5 |

9. Was the event well organised?

   | 1 | 2 | 3 | 4 | 5 |

10 Were facilities adequate for the purpose?

   | 1 | 2 | 3 | 4 | 5 |

11 Do you regard this event as a worthwhile investment of your time?

   | 1 | 2 | 3 | 4 | 5 |

12 We would welcome any further comment you might wish to make about this event/ experience/opportunity.

13 Has this event suggested a need for any further staff development courses? (Please specify)

Figure 7.12

Example of a participant evaluation questionnaire Note: A 'training event' is any learning opportunity or experience for practitioners in contact with learners in practice placements and for learners in contact with practitioners in practice placements.

Figure 7.13

Guidelines for the review of learning experiences

PRACTITIONER, TEACHER AND LEARNER GUIDELINES FOR THE REVIEW OF LEARNING EXPERIENCES

	Low				High
1. Are the learning outcomes clear, understandable and realistic? Do they describe what the learner proposes to learn?	1	2	3	4	5

	Low				High
2. Are there any other outcomes which should be considered?	1	2	3	4	5

	Low				High
3. Do the learning strategies seem reasonable, appropriate and efficient?	1	2	3	4	5

	Low				High
4. Are there other strategies or resources which could be utilised?	1	2	3	4	5

	Low				High
5. Does the evidence of accomplishment seem relevant to the various outcomes and is it convincing?	1	2	3	4	5

	Low				High
6. Is there any other evidence that could be sought?	1	2	3	4	5

	Low				High
7. Are the criteria and means for validating the evidence clear, relevant and convincing?	1	2	3	4	5

	Low				High
8. Are there other ways of validating the evidence that should be considered?	1	2	3	4	5

	Low				High
9. Are the key factors and 'dynamics' explicit in the curriculum and assessment documents?	1	2	3	4	5

FURTHER READING

Armitage, A., Bryant, R., Dunnill, R. *et al.* (1999) *Teaching and Training in Post-Compulsory Education*. Milton Keynes, Open University Press.

Ashcroft, K. and Foreman-Peck, L. (1994) *Managing Teaching and Learning in Further and Higher Education*. London, Falmer Press.

Atherton, J. (2000a) *Assessment* (on-line). Leicester, De Montfort University. Available at *http://www.staff.dmu.ac.uk/~jamesa/teaching/assessment.htm* (accessed 7 February 2001).

Atherton, J. (2000b) *Marketing* (online). Leicester, De Montfort University. Available at *http://www.staff.dmu.ac.uk/~jamesa/teaching/marking.htm* (accessed 7 February 2001).

Atherton, J. (2000c) *The Problem of Assessment* (online). Leicester, De Montford University. Available at *hhtp://www.staff.dmu.ac.uk/~jamesa/teaching/assess_problem.htm* (accessed 7 February 2001).

Downie, N.M. (1967) *Fundamentals of Measurement: Techniques and Practices.* New York, Oxford University Press.

Ecclestone, K. (1995) *Understanding Assessment.* Leicester, National Institute of Adult Education.

Jenkins, D. and Shipman, M.D. (1976b) *Curriculum Evaluation: An Introduction.* London, Open Books.

Smith, E. (2001) *Assessment in Adult Education* (online). New York, Hudson River Center for Program Development. Available at *http://www.nyadulted.org/prodevg2.htm* (accessed 7 February 2001).

8 QUALITY ASSURANCE AND IMPLEMENTING CHANGE

Learning outcome

To be achieved through the process of self-directed study, teacher/mentor support and sharing learning with fellow students.

By the end of this chapter you will be able to:

- define quality assurance
- discuss the importance of maintaining quality audits in education
- describe the main elements of standards and criteria
- examine the FENTO and ILT standards and discuss how they influence curriculum design, planning development and quality standards
- explain how quality assurance helps implement change.

QUALITY ASSURANCE IN EDUCATION

The theorist and researcher have to approach the issue of curriculum demands in two ways. First to try to help educational institutions and teachers/lecturers respond nationally to specific demands that are being made on them, because that is something that affects the quality of education and that cannot be postponed. Second, to work at illuminating the conditions that give rise to demands for accountability and at characterising the connotations of the demands and the problem itself. The theorist and researcher recognise one of the fundamental dilemmas inherent in all educational systems. On the one hand what colleges teach is some kind of public possession contingent on political climates; on the other, the curriculum is also the possession of individuals, those who teach it and those who experience it. The tension between those contrary claims, the national and public, the local and private, admits of no final resolution; this has to be found according to place and time. The role of quality assurance and its process is to help institutions to find a resolution that fits each case; it will be unique, not universal nor one of a standard set. Though what is decided will represent, ideally, a consensus, it need not be a crude compromise.

Below are some public statements regarding the quality state of our educational system.

> *Our universities and colleges are second to none, with a world-class reputation. (Baroness Blackstone, Minister for Education and Employment, 1999)*
>
> *In a world of lifelong learning, British education is a first-class ticket for life. (Tony Blair, Prime Minister, 1999)*
>
> *Our record in winning major science awards is proof of the excellence of our universities. (Department for Education and Employment, 1998)*

The results of successive Research Assessment Exercises show the increasing quality of research taking place in Scottish higher education. (Scottish Higher Education Funding Council, 1997)

QUALITY: THE FACTS

- With 1 per cent of the world's population, the UK undertakes 5 per cent of the world's research, produces 8 per cent of the publications and receives 9 per cent of the citations.
- UK scientists were responsible for sequencing one-third of the international Human Genome Project, which was completed in 2001.
- In 1996 81 per cent of learners in the UK completed their first degrees successfully. In the OECD, only Japan had a higher rate of completion.
- After inspections of more than 2,000 academic departments throughout the UK since 1992, the quality of the education observed has been rated as either excellent, satisfactory or approved, with very few exceptions.

Productivity

- Higher education learner numbers doubled between the late 1980s and the late 1990s, totalling almost 1.9 million in 1998/99.
- In the 1990s, the economic productivity of higher education staff increased three times as much as the service sector average, 6.5 per cent per annum against the service sector average of 2.2 per cent.
- The number of overseas learners (excluding other EU learners) coming to the UK has trebled to 99,000 since the beginning of the 1980s.

Employment

- In many regions higher education is a major employer. There are currently just over 300,000 staff in the sector – around 1.2 per cent of the UK workforce.
- Higher education as an industrial sector has the third highest use of temporary employment in the UK. Casual bar staff have more job security than academics working in Britain's universities.
- 94 per cent of researchers employed by universities and colleges in the UK work on temporary contracts.

(Source: AUT *Facts & Figures 2001*)

QUALITY: THE ISSUES

The issues of good practice and quality assurance have been brought together in two research projects conducted by de Wit (1992), who writes that 'Although there is no agreed definition of quality, there are several key themes in the current debate, which focus attention on the whole network of resources and procedures' (p.7). These themes are

- fitness for purpose
- the need for a strategic approach
- meeting customers' expectations

- a cycle of continuous improvement
- a cohesive system of interconnected processes.

These studies attempt to draw together in a practical manner some of the main issues that are generally agreed to constitute quality in adult education. De Wit (1992) provides a practical checklist:

- policy
- staff
- courses
- marketing
- teaching and learning
- outcomes.

Some recent initiatives

FENTO standards

Quality is also an issue raised by FENTO in relation to setting the standards for FE teachers (see Figure 8.1 for an example of the standards). FENTO's (2001) paper 'Towards a more qualified profession' refers to the government's pledge to improve the status of FE teachers. It states that all newly appointed teachers will from September 2001 be required as part of their contract of employment to hold or work towards nationally recognised teaching qualifications. Colleges will be responsible for meeting the staff development requirements of existing staff. However, there will, according to the Secretary of State, be 'no uniform qualification requirement' as teachers have different development needs depending on their experience, their abilities and the changing nature of further education. The government has allocated up to £80 million from the Standards Fund in 2001/2002 in order to fund qualifications for new entrants to the profession, and a 50 per cent matched funding for continuing professional development (CPD) for existing teachers. Local learning and skills councils will require colleges to assess the development needs and produce an action plan setting out how a college proposes to meet them. Courses leading to FE teaching qualifications will be inspected by Ofsted (see chapter 1).

The ILT

We also have seen that the Institute for Learning and Teaching in Higher Education, which is a membership organisation open to all those engaged in teaching and learning and supporting learners in higher education, also wishes to share its objective of 'improving the status of teaching as a professional activity'. The ILT's aim is to improve the experience of learning, support innovation and become a forum where academic practitioners can learn from each other and from the best research on all aspects of teaching and learning.

The ILT was launched in June 1999 as a result of recommendations in the Dearing Report on higher education (Dearing 1997). Activities of the organisation focus on:

- accrediting programmes of training in higher education
- providing support for those engaged in facilitating learning and teaching

THE STANDARDS

The standards consist of the following three main elements:

- Professional knowledge and understanding
- Skills and attributes
- Key areas of teaching.

Professional knowledge and understanding

The knowledge and understanding required to perform effectively as an FE teacher are arranged in three categories:

- *Domain-wide knowledge* applicable across all areas of professional practice
- *Generic knowledge* relating to each standard
- *Essential knowledge* relating to specific aspects of each standard.

The *domain-wide knowledge* is listed here. *Generic knowledge* appears in the introduction to each of the key areas of teaching. *Essential knowledge* is listed under each of the standards within the key areas. FE teachers and teaching teams should have *domain-wide knowledge* and critical understanding of:

a. The place of FE within the wider context
b. The aims, objectives and policies of the organisation in which the teacher works
c. Professional knowledge in their own subject area
d. Learning theory, teaching approaches and methodologies
e. Social and cultural diversity and its effect on learning and on curriculum development and delivery
f. The social, cultural and economic background of individual learners and the implications of this for learning and teaching
g. Ways of ensuring that linguistic diversity is valued and accommodated within the strategic plan of the organisation
h. Current national and international initiatives and how they are interpreted within the strategic plan of the organisation.
i. Current developments within their own specialist vocational or academic area of expertise and ways of keeping up to date with such developments
j. The concept of inclusive learning
k. Learners' entitlements and issues related to the autonomy of the learner
l. The broad range of learning needs including the needs of those with learning difficulties and/or disabilities and the facilities and arrangements that are available to help meet these needs
m. The characteristics of effective learning
n. How to measure effectiveness against a diverse range of quality indicators
o. What constitutes best professional practice
p. Ways of analysing and using key information to inform teaching and learning
q. Effects of change on the FE sector and teachers' own practice
r. Methods of assessment
s. Information technology and how it can be used to extend and enhance learning
t. Ways of ensuring the currency and effectiveness of technical and educational competence and sources of professional development
u. Models of curriculum development and how they can be applied in their own area of work
v. Sources of funding and teachers' own contribution in accessing such funding.

Figure 8.1   Example of FENTO standards (FENTO 2001)

- commissioning research and development in learning and teaching practice
- stimulating innovation.

Benchmarking statements

Another example is that of the benchmarking statements drawn up by the Quality Assurance Agency for Higher Education (reproduced in SWAP 2000) (see Figure 8.2), which provide the means for the academic community to

KNOWLEDGE AND UNDERSTANDING

Threshold Learners will demonstrate:	Modal Learners will demonstrate:	Best Learners will demonstrate:
Awareness of the underlying values and principles relevant to Education Studies	An awareness of the underlying values and principles relevant to Education Studies and a developing personal stance which draws on their knowledge and understanding	A good awareness of the underlying values and principles relevant to Education Studies and a developing personal stance which draws on their knowledge and understanding
Knowledge of the diversity of learners and the complexities of the education process	A good working knowledge of the diversity of learners and the complexities of the education process	A comprehensive and critical understanding of the diversity of learners and the complexities of the educational process
An awareness of the different contexts in which learning can take place and the range of different roles of participants in the learning process (including learner and teacher)	A good understanding of the complexity of the interaction between learning and contexts and the range of ways in which participants (including learners and teachers) can influence the learning process	A well-developed understanding of the complexity of the interaction between learning and contexts and the range of ways in which other participants (including learners and teachers) can influence the learning process
Some understanding of the societal and organisational structures and purposes of educational systems	A good understanding of the societal and organisational structures and purposes of educational systems and the possible implications for learners and the learning process	Critical insight into the societal and organisational structures and purposes of educational systems and the possible implications for learners and the learning process
The ability to identify relevant theoretical and research-based primary and/or secondary sources and to use these appropriately in their study to extend their knowledge and understanding	The ability to select a range of relevant primary and secondary sources, including theoretical and research-based evidence, to extend their knowledge and understanding	The ability to select from a comprehensive range of relevant primary and secondary sources, including theoretical and research-based evidence to extend their knowledge and understanding

Figure 8.2 Benchmarking statements (from SWAP 2000)

APPLICATION

Threshold Learners will demonstrate:	Modal Learners will demonstrate:	Best Learners will demonstrate:
A basic ability to analyse educational concepts, theories and issues of policy in a systematic way	An ability to analyse critically educational concepts, theories and issues of policy in a systematic way	A well-developed ability to analyse educational concepts, theories and issues of policy in a systematic way
A basic ability to identify potential connections between each of the aspects of subject knowledge and their application in educational policies and contexts	A developing ability to identify and reflect on potential connections and discontinuities between each of the aspects of subject knowledge and their application in educational policies and contexts	A well-developed ability to identify and critically reflect on potential connections and discontinuities between each of the aspects of subject knowledge and their application in educational policies and contexts
Some ability to accommodate to new principles and understandings.	An ability to accommodate to new principles and understandings. This would include a developing ability to suggest ways forward and potential changes in practice.	A well-developed ability to accommodate to new principles and understandings. This would include the ability to formulate appropriate and justified ways forward and potential changes in practice using a range of evidence.

REFLECTION

Threshold Learners will demonstrate:	Modal Learners will demonstrate:	Best Learners will demonstrate:
A basic ability to reflect on their own value system	The ability to reflect on their own value system	A high level of ability to reflect on their own value system
A developing ability to question concepts and theories encountered in their study	The ability to use their knowledge and understanding critically to locate and justify a personal position in relation to the subject	The ability to integrate their knowledge and understanding critically into a personal position which shows depth and originality in relation to the subject
A basic understanding of the significance and limitations of theory and research	A sound understanding of the significance and limitations of theory and research	A critical understanding of the significance and limitations of theory and research

Figure 8.2   Continued

TRANSFERABLE SKILLS (1)

	Threshold Learners will:	Modal Learners will:	Best Learners will:
Communication and presentation	Be able to communicate adequately in speech and writing using some specialist vocabulary	Have the ability to organise and articulate opinions and arguments in speech and writing using relevant specialist vocabulary	Have a practised ability to organise and articulate opinions and arguments in speech and writing in a diverse range of relevant contexts showing confident use of specialist vocabulary
Information and communications technology	Have an ability to use ICT in their study and other appropriate situations	Be competent users of ICT in their study and other appropriate situations	Be competent users of ICT in their study and other appropriate situations and be able to judge where the use of ICT is not appropriate
Application of numbers	Have an ability to interpret simple graphical and tabular presentation of data and to collect and present numerical data	Have a well-developed ability to interpret graphical and tabular presentation of data and collect, use and interpret numerical data as appropriate	Have a well-developed ability to interpret graphical and tabular presentation of data in a critical and constructive way, to collect and present numerical data and to use graphical and tabular information appropriately
Working with others	Have a basic ability to collaborate and plan as part of a team, to carry out roles allocated by the team and to keep to agreed responsibilities	Have the ability to collaborate and plan as part of a team, to carry out roles allocated by the team and take the lead where appropriate and to fulfil agreed responsibilities	Have a well-developed ability to work effectively as part of a team, including working through difficulties and conflicts

Figure 8.2   Continued

TRANSFERABLE SKILLS (2)

	Threshold Learners will:	Modal Learners will:	Best Learners will:
Improving own learning and performance	Have a basic understanding of their own preferred learning styles and strategies and work with these to organise an effective work pattern including working to deadlines	Have the ability to articulate their own preferred learning styles and strategies and actively manage their development to organise an effective work pattern including working to deadlines	Have a well-developed ability to articulate their own preferred learning styles and strategies and actively manage their development, to reflect on their learning styles and strategies in the light of learning theories and to work with these to organise an effective work pattern including working to deadlines
Analytical and problem-solving skills	Have a basic ability to use relevant empirical and theoretical data in addressing tasks and formulating possible actions	Have the ability to process and synthesise empirical and theoretical data, to create new syntheses and to present and justify a chosen position having drawn on relevant theoretical perspectives	Have a well-developed ability to process and synthesise empirical and theoretical data, to create new syntheses and to present and justify a chosen position having drawn on relevant theoretical perspectives

Figure 8.2   Continued

describe the nature and characteristics of programmes in a specific subject. They also represent general expectations about the standard for the reward of qualifications at a given level and articulate the attributes and capabilities that those possessing such qualifications should be able to demonstrate. Subject benchmark statements also provide support to institutions in pursuit of internal quality assurance. They enable the learning outcomes specified for a particular programme to be reviewed and evaluated against agreed general expectations about standards. This fits within the QAA framework. Benchmark statements in, for example, education studies are aimed at those involved in designing, approving and validating courses; external examiners and those concerned with assessment, moderation and monitoring; learners who may wish to select and/or evaluate subjects or programmes; and interested members of the public, including potential employers of learners who have completed programmes of education studies. These benchmark statements could be drawn on for the design of other programmes, for example in youth and community education.

Subjects to be studied are in a constant state of change and development, so the statements are not related to specific subject content but are grouped within the following cross-subject strands: Knowledge and understanding, Application, Reflection and Transferable skills. The example in Figure 8.2 is designed for learners who are undertaking education studies as part of a teacher training programme.

PHILOSOPHY FOR A QUALITY SERVICE

This section examines two of the philosophies that underpin many of the issues related to quality. There are a variety of possible ways of examining quality, but the two described here are Maxwell's dimensions of quality and the Donabedian approach.

Maxwell's dimensions of quality

Robert J. Maxwell (1984) put forward six dimensions of quality. These dimensions are one way of grouping issues related to the quality of a service provided. They can be used as a starting point in looking at quality, and can be modified and developed to reflect local requirements and perspectives, as indicated by the examples below.

1 Access
To include both geographical convenience and timeliness of access
Do all learners have reasonable access to services, for example in terms of geographic convenience, waiting time for entry to course, physical design of buildings and availability of transport?

2 Equity
The provision of education/training service on the basis of measured rather than any other personal characteristics
Are services provided evenly regardless of the types of and ability of learner and their cultural, racial or social background?

3 Relevance to need
The extent to which the package of services provided for a defined population meets their education/training needs
Is service provision based on the real education/training needs of the population served? Is there over-provision of one type of service, or are there gaps in others?

4 Social acceptability
The extent to which the service meets the expectations of the users, e.g. the interpersonal and environmental aspects of education/training
Is the way in which the service is provided acceptable to the population it is intended to serve? Is it consistent with the cultural and religious values of all its learners and/or clients?

5 Efficiency
The best use of resources, money, people, buildings and equipment

Are services provided as efficiently as possible within the resources available? Are they cost-effective and appropriately staffed?

6 Effectiveness
The balance of education benefits for an individual person, plus the avoidance of intervention which is inappropriate or useless for the individual person
Do the services provided actually attain the intended benefits and outcomes in terms of the education/training of the population served?

Maxwell's dimensions provide a broad framework within which the quality and standards could be examined.

Study problem

Examine your own course and apply the above questions to your course.

The Donabedian approach
Avedis Donabedian (1986) developed a conceptual approach for the examination of how an organisation (any organisation) functions. You will probably be familiar with this as a concept often used in developing standards (see Figures 8.3 and 8.4 for examples). (You will already have come across this model in chapter 4 (Figure 4.10) in relation to mentoring.)

Structure
The structures of an organisation include the skills of the staff, the buildings and premises and the equipment that the organisation makes available.

Process
The processes are the methods which are adopted by the organisation to provide its services, or in its production processes.

Outcome
The outcomes are the combined results of the structures and processes of the organisation in the production of its products or services.

Therefore, in education:

- *Structure* is the resources required to provide quality education; the environment within which that is provided; the facilities made available; the staff skills available; the equipment (e.g. video, power point, overhead projection, etc.) made available; and the documentation of procedures, policies and guidance to staff.
- *Process* is the actual procedures and practices implemented by staff in their delivery and evaluation; and the monitoring, evaluation and actions to adjust the provision of education.
- *Outcome* is the effect of education received by learners as a result of teacher intervention; the benefits to learners resulting from the provision of learning opportunities; and the costs to the organisation of providing courses.

Figure 8.3

A method of identifying
educational standards

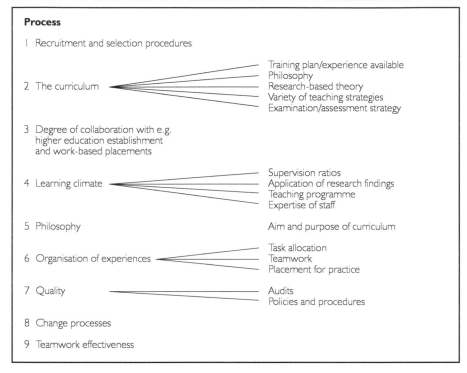

Structure

Structure pertains to the environmental and resource characteristics of the system and includes the following:

1　Buildings ───────────────── Number of sites
　　　　　　　　　　　　　　　　Locality/proximity

2　Resources ───────────────── Library/audio-visual aids equipment

3　Size ───────────────── Number of learners
　　　　　　　　　　　　　　　　Types of Courses

4　Organisation and management
　　of the school

5　Staff ───────────────── Staff/learner ratios
　　　　　　　　　　　　　　　　Qualification/personal development

Process

1　Recruitment and selection procedures

2　The curriculum ───────────── Training plan/experience available
　　　　　　　　　　　　　　　　Philosophy
　　　　　　　　　　　　　　　　Research-based theory
　　　　　　　　　　　　　　　　Variety of teaching strategies
　　　　　　　　　　　　　　　　Examination/assessment strategy

3　Degree of collaboration with e.g.
　　higher education establishment
　　and work-based placements

4　Learning climate ─────────── Supervision ratios
　　　　　　　　　　　　　　　　Application of research findings
　　　　　　　　　　　　　　　　Teaching programme
　　　　　　　　　　　　　　　　Expertise of staff

5　Philosophy ────────────── Aim and purpose of curriculum

6　Organisation of experiences ─── Task allocation
　　　　　　　　　　　　　　　　Teamwork
　　　　　　　　　　　　　　　　Placement for practice

7　Quality ───────────────── Audits
　　　　　　　　　　　　　　　　Policies and procedures

8　Change processes

9　Teamwork effectiveness

Outcome should be the ultimate validator of the educational process. However, many factors influence outcome which may not be known immediately; Figure 8.4 therefore includes two additional columns for information on monitoring/evaluation and other comments.

This conceptualisation has been used to facilitate the examination of quality in a multidisciplinary setting, as it provides a framework which allows for different interpretations by different service delivery agencies or organisations.

Maxwell and Donabedian provide only two possible approaches to the examination of quality. Your own college may be pursuing another approach. Other examples are given later in this chapter.

Positive outcomes

1 Numbers of learners reaching qualification

2 Achievement of goals

3 Safe, competent practitioner

4 Staff morale

5 Specialist knowledge and expertise

Negative outcomes

1 Wastage rates

2 Non-achievement of goals

3 Staff/learner morale

STATEMENT

The teacher will introduce the learner to the concepts of research/research appreciation in preparation for writing research-based essays.

Stucture	Process	Outcome	Monitor/evaluate	Comments
Formal teaching sessions	During the course the concepts or research, research methodology and research appreciation will be introduced. These sessions will be developed and evaluated throughout the training programme to a level determined by the level of training/course requirement.	The learner will gain an insight into the meaning of research and its application.		
Field work	The learner will be given the opportunity to gain experience in collecting and analysing data, using the following research techniques: • questionnaires • interview schedules • observational studies	The learner will gain an insight into three methods of collecting information, to begin to develop an awareness of research appreciation. The level at which the learner is finally expected to arrive is defined as follows:		
Teaching will be supported by relevant/up-to-date research material		1 identify the purpose of the research 2 formulate opinions about research findings		

Figure 8.4 Standard setting

MEASURING OR ASSESSING QUALITY

It is clear that quality is intangible and cannot be *accurately* measured. This section examines how aspects of quality *can* be measured and how some form of quality assessment can therefore be carried out.

The definitions and relationships given in this section reflect only one view of how quality can be examined. The definitions used may not be consistent with those that you are familiar with or may come across in your working life. They do, however, provide one way of looking at quality.

Standards and criteria

Professional staff are trying to move away from the traditional ways of assessing quality towards a more dynamic style; moving away from the techniques of examining past deficits towards a proactive, forward-looking approach (see Figure 8.5):

- Where are we now?
- Where do we want to go?
- How do we get there?

If this approach is to be successful, the organisation has to *monitor* quality, and if it is to be monitored effectively, quality has to be measurable.

Figure 8.5

The standard-setting cycle (Downie 1967, p.11)

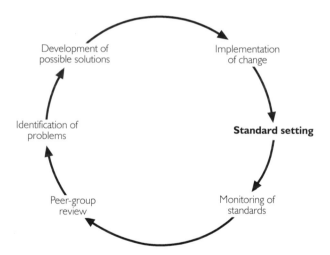

What is a standard?

- An agreed result
- A tool used in quality audit
- Agreed levels of performance
- A known quantity/quality of service or production (e.g. education, training, staff development)

The use of standards as agreed levels of performance is considered in the following section.

Approaches to quality

Because quality itself cannot be accurately measured, it tends to be broken down into component parts. Such component parts may be called *standards*, each standard reflecting an element of the quality provided. These standards, even taken in their entirety, will be unable to totally define the quality of the education provided.

Standard: An agreed level of performance negotiated within available resources
If the standard is not capable of direct measurement, it can be broken down into a number of more definable components – *criteria* – which relate to the standard. These criteria will always be measurable.
Criteria: Measures of the achievement of a standard

Once the criteria have been set, it will be possible to determine whether or not they have been achieved.

The relationship between quality, standards and criteria is shown in Figure 8.7 (p.210). This shows how quality can be described by a series of standards which can in turn be broken down into a series of criteria (see also chapter 4).

Why standards should be written

Writing, maintaining and monitoring standards is a useful way of defining the work in a given area, be it clinical, educational or clerical. If this is done well, the process and outcome of writing standards will support the ideology that exists in a unit or will help form one where none exists. By maintaining and adhering to the standards the quality of the work in the defined areas can be measured.

Standards have many benefits:

- They can form the basis of a quality audit, being both formative and summative.
- Written well they will be understood by people outside the department.
- They can be used as a source of information when defining jobs, projects, action plans and service provision, or during an individual performance review (IPR).
- They help us to explain the service we provide.
- They are a quality tool designed around the individual unit.

Standards: a SWOT analysis

Standards need to be monitored and evaluated; one way of doing this is to carry out a SWOT analysis, i.e. an analysis of strengths, weaknesses, opportunities and threats.

Strengths

- Standards can unify a group, reduce confusion and direct attention to what is important.
- Because standards are written by those who will achieve them they are owned by the authors. Because they are ratified by the manager no control of the service is lost.
- Being dynamic new standards can be initiated by management so they

are leading the developing service. They can also be initiated by service staff.

- They can be introduced into any setting.

Weaknesses

- Because standards are dynamic they require updating, and so will the monitoring tool.
- Managers have to spend quite a lot of time stressing their importance.
- Individuals may ignore them if allowed to.
- Where standards involve agencies outside the teacher's control it is difficult to spend enough time with the people involved to get their cooperation.
- They are based on a rational approach to work, but people are not rational all the time.
- Because they are written by the people expected to achieve them standards need to be 'sold' not imposed.

Opportunities

- Standards help to define the service, so helping management define corporate goals and explain the service it provides. Thus they demonstrate to general management in a rational way the use of resources at present and enable the use of resources in the future to be forecasted.

Threats

- In helping to define projects/jobs and action plans, weak areas in people's jobs are exposed.
- Some people do not like to have their job defined and will attempt to hinder this approach.
- Knowledge about the work is power which can be used by everyone.
- Managers may have to support the idea of standards against people whose work they affect adversely.

Indicators

An indicator is a measure that provides comparative data, a non-judgemental 'signal' which can be used to compare differences in numerical data over time or between locations. There are two main types of indicator:

1 an indicator which compares data for a specified time period for several discrete places of activity
2 an indicator which compares data for a single place of activity through a series of different time periods.

Both types of indicator can be used in assessing, monitoring and comparing quality.

College performance league tables are one example of comparative data, showing for instance the percentage of learners who get a first class degree at one college compared with another.

Goals and targets

The concepts associated with the terms *goals* and *targets* are related, and these terms are sometimes used interchangeably within the literature. Other frequently used and often interchangeable words are *objectives*, *aims* and *missions* (see Appendix 4). These have already been discussed in chapters 3 and 4 (see also Appendix 1).

A goal and a target are defined below. The definitions are general in nature and you may find they are used differently within the literature.

Goal: a level of performance stated as an aim
Target: a specific level of performance stated as an aim to be achieved within a given timescale and within given resources

Using these definitions a goal may be periodically reviewed:

- Have we improved the use of resources?
- Could we further improve their use?

During this review process further types of goals might be identified:

- Should we examine the use of resources in the same way as we have examined learners' outcomes?

A target has to be reviewed; that is its purpose. If targets have been set it will be necessary to assess whether they have been attained. This review process will not only look at whether past targets have been achieved but may need to reset the targets in the light of the review. This fits well with the audit cycle (Figure 8.6).

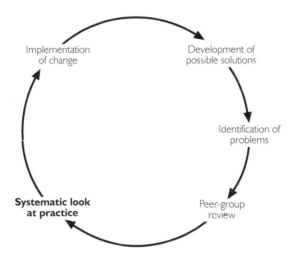

Figure 8.6

The audit cycle

Figure 8.7 shows one view of the relationships between quality, standards, criteria, targets and indicators. Quality can be broken down into standards, which can in turn be broken down into criteria. The indicators provide information about the standards and criteria set but they are also determined by the standards and criteria; thus there is a two-way arrow between them.

Figure 8.7

The relationship between
quality, standards, criteria,
targets and indicators

Study problem

- Select an issue pertinent to your current working environment.
- Use one of Maxwell's dimensions (see p.202) and define an appropriate standard and three or four relevant criteria.
- Define an appropriate standard and three or four criteria for Donabedian's structure (see p.203).
- Take up to 15 minutes on this exercise, longer if you would find it of value.

FRAMEWORK FOR QUALITY ASSURANCE AND MANAGEMENT

Here we draw together some of the issues from the preceding chapters.

Assessing, monitoring and improving quality needs a framework if it is to be a success. If standards are set, targets/goals determined, and indicators defined, the organisation needs to know what has been achieved and what needs to be redefined or reset.

An evaluative cycle of some type is one of the most effective ways in which this can be achieved – see Figure 8.8. Such cycles may be described in many ways, for example feedback loops, or in this case a quality cycle.

The main purpose of defining standards might be to assess the current quality of service provision or to monitor these standards against predetermined targets, or both. Whichever it is, the ultimate aim is to improve the quality of education provision and the outcomes from curriculum development interventions.

Information and monitoring

The use of information in the processes of monitoring raises issues that are generally applicable to all forms of monitoring where monitoring is defined as *the continual surveillance of a defined area of activity or performance*.

If we are to judge whether the service on offer is one of quality, we first have to define the present position of the organisation with regard to the standards it has determined. Once the current position has been determined the organisation can look at ways of moving towards a higher quality service. As already pointed out, if quality is to be either assessed or monitored something has to be measured. It is the standards that are measured either directly or, more usually, indirectly through the criteria established.

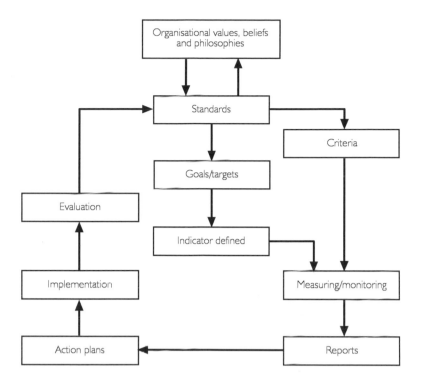

Figure 8.8

The quality cycle or review process
(See Appendix 4 for an example of a statement of organisational values, beliefs and philosophies)

Figure 8.9 shows the process of monitoring.

Study problem

- What do we want to monitor?
- What is the information required to monitor?
- What data are required to be collected?
- What data do we need to change standards?
- What data do we need to develop new criteria?

Levels of monitoring

There are two broad levels at which monitoring may be adopted:

- *macro level:* wherein the overall service provision is monitored, adopting a 'broad brush' approach
- *micro level:* wherein specific elements or aspects of service provision are monitored.

Macro level

Macro-level monitoring provides a broad overview, either of one specific area or of a range of interrelated areas. The data for an entire department or unit are aggregated and assessed.

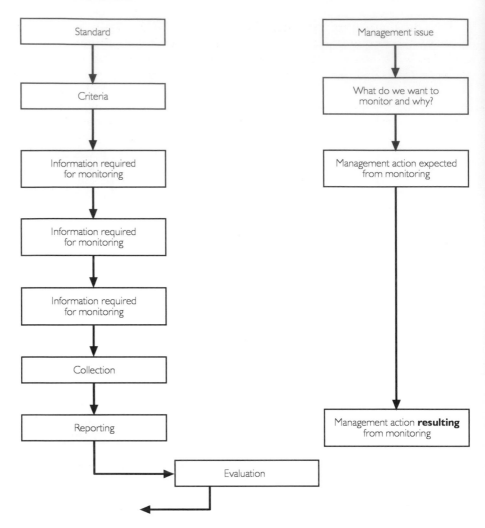

Figure 8.9

The process of determining information requirements for monitoring

Micro level

Micro-level monitoring gives a greater amount of detail about an area, subject or aspect of service provision. An area might be a department or a unit, a subject or speciality; an aspect might be indicators such as examination rates.

Study problem

Think of two examples for each of:

1 information at a macro level
2 information at a micro level.

Whether it is macro- or micro-level data that are being used depends on the situation being reviewed. Similarly, the data/information required to carry out a review have to be appropriate to the situation being reviewed.

Education managers are often faced with the requirement to monitor what is happening in their institutions. This monitoring might be concerned with levels of activity, the quality of service provided, the expenditure against budgets, the level of staff absence, or any other management issue. To be able to monitor the areas for which they are responsible in great detail, for every aspect that could be monitored, would require very large volumes of information to be analysed. The approach adopted by most managers is to:

1 limit the areas which they monitor
2 monitor at a macro level to identify any potential problem areas
3 if problem areas are identified then monitor at a micro level to identify specific problems.

To monitor at a macro level may require different sets of information and different analysis techniques than the more specific micro-level monitoring.

Data collection and processing

To be able to actually measure performance against standards and criteria, it is a prerequisite that there should be some form of data that can inform about the standards. These data have to be collected and processed into information for the purposes of assessment or monitoring. If the data cannot be collected or are too costly to collect, then the standard may exist but it may not be possible to monitor or assess it. Assuming that the data can be collected, these still require analysis to be transformed into the information that will provide the indicators designed to assess or monitor the criteria and/or the standards. If the information is to be used to monitor then it will be with regard to a set of criteria or targets that have been previously established.

The collection of data may be very informal in nature or it may be very formalised. For example:

Informal data collection could be carried out by walking into a classroom to assess the work that is being carried out. You may look for instances of unsafe practice in the laboratory, or aspects of the environment that are not conducive to a pleasant learning atmosphere; for instance unfriendly or overly brisk attitudes of the teacher. You may find examples of good practice which you would like to see implement elsewhere.
Formal data collection might be the number of learners attending classes on a regular basis or examination results.

In examining quality many of the current formal systems of data collection provide little useful information for those wishing to measure and assess the quality of services provided by education institutions. The challenge for those wishing to assess and monitor quality is to devise different formal and informal systems. To do this they may need to consider such issues as:

● Why is this information required?
● Who requires this information?
● Will these data provide the information required?
● How reliable will these data be?
● Are these data available?

- How costly will it be to collect these data?
- How costly will it be to process these data?

Specific examples of different data processes for monitoring could be

- learner performance tables
- QTA and QAA results
- quality of resources as perceived by staff and learners.

Standards of information

The question of how information on quality should be used must reflect the overall approach to quality management. Staff must feel that the information is being used in a positive and useful manner. They should be able to see its relevance and be able to identify the benefits to the service deriving from the use of information.

The standards of the information itself have to be a key objective of the organisation. If these data are to be used as information in management processes such as the quality cycle they should be:

Valid	They measure that which they are intended to measure.
Appropriate	They should give the user what is needed.
Available	Users should have ready access to the data.
Acceptable	The data should be understandable.
Accurate	The measure is correct.
Up to date	The data are the most recent.
Timely	The information is supplied in time for action to be taken.

Sources of information

There are many sources of information within the education service which can be used when looking at the quality of the organisation and the quality of education it provides in its broadest sense. Some of this information is required by government departments, some by the various tiers within the LEA, FENTO (college), the UKCC (Nursing and Midwifery Council) for nursing and midwifery, HMP for the prison service, etc., routinely, whether on a weekly, monthly or yearly basis.

Some information is generated at a local level, as a matter of routine, for local use rather than for others (i.e. higher tiers of the organisation). This includes:

- individual performance reviews
- complaints and 'thank you' letters
- staff surveys
- customer satisfaction surveys
- peer and self-assessment, as part of audit systems
- personnel data.

Other information sources include those which are published on a yearly or more infrequent basis. Some of these are formal statutory requirements and so should be readily available:

- annual reports

- publications of the Office of Population Censuses and Surveys (OPCS)
- research papers.

The lists above indicate the actual sources of much valuable information and data. The following suggests some useful contacts you may try approaching to reach these sources:

1   for work-related data, for example learner activity, occupational courses:
    - your line manager
2   for work-related information which is professionally related, such as recent research material or differing methods of teaching, assessment, etc.:
    - your line manager
    - your colleagues
    - librarians
    - senior staff
    - universities and colleges of HE
    - community colleges.

The way in which quality assurance and quality management are introduced to any organisation influences the outcome of implementation. This type of initiative often meets more resistance than others because the impact of changes – both expected and actual – tends to be 'global': the whole organisation from senior management to the most junior member of staff can be affected.

If quality assurance and quality management are introduced as an integral component of the curriculum and culture of an organisation, they are likely to be successful. All staff must view the assurance of quality as *key* to their role in providing education and training. They must also feel that their contributions are important to the organisation.

To achieve this:

- Quality must be seen as a key priority (not an optional extra).
- It must be comprehensive (covering *all* staff groups).
- It must be an ongoing process.
- Each quality initiative must have regard for other elements of the education/training process.
- A proactive approach is required – quality must become an inherent part of the planning and management framework of any curriculum.

A reactive approach to quality may at times still be required; you will have to respond to issues as they arise.

Introducing a quality assurance programme

The steps to be taken

It will be clear from what you have read already that the important steps to be taken when introducing a quality assurance programme into the curriculum include some or all of those shown in Figure 8.10.

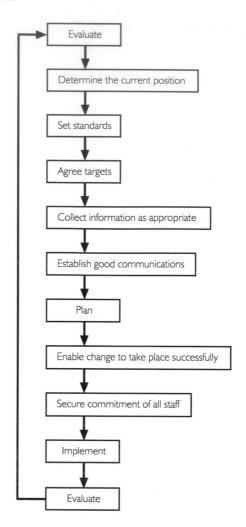

Figure 8.10

Steps in introducing a quality assurance programme

Study problem

Some of these steps have been discussed already throughout this book. You may want to take another look at these issues before going on to the next section and remind yourself of their importance.

Defining the current position

Defining the current position is the first step. This is also part of the audit cycle (Figure 8.6, p.209). It enables teachers and managers to appreciate what is currently taking place. It also establishes the baseline which can be used to assess the level, the direction and the effects of the change desired and expected when the quality assurance programme is introduced. Defining the current position may entail the collection/collation of substantial quantities of data and information.

Determination of the current position may generate different reactions and responses from different people within the organisation. Each member of staff will have their own perspective of quality. This will be heavily influenced by their role in the organisation, their level of responsibility, their training, their professional standing and their ideologies.

In order to limit the development of negative attitudes during the assessment of the current position, it is important that all staff understand not only the methodology being adopted but also the purpose for which the information is being collected. Without this, some staff may feel that because they are being questioned about the quality of training they provide, and that there is concern about their professional ability.

A number of methods can be used to assess the current position:

1 *Checklists:* lists of existing standards and of existing provision
2 *Audit tools:* to give a baseline of the current service provision
3 *A review and evaluation of existing policies and procedures:* This will give an overview of the documented intentions to provide education/training, appraisals and individual performance review (IPR)
4 *Performance indicators:* These may suggest that in-depth analysis is required.

Communication networks

Good communications are essential if staff and users of a service are to understand and share the quality initiatives that are to be introduced. To achieve good communications within an organisation requires the identification of those staff who need to be informed. These staff should form a communication network. The identification of this network should address who is involved, who should be involved and how much they need to know. The people in the network need to understand the rationale for the network and the importance of their role within it.

Quality is a 'global' issue in which teachers and other staff from almost every department and function need to be involved. All staff groups should be taken into consideration when identifying the network. Examples would include:

- management
- training and education
- professions allied to training/education
- support services
- professional and technical
- library services.

All staff groups are interrelated – they cannot function in isolation if they are to provide quality courses effectively. In their contribution to the provision if education/training each group depends on specific functions carried out by several of the other groups.

Why should staff be involved?
The holistic nature of quality assurance means that all groups of staff need to be involved. They need an understanding of the overall concept of quality assurance, how it will affect them and their role in the quality assurance

programme. Staff have to see that they are valued and that quality assurance is a shared and common vision, perceived by all as the norm rather than the exception. They also need to understand the value of the quality assurance programme to themselves, the learners, other staff and the organisation.

Circulating examples of good practice both benefits and encourages others. It motivates the successful to higher endeavours and passes on experience without being negative to the 'not so successful'. Another tangible effect is that it reduces the cost of duplication of effort; it encourages 'getting it right first time' as a way of thinking. Common language and shared values are encouraged by good networking, which in turn develops a feeling of common purpose. Without good networks people will work in isolation, pulling in different directions or wasting time 'reinventing the wheel'.

Who should be involved?

The question who needs to be involved is directly related to the question of *what do they need to know*. The principle of Total Quality Management (TQM) is that staff should have access to whatever information they need.

Figure 8.11 shows the external and internal functions of the education system which influence the quality of teaching, learning, assessing and evaluation.

Figure 8.11

External and internal influences on quality

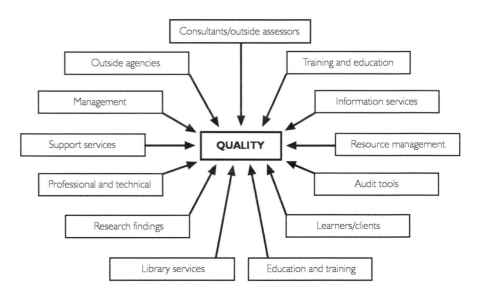

In some industries all levels of staff have access to all operational and quality assurance information. So why not you?

Study problem

Try completing the following checklist for your communication network. In the first column tick those people with whom you already communicate and in the second those with whom you think you should communicate, particularly if you were to introduce a quality assurance programme as part of your new curriculum. Add to the end of the list any other people with whom you think you should communicate.

Checklist of those with whom we need to or should communicate

	Already communicate with	Should communicate with
Staff		
Teaching teams		
Education/training development officers		
Other specialists		
Senior staff		
Research group		
Standards group		
Advisers/outside assessors		
QTA, QAA personnel		
Support staff or PAs		
Support services		
Portering, AVA officer		
Catering and domestics		
Finance		
Computing/information services		
Other resources		
Management		
Senior managers		
Business managers		
Information services personnel		
Personnel department		
Other		

Enabling implementation

Effective implementation of quality assurance programmes can only be ensured if they are integrated within the management process. This in turn requires leadership which responds to the changing environment; a leader with a positive, forward-looking and responsive approach to change, who, in addition, has a belief in the philosophy of quality management. The leader might be a project manager or a senior manager such as the professor or head of department; indeed any member of staff may attempt to lead change within the organisation or their part of that organisation.

The leader must act as a *change agent* who enables the introduction of quality assurance. They must have an understanding of the management of change and how to enable staff to cope with change. The three phases to enable change were described by Lewin (1958) as being:

Unfreezing: getting staff to leave previous practice
Changing: introducing the new practice
Refreezing: consolidating the new practice

In the first phase (unfreezing) the leader has to identify and overcome resistance to the proposed change.

Unfreezing

Most people are not resistant to the notion of change if they can perceive personal benefits arising from it. For instance, if you offer staff better working conditions, higher pay, shorter hours, access to free books, paid sabbatical leave, an exciting new curriculum, how many do you think will refuse? Not many, one would suspect. Equally, most people will not be resistant to change if they can perceive benefits for other people – as long as they incur no personal costs. Few people would object to changes if they felt no resources were being diverted away from themselves.

Resistance to change does tend to develop when people perceive that they may incur personal costs as a result of change – for example:

- loss of status
- loss of responsibility
- reduction of pay
- changes in the 'values' of the organisation within which they work
- loss of personal 'value'
- loss of personal power.

How many times do we hear teachers say that they or their work are not 'valued'?

Regrading staff or restructuring the curriculum may be beneficial to a number of staff, the organisation and/or its learners/clients. However, the individuals involved in the change will tend to resist if they can only perceive that they may lose responsibility, to which they believe themselves entitled. Resistance to change may also develop when people are unclear about the nature of the change itself. For example, the introduction of staff appraisal or performance-related pay may cause anxiety to staff.

However, if these benefits cannot be clearly defined staff may feel that there are hidden issues; for instance they may feel that the philosophy and values that have previously driven the curriculum may also change.

Resistance to change may appear to be global, but it is more likely to be vested in a few individuals, or in groups which have been influenced by these individuals. Staff may have genuine cause to be concerned about proposed changes; these range from being comfortable with their present position to a fear of not being able to cope with new ideas and the practices and demands of the new curriculum.

Study problem

What might hinder the process of achieving standards?

Positive approaches to unfreezing include the following.

1 Participation
Get staff to contribute to the change process by giving them a sense of ownership over the developments. Participation enables staff to gain an understanding of the proposed developments and an opportunity for those implementing the changes to determine more rapidly potential problems areas.

2 Removing the threat
If staff feel threatened by proposed developments these fears will need to be overcome if their wholehearted cooperation is to be provided. One way of balancing real or imagined threats is by offering direct or indirect incentives. However, such methods may result in cooperation for the wrong reasons, and may become expensive.

3 Explaining the benefits expected
Clearly explaining the expected benefits from the developments proposed will assist in enlisting the participation of all staff, and gain the enthusiasm of possible champions/gatekeepers. If there are no clearly identifiable benefits, or at least reasons, for the proposed changes you may wish to query why it is proposed to implement them.

4 Communication
It is necessary to ensure that there is an effective and efficient communication system which keeps all staff and leaders informed. If staff are participating in the changes it is important to ensure that they feel their contributions are being considered and valued. Lack of communication between those staff leading and implementing change and those staff required to undergo change can cause many difficulties, for instance disillusionment.

5 Identifying training and education needs
Often the training and education required to effect change is a matter of increasing staff awareness and providing them with information. A full analysis of staff training needs is not usually required unless the change is very significant to the organisation. As change is implemented the review process will

often highlight the developmental and training needs of individuals and groups of staff.

If the proposed developments require staff to alter their current working practices, or to develop new ones, it is essential to ensure that they have the necessary skills to effect the changes required of them. Failure to provide adequate training and education may result in frustration, and therefore negative feelings about the changes taking place. Many teachers do not realise that new curricula can add to their already busy day, until it is too late.

6 Identifying the champions and gatekeepers

The champions or gatekeepers are those who will rise to the challenges and take others with them. They need to be identified and provided with any developmental training that may be required. If they understand the requirement for change, their actions and behaviour will help to effect curriculum and cultural changes, and they could become the basis of a pyramid training strategy.

A pyramid training strategy is one where the experts and enthusiasts are trained so that they can train their own staff. Such a strategy puts the ownership of change firmly in their hands, thereby increasing their enthusiasm. It encourages the local development of a corporate culture in a way that classroom-based teaching cannot.

It may be that these champions are also the key opinion leaders; if they are not, these opinion leaders need to be identified and their support enlisted.

7 Identifying the most resistant staff

Try to ensure that the staff most resistant to change understand the benefits expected from the implementation of the proposed developments. They should perceive the benefits to themselves, to other staff, to the organisation and to learners. Listen to their concerns and remain open to their suggestions. People who resist change may, when invited to make a contribution, begin to feel their contributions are valued and allow themselves to become a part of the change process. They often discover new skills which have been hidden under the old curriculum.

During the next two phases, *changing* and *refreezing*, there are further potential problems.

Changing and refreezing

1 Staff who cannot cope with the change

This may be for a number of reasons:

- There are other priorities on their time.
- They cannot comprehend their role in the change.
- The change challenges their self-image or professionalism.
- They feel incompetent and stressed.

These issues have to be addressed, so we need to allow time during these phases to deal with such problems.

2 Innovations which fail to live up to expectations

When introducing multifaceted solutions such as quality assurance programmes to a new curriculum, not all of them can be expected to be as successful as you would expect. Some part of the programme may lead into dead ends. If you recognise that the programme, or a part of it, is doomed to failure, it is far better to communicate the problems to the staff, and be open to new suggestions.

Once changes have been successfully implemented staff should be able to *build on success*. The introduction of successful, innovative, quality measures will serve as an example to others to show what can be done and that the intended benefits are not mere rhetoric. One way to build on success is to publicise, or promote, examples of good practice. These examples might be derived from external or internal sources; they should be circulated appropriately throughout the organisation and should highlight the benefits to learners, to staff and to the organisation. A major part of building on success is to evaluate effectively the reasons why changes have been successful and if necessary why they have not proved as successful as had been hoped.

Evaluating the implementation of the change process can point the way to:

- maintaining the benefits already derived
- attaining further benefits
- deriving benefits when implementing future changes.

Rationale for quality assessments

The further and higher education sectors have undergone a period of rapid and continuous change over the past ten years, the pace of which has accelerated since the incorporation of FE/HE colleges in 1993. From 1995 onwards some colleges were faced with closure while others continued to grow and merge to form larger institutions offering new courses at quality standard. The evaluation of the change process will require consideration of the procedures for monitoring, providing feedback and establishing control. The method of evaluation adopted needs to be carefully planned, and the evaluation team, who will validate, assess and monitor the change, needs to be carefully selected.

The quality mechanisms imposed through funding council assessment inspection processes and through quality assessment committees place further demands on colleges and universities to prove that they are up to the job of educating and training learners. Colleges are now inspected every four years and are graded against a five-point grading scale, to identify their strengths and weakness in the following aspects of cross-college provision:

1 responsiveness and range of provision
2 governance and management
3 learner recruitment, guidance and support
4 quality assurance tools
5 resources.

Educational institutions are large, busy, complex and dynamic places to learn in, with a diverse learner population of all ages. It is therefore vital that all staff have knowledge of their curriculum and how quality issues fit into that curriculum. (A good example can be found in Appendices 1 and 2.)

QUALITY ASSURANCE IN THE FUTURE: SUBJECT REVIEW

The first round of the Quality Assurance Agency's Subject Review is beginning to focus minds across the academic community. Social policy and social work will be amongst the first subjects to be reviewed under the new framework. The following explanation of Subject Review is based on information provided by Hilary Burgess, Learning and Teaching Adviser, Social Policy and Social Work Leaning and Teaching Support Network (SWAPltsn).

What is Subject Review?

Whilst the primary responsibility for standards lies with each higher education institution, the funding councils have a statutory responsibility to ensure that the quality of education is assessed. The QAA takes on this role, on behalf of the four funding councils.

'Academic Review' was introduced in Scotland for the academic year 2000/1, and in the rest of the UK from 2001/2. It brings together 'Institutional Review' (formerly known as 'Audit' or 'Continuation Audit') and 'Subject Review' (the old Quality Assurance (QA) or Teaching Quality Audit (TQA) process), thus providing both horizontal and vertical perspectives on higher education.

How does Subject Review fit with other QAA initiatives?

The QAA's overall policy framework aims to make the intended and actual outcomes of learning (a) more explicit, and (b) linked to appropriate institutional and external reference points. Subject Review (SR) is central to this framework. Some other elements of the policy are shown below, along with their link to the SR process.

National Qualification Frameworks (one for Scotland, one for the rest of the UK), on which institutional awards can be positioned. In SR reviewers will judge whether the outcomes for a programme are appropriate for the award offered.

Programme Specifications, which describe the main learning outcomes for a programme and how these are to be achieved. Programme specifications will be central to SR, and will be attached to the self-evaluation documents.

Subject Benchmarking: information from the 42 subject benchmarking groups. These will be used as reference points for curriculum design and assessment in SR.

Codes of practice: Codes on many aspects of HE have been produced by the QAA (with others soon to arrive). Those likely to be used as a point of reference by reviewers in SR include:

- assessment of learners
- external examining and programme approval
- monitoring and review.

When will the review take place?

The QAA will work in cycles of six years, broken down into two periods of three years. The majority of SRs for social policy and social work will take place in the first three-year period, with the exception of departments linked to health sciences, which will usually be in the second period.

In the year preceding each period, all institutions will complete a form to outline the subjects offered, the programmes for consideration under each subject heading, estimated numbers of full-time-equivalent teachers for each programme and the preferred timing for the review of each subject.

The QAA is currently agreeing plans with each institution for the scope and timing of academic reviews for each institution. Where possible this will accommodate preferences for timing, and ensure that reviews coincide with scheduled internal reviews or accreditation visits by professional bodies.

What form will the review take?

The shape and intensity of subject review will vary between institutions. If, following institutional review, the QAA has confidence in an institution's ability to assure quality and standards, a lighter touch may be expected, but where there is no convincing evidence of robust and effective systems, greater intensity may be necessary. Additionally a sample of SRs may be conducted at 'standard intensity'. Since in the early days few institutional reviews will have been conducted using the new format, the QAA has prepared initial institutional profiles, and is discussing with each institution the overall approach to the intensity of review.

The review team, composed of selected and trained peer reviewers, may compress its energies into a single visit, or spread the visits over a period of time (e.g. 6–12 months). As yet, there is little information about how this is being approached and the relative merits of different methods.

The review team will:

- consider the self-evaluation document
- hold meetings with staff and learners (and potentially external examiners)
- observe key meetings (e.g. programme reviews, validation events)
- sample assessed learner work.

Whilst they have the right to observe teaching, this may not be necessary if the institution can demonstrate that effective mechanisms are in place to assure the quality of teaching, and that learner feedback indicates there are no significant deficiencies.

How will Subject Review relate to previous TQA/QAA methods and outcomes?

The new system replaces two previous methods used for assessing quality. Those who have been in higher education long enough will recall the 1994–5 exercise in social work and social policy, in which departments were rated 'excellent', 'satisfactory' or 'unsatisfactory'. Not all departments had the pleasure of a visit, as some were reviewed only by the self-evaluation document (SED). This system was replaced by the (in)famous 24-point scale, in which departments submitted an SED, had a three-day visit and were then rated out of 4 in relation to six aspects of provision:

- curriculum design, content and organisation
- teaching, learning and assessment

- learner progression and achievement
- learner support and guidance
- learning resources
- quality management and enhancement.

Provided that each aspect was graded 2 or better, the quality of the education was approved.

In a recent statement ('Delivering lightness of touch'), the Secretary of State announced a further change to the process outlined by the QAA, in which the move towards lessening the burden of review is taken a step further. The new approach suggests that external review will take place in all departments or schools that achieved a rating of less than 21 points (three 4s plus three 3s) in the last system, and those not achieving excellent rating in the pre-1995 assessment. However, only a sample of departments that achieved a rating of 21 or over (1995–2001 methodology) or an excellent rating (pre-1995 methodology) will be externally reviewed. This sample may be about 25 per cent of eligible departments in a given institution. All departments will still be expected to produce a full self-evaluation document for the QAA, with a summary for publication. It seems that there are many details of this most recent development to be worked out; for the most up-to-date information see the SWAPltsn website (www.swap.ac.uk).

What goes into the self-evaluation document (SED)?

SEDs again form the basis of Subject Review, and must demonstrate that a subject provider has evaluated:

- the appropriateness of the academic standards set for its programmes
- the effectiveness of the curriculum in delivering the intended outcomes of the programmes
- the effectiveness of the assessment in measuring attainment of the intended outcomes
- the extent to which the intended standards and outcomes are achieved by learners
- the quality of learning opportunities provided for the learners.

Reference should also be made to any relevant QAA codes of practice.

The structure for the SED is given in Annex C of the *Handbook for Academic Review* (see www.qaa.ac.uk). Peer reviewers test the statements made and make judgements about the appropriateness and effectiveness of the provision. The intended outcomes will be considered in relation to the relevant benchmarking statement, and programme specifications will be important in clarifying what is taught.

What judgements will be made?

In relation to standards, a single threshold judgement will be made. Reviewers will either

- have *confidence* that the standards are satisfactory and that they will be maintained, or
- have *limited confidence* that standards can be maintained.

In the latter case, reviewers will identify areas where improvement is needed, and the provider will prepare an improvement strategy, the implementation of which will be monitored by the QAA, followed in some cases by a further review within a calendar year. If standards continue not to be achieved, funding is potentially at risk.

In relation to the *quality of learning opportunities*, separate judgements will be given for

- teaching and learning
- learner progression
- learning resources.

Each of these will be judged as *failing*, *approved* or *commendable*, with a narrative identifying strengths and weaknesses. If provision is found to be failing in any one area, provision overall will be designated as failing, and another visit will take place within a year. In the *commendable* category, reviewers may also identify *exemplary* provision, which represents sector-leading practice, is worthy of dissemination to and emulation by other providers and makes a significant contribution to the success of the provision.

What can be done to prepare for Subject Review?

- Familiarise yourselves with the relevant benchmarking statement or statements, and consider where your programmes sit in relation to these.
- Read the subject overview reports from the previous review of social policy and social work.
- Consult your institution about its plans for the timing and formats of reviews.
- Prepare programme specifications for each programme (your institution may be evolving a standard format).
- Review your own mechanisms for quality review: how could these be enhanced?
- Think about setting up peer observation of teaching.
- Consider your departmental teaching and learning strategy and assessment strategy.
- Think about which of the QAA codes of practice may be relevant to your department.
- Attend relevant training organised by your institution, SWAP or other bodies.
- Don't panic!

AUT (1999a) *Higher Education in the New Century*. London, AUT.

AUT (1999b) *Analysis of Labour Force Survey Data*. London, AUT.

AUT (2001a) 'Now is the time to spend on people' (Pay claim 2001–2), Table 3. Available at *http://www.aut.org/uk/pandp/index.html*

AUT. (2001b) 'Now is the time to spend on people' (Pay claim 2001–2), Section 6. Available at *http://www.aut.org.uk/campaigns/index.html*

Bett, Sir Michael (1999) *Independent Review of Higher Education, Pay and Conditions*. London, Stationery Office, para.21.

CBI (1994) *Quality Assessed: The CBI. Review of NVQs and SVQs.* London, CBI.

Cookson, C. (2001) 'UK scientists responsible for third of genome project'. *Financial Times* 13 February, p.2.

Court, S. (1996) 'The use of time by academic and related staff'. *Higher Education Quarterly* 50(4): 237–60.

De Wit, P. (1992) *Quality Assurance in University Continuing Vocational Education.* London, HMSO.

Donabedian, A. (1980) *The Definition of Quality and Approaches to Its Assessment.* Ann Arbor, Michigan.

Donabedian, A. (1986) 'Criteria and standards for quality assessment'. *Quality Review Bulletin* 12(3): 99–100.

FEFC (1996) *Quality and Standards in Further Education in England. Chief Inspector's Annual Report 1995–96.* Coventry, FEFC.

Greater London Group (1996) 'Higher education productivity' (draft report), p.3.

HESA (2000) *Learners in Higher Education Institutions 1998/99.* Cheltenham: HESA, Table A.

Lewin, K. (1958) 'The group reason and social change'. In E. Maccoby (ed.), *Reading in Social Psychology.* London, Holt, Rinehart and Winston.

Maxwell, R. (1984) 'Quality assessment in health'. *British Medical Journal* 12 May: 1470–2.

Muller, D. and Funnell, P. (eds) (1991) *Delivering Quality in Vocational Education.* London, Kogan Page.

Oakland, J.S. (1989) *Total Quality Management.* Oxford Heinemann.

OECD (1998) *Education at a Glance.* Paris: OECD, p.198.

Sainsbury, Lord (Minister for Science) (1998) Speech at the British Association Festival of Science, Cardiff University, 7 September.

For further information on the QAA and Subject Review, consult the QAA website (http://www.qaa.ac.uk) and SWAP's website (www.swap.ac.uk), which includes examples of programme specifications for social policy and social work and a range of other materials relevant to the QAA and Subject Review.

CONCLUSION

9

We seem to exist in a hazardous time,
Driftin' along here through space;
Nobody knows just how we began,
Or how far we've gone in the race.
(Ben King, 'Evolution')

Our progress as a nation can be no swifter than our progress in education.
(John F. Kennedy)

While this book attempts to cover the main issues involved in curriculum studies, the reader is strongly advised to read further about other essential ideas derived from earlier influences from which new areas have been developed. For example:

- values and the curriculum
- ideologies of education
- management of schools/colleges
- policy analysis: social and political context
- evaluation research
- management of theory and knowledge of curriculum
- culture and the curriculum.

It is often argued that the field of curriculum studies is distinguished by its concern with practicalities and may be eclectic in its search for theoretical support. Lawn and Barton (1981) argued that there are contradictions in this account of the development of curriculum studies and suggested that pragmatism and eclecticism seem oddly matched with the prevailing technical determinism of rational curriculum planning, received knowledge, research development and dissemination models. The problem does not arise where there appears to be a clear relationship between industrial change and educational reorganisation, as appears to be the case in the USA and Germany. The question to be answered is not so much whether the gap between curriculum studies based on or dominated by managerial influence and a curriculum practice controlled by teachers is widening, but rather whose purposes curriculum studies serves and what the relationship is between theory and practice within it (Lawn and Barton, 1981).

Petter (1970) argued for curriculum balance and claimed that the true balancing agent lies not in the subject content but in the methods and approaches of the teacher and the teacher's interaction with students, and that the way in which something is taught affects profoundly the form that it assumes in the consciousness and behaviour of students. Kelly (1986) suggested that

interpretation of balance do[es] not always begin from consideration of the knowledge-content of the curriculum but from a concern for the experiences of the student and that our search for educational balance points us away from a rationalist epistemology and, indeed reinforces the claim that it is a too ready acceptance of and adherence to that kind of epistemological stance which is at the root of much of the confusion in this area – a confusion in theory which inevitably results in a corresponding confusion of practice. (p.149)

The balance we should be seeking is not a balance of subject content, but a balance of experiences for the student. Balance in education must be recognised as relative, taking its meaning almost entirely from the value system of the person using it. Kelly (1989) argues:

We will all have our own view of what constitutes a balanced curriculum and what that view is will in turn depend on what we see as the fundamental principles of education. We must begin, therefore, by recognising this and noting the essential and problematic value element in all educational debate. (p.230)

Study problem

With a fellow student discuss the following: What are the most suitable approaches to adopt to educational or curriculum planning?

There are at least three different starting points, as listed below. Indicate their order of priority in the boxes. This will give you a rationale for your approach. If your order differs from your fellow student's you will need to debate your differences and why each of you has adopted your approach.

Starting points	**Priority**
Concern with the transmission and the acquisition of certain kinds of knowledge	☐
Concern with certain end-states to be reached	☐
Concern with the forms of development to be promoted	☐

Take time to read the following, on the purpose of the curriculum as a whole.

Stephenson (1988) suggested that a programme should reach the parts of the person that other courses miss. Rogers (1983) claimed that the curriculum should develop a climate of trust in the classroom in which curiosity and the natural desire to learn can be nourished and enhanced. Giles (1989) argued that the curriculum should use the field experiences of all students in ways that are both individualised and generalised. Rick (1972) saw the curriculum as a re-vision, the act of looking back, of seeing with fresh eyes, of entering an old text from a new critical direction. Wildemeersch (1989) suggested that there should be a growing emphasis on education so that it is 'a political, a curricular, reactive, and consumer-oriented enterprise which casts the educator in the role of marketing expert and technician of the teaching–learning machine (p.51). Finally, Lawton (1979) was keen to remind us that curriculum studies is not a field of educational enquiry to specialise in for those who want a quiet life in an ivory tower; it is a rather aggressive world in which even jokes about the curriculum tend to have a cruel edge.

Here are four basic questions you need to ask relating to the curriculum:

1   What is the purpose of the curriculum?
2   What subjects are to be included?
3   What learning experiences and college organisation are to be provided?
4   How are the results to be assessed/evaluated?

Curriculum planning should involve the following:

1   a systematic strategy and a step-by-step methodology which allows for logical and ordered planning
2   a national scheme of planning for the various elements
3   a method for developing these elements and relating them to each other
4   aims, goals and objectives which should be creative, avoid rigidity and encourage flexibility
5   a process by which all students are motivated to learn.

Study problem

To consolidate your own understanding of the curriculum imagine you are about to design a new curriculum.
1   Study the checklist below and use it to analyse your curriculum proposals.
2   Use this checklist as an example to map out your own concept of a curriculum and its content.

CHECKLIST FOR YOUR CURRICULUM

Your checklist should be applied to a specific curriculum or part thereof.

Give the title here:

The purpose of this checklist is to help you to analyse your curriculum proposals and to assist in their eventual realisation and presentation.

Please consider each factor and rate the application attached to it. More than one option may be applicable, or you wish to write in other specific factors which apply to your proposal.

FACTOR	APPLICATION	Please tick		
		Applies in full	Partly applies	Does not apply
SCOPE	National			
	Regional			
	Local/institutional			

FACTOR	APPLICATION	Please tick		
		Applies in full	Partly applies	Does not apply
SCALE	System-wide			
	Industry sector			
	Scheme			
	Course			
	Module/unit			
	Lesson			
FOCUS	Student-centred			
	Subject-centred			
	Vocation-centred			
	Professional-centred			
BASIS	Subjects			
	Discipline of knowledge			
	Praxis – for practice			
	Experience			
	Basic skills			
	Process skills			
	Specific occupational skills			
CONTROL	Teacher control			
	Student control			
	Institutional control			
	Employer			
	Government			
	Professional body			
	Examination body			

FACTOR	APPLICATION	Please tick		
		Applies in full	Partly applies	Does not apply
LEVEL	Pre-professional			
	Pre-vocational			
	Foundation			
	Basic occupational			
	Advanced			
	Post-advanced			
LEARNING	School/college based			
	Work based			
	Cooperative, i.e. college and work based			
	Open learning			
	Distance learning			
DERIVATION	Examination body			
	College Board of Studies			
	Consultation with industry			
	Consultation with students			
	Teacher determined			
	Research based			
	Precedent based			
MARKET	Demand led			
	Supply led			
	Responsive			
	Reactive			
	Proactive: marketing			
	Full cost			
	Subsidised as a public service			

Appendix 1   Sections from a PGCE course guide 2000–1

Quality policy

Quality assurance

The quality of your educational experience and your preparation as a beginning teacher are of paramount importance in the design and implementation of the PGCE programme and are a primary goal of all those who contribute to it. It is the responsibility of each person who teaches on or otherwise contributes to the scheme to take personal responsibility for the quality of their contribution to the provision of students' educational experience. It is the responsibility of the Course Director, within the framework of Departmental structures and processes, to monitor the programme drawing on, for example, student evaluation data and feedback given via the staff–student panel.

As a student on the programme and as an intending teacher you are expected to aspire to the standards of the programme, to complete work on time and to a high standard, and to maintain a professional attitude towards other students and tutors.

Detailed procedures are set out in a separate **procedures document** which provides information on:

- Evaluation
- Staff–student panel
- Board of Studies

Course evaluation

You will be asked to evaluate your experience on the PGCE and these data will be taken into account in the design, content and delivery of the programme. A summary of evaluation data will be posted on the PGCE noticeboard.

Staff–student panel

The staff–student panel is a formal committee with representatives on the Board of Studies. The panel will meet according to the schedule set out in the calendar and, if necessary, at other times. The principal roles of the staff–student panel are: to raise with the Board of Studies matters relating to the content of the scheme of study; to be consulted on proposed major changes to schemes and content; to comment on processes for obtaining feedback including the effectiveness of student questionnaires; and to contribute to the annual review.

Minutes of the meetings will be posted on the PGCE student noticeboard.

The Board of Studies

The PGCE Board of Studies is responsible for the scheme of study on which you have enrolled, for ensuring that procedures exist for monitoring of student progress, and will note and discuss student cases.

Assessed work

Unit tasks

You have to complete FIVE short written assignments (Unit Tasks) of about 1000 words each. Copies of Unit Tasks, which includes the task, the assessment criteria and a record sheet will be given out by tutors and should be handed-in by the dates set out in the attached schedule of assessment. Unit Tasks should be given or posted to the Course Secretary (not your tutor) on or before the set dates. The deadline for submission is 1600 hours.

Teaching practice, teaching project and learning journal

Details of the teaching project and the learning journal are given in the 'Teaching Practice Guide for Students and College Mentors'. This includes a copy of the teaching appraisal form used to comment on lessons and a report form to be completed by your placement college. There is also a 'Guide to the Assessment of Teaching Effectiveness'. Together, these indicate the range over which your practical abilities will be judged. You are also required to maintain a record of your teaching hours on the attendance form. A copy of the report form and criteria on which your teaching project and learning journal will be assessed are provided in the teaching practice guide.

The learning journal will be monitored in at least three stages and the final entries posted to your visiting tutor. Your entries should be posted to **your visiting tutor** to reach him or her by the agreed dates and the final entry by Friday, (date).

The teaching project will be monitored by your visiting tutor when he or she visits you on teaching practice. Please, therefore, have it available and ensure that it is up to date. The completed teaching project should be handed to or posted to **your visiting tutor** by Friday, (date).

ICT module assessment task

You are required to use and evaluate or design, use and evaluate either a flexible learning or ICT package. Details of what is required will be given in a lead lecture. This should be posted to the ICT Coordinator by Friday, (date).

Negotiated assignment

This is an extended essay of about 4000 words. Details of what is expected of you will be given in a lead lecture. At this time, you will be issued with a proposal form which you should complete and take with you to an interview with your personal tutor. A copy of the record sheet and general criteria for assessment will also be given to you.

The record sheet and the completed contract form must be attached to your written work before handing in. These should be posted to your personal tutor.

You might be asked to present your assignment as part of a conference. Remember to keep a copy for your own use. The finished assignment should be posted to your **personal tutor** by Friday, (date).

Portfolio of evidence

There is no formal assessment requirement for you to keep a portfolio of work. However, you might wish to maintain a record of lectures, seminars and workshops, together with a contemporary archive of issues in FE/HE taken from the media. This would provide a further record of your professional development and a record of achievement which you could offer to show prospective employers at job interviews.

LEARNING AND TEACHING

As teachers, an overriding concern is to develop the knowledge, understanding, skills and attitudes of others. We have, therefore, to be concerned not only with the process of teaching and becoming a teacher, but also with the outcomes of the enterprise seen in terms of other people's learning. We have to ask ourselves questions about our own development and about others' learning. With this in mind the PGCE course is built with three key and inter-connected ideas in mind, and which provide the course with a coherent framework. These are:

- the development of you (self) as a learner
- your initial preparation and professional development as a beginning teacher
- your responsibility to the students you teach to be an effective teacher and to promote effective learning.

You join the course as an adult learner, having had considerable work and/or life experience. An appropriate adult learning model is adopted in the design of this course and within a given framework. You will take responsibility for your own learning. You will negotiate with personal tutors, write unit tasks, personal portfolios, learning journals, participate in seminars and consult with experienced teachers and senior staff in the workplace during supervised teaching practice. For this reason we introduce you to the principles and practice of adult learning.

The following assumptions, values and beliefs relate to how adults learn and the conditions under which they learn. The statements emerge largely from the growing literature on **andragogy** but they have been extended by tutors experienced in working with adults. They are offered not as a prescription but as a set of ideas for you to consider and, in time, to accept or reject. In general, it is assumed that adults learn best when they:

- **Are involved in negotiation**: negotiation and evaluation should be continuous and there should be a mechanism for mutual planning. Should adults accept a share of the responsibility for planning, implementing and evaluating their own learning?
- **Derive their own goals**: to what extent do adults need to derive their own goals from their own practice, experience and future needs?
- **Diagnose their own needs for learning**: how can adults be helped to diagnose their own learning needs?
- **Accept that learning is an internal process**: is learning something that occurs 'inside' the adult or something that the teacher 'does' to them?

- **Become autonomous:** how can the adult learner be enabled to move from a state of dependency (on the teacher as 'appointed leader') to one of inter-dependency and autonomy?
- **Have responsibility for learning:** to what extent should adults have and be prepared to take responsibility for their own learning?
- **Share ideas and feelings:** in what ways can adults be encouraged to share their ideas and feelings with others? What can the teacher do to help build the sense of trust and membership that will enable sharing to take place?
- **Experience openness, trust, respect, commitment:** what characterises a classroom which emphasises equality, mutual trust and respect, mutual helpfulness, openness, care, commitment, freedom of expression and acceptance of differences?
- **Are in a climate conducive to learning:** how can teachers establish a suitable 'climate' conducive to learning?
- **Are able to accept uncertainty:** how easy is it to convey that some questions don't have answers?
- **Can create knowledge:** how is it possible for learners to understand that knowledge is something that can be created as well as used and to recognise that not all knowledge comes from 'authoritative sources'?
- **Make use of their experience:** adults may have a highly structured understanding of the world created over a lifetime which can enhance or inhibit learning. How can teachers tap into this 'reservoir' of experience? How can long-established habits, assumptions and beliefs be challenged?
- **Reflect upon experience:** how can adults be encouraged to reflect upon their own experience and praxis and use this as a source of learning? How can they be encouraged to reflect upon and change their own and other people's learning processes?
- **Learn from problems:** to what extent can learning draw on problems and issues which are grounded in the social and professional interests of learners?
- **Are involved in activity-based work:** how can adults be helped to move from passivity to activity in their approach to their own learning? Do they learn best when they are actively involved in the learning process?

Overall the course will provide opportunities for *you* **to:**

- make the transition from being an expert in a subject to becoming a professional teacher in the post-16 sector
- acquire knowledge of relevant educational theories of the post-16 system
- study teaching within the social, psychological and philosophical context and relate these to changes in the provision of education and training
- develop the strategies, tactics and expertise necessary for planning, preparing, implementing and evaluating teaching and learning activities for the subjects and classes you will be expected to teach
- identify barriers faced by learners in education and training such as disability, age, race and gender and promote professional practice that recognises and values diversity
- respond to the educational needs of the older adolescent and adult learner
- develop confidence in your professional knowledge, develop a personal

philosophy of education and commitment to and critical awareness of your professional situation

- plan teaching and learning (practical and theory lessons, workshops, open learning situations, teacher and student-led activities) to meet learners' needs
- use a range of information communication technologies, media and methods to support teaching and promote learning
- assess student learning, and achievement, using an appropriate range of assessment techniques
- practise and develop a range of professional skills and techniques associated with an effective teacher, instructor or facilitator of learning
- demonstrate effectiveness as a specialist teacher and reflective practitioner
- use opportunities to enhance your own learning and develop skills and strategies to facilitate other people's learning
- investigate an aspect of an organisation and understand the context in which education and training takes place
- be enterprising and respond positively and effectively to change
- evaluate your own effectiveness and students' learning experiences.

Our curriculum model places great importance on adult learning, reflective practice, group activity through an integration of the following themes:

1. Exploring the Foundations of Learning and Teaching
2. Planning for Effective Teaching and Learning
3. Strategies and Approaches for Effective Teaching and Learning
4. Further Education Today
5. Assessment and Evaluation of Learning
6. Teaching Practice.

Theme 1: Exploring the Foundations of Learning and Teaching

1.1 Overview: What is learning?
1.2 Communication and the teacher
1.3 Sociological perspectives 1: an overview
1.4 Learning, instruction and the individual
1.5 Sociological perspectives 2: the hidden curriculum
1.6 Memory and attention (What do teachers need to know about these?)
1.7 Sociological perspectives 3 (How can we explain the differential attainment of different groups of learners?)
1.8 Motivating learners (How can teachers maintain students' motivations?)
1.9 Counselling in education
1.10 Time and learning
1.11 Classroom management

1.1 Overview

For effective teaching to take place it is essential that teachers understand the nature of learning and the learning process, and are aware of the factors which can promote or inhibit learning. There is a need to be familiar with theories of learning and recent research which sheds light on how learning takes place in the classroom and other sites of learning. This lecture provides an overview which sets the scene for psychological and sociological perspectives on learning, identifies the need for careful lesson planning and suggests that teachers should utilise a variety of approaches to teaching and learning. (The Unit Task will be launched in this lecture.)

1.2 Communication and the teacher
This session looks at how both teacher and student can become effective communicators and acts as a key focus for the remainder of the course.

1.3 Sociological perspectives 1: an overview
It has been argued by some educationalists that the role of the sociologist of education is to examine, to question, to raise doubts about, to criticise the assumptions on which current policy, current theory and current practice are based. However there has never been a unanimous view on the kinds of questions that are posed as different theoretical approaches have resulted in different kinds of social research. The sociological perspectives that are used by sociologists lead them to ask different sorts of questions and to use different research methods thereby producing different kinds of evidence.

This lecture will provide a brief overview of some of the *main* sociological perspectives that have influenced the research agenda in the sociology of education. The session will identify and discuss some of the ways in which these perspectives have shaped our understanding of schools, education and training.

1.4 Learning, instruction and the individual
Many contemporary psychologists would agree that learning in the individual takes place by making connections between new information and unique and existing networks of prior knowledge, through opportunities to apply new learning to authentic tasks or problems, and through engaging in social interactions with other students about content. This kind of view of learning is known as 'constructivist'. In terms of instruction, it means that effective instruction is not just good teaching. According to Robert Slavin, effective instruction ensures adequacy in quality, appropriateness, incentive and time use.

1.5 Sociological perspectives 2: the hidden curriculum
Like all formal organisations, schools and colleges have relationships which are not officially laid down in the rule books and syllabuses. The idea of the 'hidden curriculum' or what some educationalists call the 'paracurriculum' suggests that students learn many values and norms which teachers are not consciously trying to teach them. There is evidence that different accomplishments are systematically rewarded among different groups of students. Schools and colleges present a differentiated hidden curriculum. Different types of student are exposed to different curricula. This session introduces the concept of the hidden curriculum and considers ways in which it is conveyed. Research evidence from classrooms and other educational settings will be used to illustrate and discuss the hidden curriculum in relation to students' social class, gender and ethnicity.

1.6 Memory and attention

Learning is not the same as simply remembering, it is an active meaning-making process. This session will explore the implications of viewing learning as an active process. Only information that has been structured, organised and reinforced by the student can pass into long-term memory. This organisation process is helped by 'doing' rather than simply 'listening'.

1.7 Sociological perspectives 3: differential attainment

This lecture will provide an overview of some research evidence which has revealed different patterns of attainment for different student groups and will examine current evidence on 'performance gaps' in the late 1990s. The lecture will show that the situation regarding examinations and assessment is complex, that where differential attainment between males and females, different ethnic minority groups and pupils from various socio-economic backgrounds exists, it may be due to numerous causes.

1.8 Motivating learners

Motivation is a pre-requisite for effective learning and the greatest challenge that many teachers face. This session will explore ways of motivating students and therefore, strategies for improving learning.

1.9 Counselling in education

Relationship skills and Counselling are part of *every* teacher's life. Counselling in education is usually subdivided into educational, vocational and personal counselling. In practice, although the emphases are different these areas are not divisible. This session will show how counselling theory offers a way of viewing constructive contact between teachers and students. 'Principles of counselling' and 'Qualities of a counsellor' will be identified to help clarify the appropriate attributes and behaviours of a counsellor. Vignettes used to illustrate 'student problems' will alert trainee teachers to the complexities and constraints of student life in the mid-1990s.

1.10 Time and learning

If quality, appropriateness and incentive are high, then more time on instruction is likely to pay off in greater learning. Engaged time – or time on task – is largely a product of quality of instruction, student motivation and allocated time. Time is important for constructivist theories since making connections with prior learning needs considerable time.

1.11 Classroom management

Classrooms are social arenas in which teachers take overall responsibility for managing learning whilst, at the same time, encouraging students to take responsibility for their own learning. The classroom is, however, an arena in which tensions and conflicts may arise both between the teacher and learners, and between learners. Whereas relevant and well-planned lessons will reduce these tensions and conflict teachers do need to be aware of a range of strategies and interventions so as to maintain the conditions conducive to learning. These sessions will explore the sorts of interactions which might arise in the classroom and offer practical advice on how to manage them.

APPRAISAL OF PERSONAL PERFORMANCE

This appraisal is to be completed during Part I by the due date. Sections 1 and 2 and desirably 3 must be self-assessed prior to arranging an appointment with your Personal Tutor.

NAME:..

SECTION 1

The key learning/teaching outcomes/tasks and targets which I successfully achieved, enjoyed and developed to my advantage are: [Please study the objectives listed in the Course Guide and in your unit tasks].

SECTION 2

The key tasks/objectives I am still working towards are:

SECTION 3   PERSONAL ACTION PLAN

I propose to set myself the following tasks/targets/to improve my learning/ performance/teaching ability and competence. (You may negotiate this section with your tutor – see tutor remarks section 4).

SECTION 4

Discuss sections 1, 2 and 3 with your tutor. Your tutor will state and record his/her pertinent observations in section 4 on your overall performance and progress.

Tutor comment:

Attendance has been: Excellent/Good/Satisfactory/Poor

Has ill health has been experienced this term: YES/NO

Date of Doctor's Certificate ....

Tutor: ....   Date: ....

I have discussed sections 1, 2, 3 and 4 and have noted the records and comments made.

Student: ....   Date: ....

APPENDIX 2   SECTIONS FROM A PGCE TEACHING PRACTICE GUIDE FOR STUDENTS AND MENTORS

TEACHING PRACTICE PERFORMANCE CRITERIA

Under the supervision of a skilled practitioner the student teacher is expected to:

Prepare and teach lessons
- plan and prioritise for learning over different periods of time
- identify appropriate learning outcomes and the means to achieve them
- select and use methods of learning and teaching suitable to different learning situations and learners' needs
- give attention to the improvement of students' communication, problem solving, interpersonal and ICT skills
- prepare effective materials for teaching and learning.

Manage learning and teaching
- manage individual and class learning
- use time and resources effectively
- develop and demonstrate appropriate relationships with learners
- create conditions conducive for learning
- involve learners in reviewing the learning process.

Assess student learning and evaluate own teaching
- plan, prepare and assess student assignments
- be familiar with a range of assessment techniques
- monitor and assess, record and profile student learning formatively and summatively
- provide constructive feedback to learners
- evaluate own teaching
- undertake self-analysis and self-criticism
- be open to criticism, act on advice and accept support
- improve own and students' abilities to observe and analyse.

Develop and maintain professional standards
- be sensitive to students as individuals and demonstrate sympathetic and positive attitudes towards them
- provide appropriate support, advice and counselling
- develop and maintain professional standards including appropriate relationships with colleagues and students
- conform to agreed codes of professional practice, including the usual contractual obligations.

Personal development
- engage in relevant research and study
- identify, interpret and apply specific subject knowledge to practice

- develop and display self-confidence, reliability and integrity
- negotiate effectively with students and other learners
- recognise the importance of continuous learning and continuing professional development.

PART A: RESPONSIBILITIES OF THE PLACEMENT COLLEGE

The object of the course is to produce a proficient lecturer for employment in a further education establishment or college of nursing and midwifery education. It is important that visiting tutors and college mentors work together in partnership to achieve this aim. Please advise us of any difficulties.

The design of a student's teaching practice programme should take into account the need for students to demonstrate that they have attempted to meet the teaching practice performance criteria and that they are able to complete the requirements of the Teaching Portfolio set out in Part B of this guide.

The student, when on teaching practice, should:

- engage in a two-week period of observation
- work the institution's terms between January 2001 and mid-June 2001 for between 15 and 18 weeks
- during the placement teach between 8 and 10 hours per week to a total class contact of between 120 to 140 hours
- be on the premises for timetabled teaching periods, to undertake preparation, marking, departmental duties, etc. to a total of at least 15 hours per week
- undertake assignments as set by the School of Social Sciences.

The placement institution is asked to:
Provide a supervising tutor/link tutor who will:

- carry out four formal teaching appraisals and give feedback (see teaching appraisal proforma)
- undertake two appraisal of personal performance interviews (see APP proforma)
- complete an interim and a summative report and pass statement (see proformas). The interim report and pass statement should be sent to the Course Secretary by March (date) and the summative report and pass statement should be sent to the Course Secretary by (date).
- meet one hour per fortnight (five meetings in total).

Provide a subject mentor who will work through a mentorship programme. An outline mentoring scheme is set out below.

Mentoring: outline scheme

A mentor will be an experienced subject specialist and a classroom teacher. A mentee will be a student-teacher who has expert subject knowledge.

The mentoring process should take into account other aspects of supervision and support which a student receives, which might or might not be given by the same person who acts as mentor. This other supervision and support includes: weekly lesson observation and informal feedback from a teacher whom the student releases from teaching duties; formal lesson supervision and assessments from the same or another mentor; two formal appraisal interviews with the professional link tutor or other person.

In the context of the Cardiff Postgraduate Certificate in Education/ Certificate in Education the role of the mentor is conceived as the means of providing specialist subject support with a practical and classroom orientation. It provides the student with an opportunity to benefit from the experience and expertise of a specialist classroom teacher who can guide the student in how best to put their ideas about teaching into practice. The overall purposes of meetings between the mentor and the student are to provide opportunities to:

- discuss classroom experiences with a view to making teaching and learning more effective
- focus on strategies to promote effective teaching and learning as appropriate to the subject
- promote critical reflection on practice.

In turn, it is suggested that these purposes can be met through a series of meetings, which address the following:

Syllabuses and schemes of work
For example, give attention to constraints and requirements of external examinations, departmental and college planning, depth and breadth of coverage.

Monitoring and assessment
For example, marking and record keeping, records of achievement, make reference to external examinations and examiners' reports, discuss the design and use of tests and marking criteria.

An exploration of subject pedagogy
For example, consider accepted ways of teaching a particular subject, how to teach the subject and the use of teaching aids including ICT.

Designing resources for effective teaching and learning
For example, how to design and use worksheets, case studies and other student-centred tasks and the application of ICT.

Evaluating teaching and learning
For example, employ methods such as the use of second marking, discuss outcomes from tests, self-evaluation and evaluation from students.

Each mentee (PGCE/Cert. Ed. student) is expected to keep a record of meetings with his/her mentor and to make reference to them in a learning journal.

NB: Those mentors interested in developing their role as a mentor are referred to a separate guide and information contained in the Mentor's Handbook. Those who undertake such mentoring may, in certain circumstances, use the credit so gained towards the requirements of the award of an MA in Education. Information is available from the Higher Degrees office at the School of Social Sciences.

Professional tutor/link tutor

The professional tutor will be an experienced member of college staff who has sufficient knowledge of teaching programmes, administration and management. In practice this role can be fulfilled by more than one person but it is hoped that students located at any one college site would be able to identify a particular person who carries responsibility for the organisation of this part of their programme.

In the context of the Cardiff PGCE the role of the professional tutor is conceived as someone who takes on the responsibility for organising a programme for students which gives them a wider insight into the functions, organisation and management of a college. In addition, this person would also have an oversight of students and ensure that monitoring and supervision of students takes place, including informal lesson observations, formal lesson observation and assessment, two appraisal interviews and mentoring of students.

It is envisaged that meetings with a professional tutor would normally take place with a group of students, thus providing the opportunity for discussion and comparison of experiences. The focus for separate sessions could include:

- organisation of the college, the college and its context
- managing the curriculum, course teams: theory and practice
- pastoral support, counselling and the promotion of core skills
- the National Grid for learning
- the quality process, the role of FEFC/OHMCI
- marketing the college
- responding to labour market needs, links with TECs, local employers and EBPs
- staff development and training
- reviewing experiences.

THE TEACHING PORTFOLIO

During your teaching practice you are required to compile a portfolio of material relating to your placement and experiences at the 'chalk face'. This will include:

1   A Teaching Project: a detailed record of six lessons
2   A Learning Journal: beginning with an account of micro-teaching to include a write-up of at least five observed lessons during the observation period, and seven fortnightly entries
3   An Evaluation of Flexible Learning/ICT
4   Unit Task E: assessment and evaluation of learning
5   Copies of key teaching practice documentation.

and each should be produced to a high standard as a reflection of your professional commitment and to demonstrate your professional development.

SUMMARY OF SCHEDULE FOR MONITORING AND ASSESSMENT

		Tasks to be completed before the end of the following months				
		Jan	Feb	Mar	Apr	May
Four formal teaching appraisals	1		✓			
	2			✓		
	3				✓	
	4					✓
Two appraisal interviews	1			✓		
	2					✓
Interim formative report				✓		
Final report/pass statement						✓
Formal meetings with subject mentor	1	✓				
	2		✓			
	3			✓		
	4				✓	
	5					✓
Formal meetings with Link Tutor	1	✓				
	2		✓			
	3			✓		
	4				✓	
	5					✓
Visiting Tutor: 1st visit				✓		
Visiting Tutor: 2nd visit						✓

Teaching Practice Register to be completed weekly.
Informal (non-assessed) observation and debriefing to be negotiated.

1 Teaching project

This should include the following:

Table of Contents

Introduction
Provide details about the 'institutional backdrop' of your placement college in order to give the reader some background and context of the college and its work. In your own words provide a description of the college and its setting including its size, location, organisation. You may use selectively maps, extracts from policy statements and the prospectus, FEFC/OHMCI reports, but do not include them in their entirety. Much of this can be completed during your observation period.

A selection of six lessons

Choose six lessons, two of which must have been observed and assessed by your visiting tutor and two by your college mentor (or other college tutor) to include in your teaching project file. The teaching appraisal forms should also be included with the lessons. You may include additional lessons to demonstrate that you have met a selection of the performance criteria listed on page 243, for example to show that you have assessed student learning.

Each of the six lessons must include:

- a description of the context for that lesson, such as class size, the level of the class, an extract from a syllabus or scheme of work, details about the teaching environment which might enhance or detract from the proposed teaching and learning, a layout of the classroom
- a detailed lesson plan (see later notes) including objectives, learning outcomes, rationale, methods (introduction, development and conclusion), examples of handouts, resources and tests
- an evaluative commentary (written after the lesson).

In addition to Unit Task E one or more of the lessons chosen should include:

- examples of assessments/tests and mark schemes, with an explanation of how you devised and used them, and should include samples of marked students' scripts.

Two or more of the lessons chosen should include:

- some samples of students' class work which illuminates some of your evaluatory comments
- an evaluation of the lesson conducted by students using an evaluation questionnaire provided by you. You should write a short commentary to summarise and explain the results and to state what, if any, action you propose to take.

Examples of students' work

Examples could include the following:

- photocopies of notes made by students in the lesson
- audio or video recording of a class or group discussion, debate or other activity, together with a written summary of the task
- annotated photographic evidence of students involved on a field trip or drama production
- photographs of students at work, together with a written description, cataloguing the stages of a GNVQ investigative project.

Please place copies (not the originals) of the teaching appraisal forms, appraisal of personal performance, teaching practice register and student declaration at the front of the teaching project file. Originals should be appropriately located in your portfolio.

It is easier to focus on *one* or *two* features when observing the experienced teacher at work. The ones listed here are useful foci for the 'beginning teacher'.

Questioning: What type of questions? How many? Who to? How does teacher respond to answers . . .? Or a student's inability to answer?

Explanations: How does the teacher set about this? Does she/he use metaphors, analogies, visual aids/models, etc. . . .?

Lesson introduction: What does the teacher do to signal the start of the lesson? What ways are used to 'introduce' the session?

Space/seating/classroom setting: Do features of the architectural setting 'shape' the lesson or teachers'/students' actions in any way?

Discipline/sanctioning/managing: How does the teacher 'contain' inappropriate student actions? (e.g. refusing to work, excessive talking, lateness, etc. . . .)

Teacher/student interactions: Are there observable differences in

(a) quantity and

(b) type

of interactions between teacher and student?

Teacher attention: Observe this over the full lesson period. To what extent is the teacher's attention on

- whole class
- groups
- individuals?

Lesson endings/conclusions: How does the teacher 'wrap up' and draw together the end of the lesson. Homework/Tasks set? Signposts for next lesson, etc.

APPENDIX 3   PROFESSIONAL DEVELOPMENT THROUGH REFLECTIVE PRACTICE: AN EXAMPLE

STUDENTS' AUTONOMY

- Each learner is encouraged to assess their own progress throughout their teaching practice.
- Each learner is encouraged to link these teaching competencies to (a) their reflective journal; (b) their teaching project.
- Read each statement of competence and ensure that the opportunity is available for you to practise and achieve that competence.
- Write a brief account in the 'self-assessment' and 'reflective comments' column of how you presume to have achieved each competence.
- Each learner is encouraged to link theory and practice and show how they applied the theory taught during the first three months of the course to their teaching practice, which starts with lesson introduction, micro-teaching, and continues into supervised teaching practice.
- Each learner is encouraged to seek help and advice from their assigned mentor whilst on teaching practice.
- Your visiting tutor will ask to see evidence of your progress while on teaching practice – please have this booklet ready for your visiting tutor.

COMPETENCY UNIT ONE: PLANNING FOR AND MANAGING LEARNING ENCOUNTERS AND EVENTS

End Competence: The participant is able to plan and implement systematically effective learning encounters and programmes. This achievement signifies that the participant has:

STATEMENT OF COMPETENCE	SELF-ASSESSMENT	REFLECTIVE COMMENTS
Utilised various strategies of Communication and Equal Opportunities in own curriculum area.		
Identified and established a consistent and responsive approach to the planning and implementation of teaching and learning in own curriculum area.		

COMPETENCY UNIT TWO: PRINCIPLES OF LEARNING

End Competence: The participant is able to plan and implement systematically effective learning encounters and programmes. This achievement signifies that the participant has:

STATEMENT OF COMPETENCE	SELF-ASSESSMENT	REFLECTIVE COMMENTS
Differentiated between broad categories of learning theory (e.g. Behaviourist, Cognitive, Humanist, Experiential)		
Identified examples of the above being applied during given teaching and learning situations.		
Derived a range of key conditions/principles and strategies which are applicable to given teaching/learning situations.		
Designed a unit of learning experiences (e.g. a lesson) which contains these conditions/strategies and application of related key principles in order to promote effective learning.		
Indicated a range of conditions and situations likely to support the learning required (concepts, skills, attitudes, etc.)		

COMPETENCY UNIT TWO: PRINCIPLES OF LEARNING (continued)

End Competence: The participant is able to plan and implement systematically effective learning encounters and programmes. This achievement signifies that the participant has:

STATEMENT OF COMPETENCE	SELF-ASSESSMENT	REFLECTIVE COMMENTS
Given examples of how differences in motivation, personality, cognitive and social development and effects affect the capacity to learn.		
Designed a range of activities which enhance appropriately the 'learning styles', 'study skills' and communication skills of learners.		
Evaluated current teaching and learning strategies operational in a given course in the light of equal opportunity and communication policies and practices.		

COMPETENCY UNIT THREE: MANAGEMENT OF LEARNING

The participant is able to create and maintain an effective learning environment. This achievement signifies that the participant has:

STATEMENT OF COMPETENCE	SELF-ASSESSMENT	REFLECTIVE COMMENTS
Stated and explained the main factors affecting the creation and maintenance of an effective teaching and learning environment.		
Applied at least three basic strategies of teaching and learning, i.e. presentation, small group interaction and negotiation/facilitation.		
Applied a set of principles of learning to the creation and maintenance of an appropriate environment for learners and/or groups of learners.		
Managed learning in a range of learning encounters using a variety of management strategies.		
Established and applied criteria for an evaluation of their management of learning and the learning environment.		

COMPETENCY UNIT FOUR: LEARNING RESOURCES

End Competence: The participant is able to design, develop and deploy learning resources effectively. This achievement signifies that the participant has:

STATEMENT OF COMPETENCE	SELF-ASSESSMENT	REFLECTIVE COMMENTS
Identified the range of audio-visual and other learning aids available within specified teaching/learning environments.		
Designed a simple learning aid to support own teaching.		
Used principles of resource-based learning to design, produce and use an advanced learning aid.		
Used a range of AVA hardware and software effectively.		
Used computer hardware with appropriate software in the teaching/learning process.		
Identified and described how the use of IT can enhance effectiveness of learning within own curricular area.		
Evaluated a selection of learning resources according to a range of criteria.		

COMPETENCY UNIT FIVE: ASSESSMENT

End Competence: The participant is able to apply appropriate assessment procedure and methods. This achievement signifies that the participant has:

STATEMENT OF COMPETENCE	SELF-ASSESSMENT	REFLECTIVE COMMENTS
Identified the purposes of assessment.		
Stated and applied basic assessment design principles.		
Differentiated between the various bases for analysing the outcomes of assessment.		
Selected and justified a range of assessment instruments and procedures in line with intended aims, objectives and/or outcomes.		
Constructed and used a range of assessment instruments.		
Designed marking schemes and checklists as appropriate.		
Designed and used assessment procedures for assessing achievements in natural surroundings (such as workplaces).		
Interpreted assessment outcomes as a means of making diagnoses and prognoses about learning effectiveness.		
Constructed and/or used mechanisms for recording assessment results (profiles, records of achievement, etc).		
Communicated feedback to learners regarding the outcomes of assessment.		
Evaluated the assessment strategies and techniques adopted for particular cohort(s) of learners.		
Analysed the significance and impact of assessment processes upon equal opportunities and the differential attainments of individual learners and groups of learners.		

COMPETENCY UNIT SIX: EVALUATION

End Competence: The participant is able to apply and evaluate the effectiveness of learning encounters and programmes. This achievement signifies that the participant has:

STATEMENT OF COMPETENCE	SELF-ASSESSMENT	REFLECTIVE COMMENTS
Described the principles and purposes of evaluation and justified planning for it in the process of planning learning events.		
Drawn up and justified checklist(s) of criteria for evaluating different types of teaching/learning encounters.		
Employed a range of strategies and investigative methods in conducting evaluations of teaching/learning encounters.		
Designed, justified and implemented a learner-centred evaluation of learning events and outcomes.		
Drawn up a procedure and criteria for evaluating a course or programme of study.		
Implemented monitoring and review procedures appropriate to a given course or programme of study.		
Collaborated with colleagues (as appropriate) to utilise the results of evaluations to improve the learning experience and process.		
Asked advice on issues of impartiality, confidentiality and integrity as these apply to the process of evaluation.		
Designed, justified and implemented a teacher self-evaluation checklist and procedure as part of an ongoing concern for appraisal and improvement of teacher/tutor performance.		

COMPETENCY UNIT SEVEN: COMMUNICATION

End Competence: The participant is able to apply and evaluate the effectiveness of learning encounters and programmes. This achievement signifies that the participant has:

STATEMENT OF COMPETENCE	SELF-ASSESSMENT	REFLECTIVE COMMENTS
Demonstrated an awareness of the factors involved in the process of communication.		
Developed the ability to communicate effectively.		
Identified and taken steps to overcome barriers to effective communication with colleagues, clients and learners.		
Shown in practice how communication varies when using different strategies and methods of teaching and learning.		
Utilised a range of types of questions in establishing and maintaining communication and facilitating teaching/learning.		
Taken action (as appropriate) to develop the communication skills of learners.		
Proposed and justified communication strategies in communication skills of learners.		
Evaluated the communication process in advance of a given event.		

COMPETENCY UNIT EIGHT: PROFESSIONAL CONCERNS AND ISSUES

End Competence: The participant is able to develop their role as professional, specialised educators on the basis of their developing knowledge and appreciation of current educational trends and developments in education and training. This achievement signifies that the participant has:

STATEMENT OF COMPETENCE	SELF-ASSESSMENT	REFLECTIVE COMMENTS
Recognised key stages and events in the development of educational provision.		
Outlined the contemporary structure of educational provision, both nationally and in their curriculum area.		
Demonstrated an awareness of the key issues and controversies in contemporary education structure, curriculum, governance, management and finance of education.		
Developed conceptions and justified personal views upon 'education', 'training', 'instruction' and 'learning'.		
Reviewed and explored different conceptions of the teaching/tutoring role.		
Developed and applied knowledge and understanding in the development of teaching and learning strategies to minimise disadvantages and deprivations with regard to class/race/gender/disability/age.		
Undertaken a sustained enquiry with a focus upon the teaching/learning process in own curriculum area.		
Planned, implemented and evaluated developmental or innovative projects in selected aspects of a teaching and learning programme.		
Identified and, where appropriate, taken on one or more ancillary roles associated with the management of teaching and learning.		

COMPETENCY UNIT EIGHT: PROFESSIONAL CONCERNS AND ISSUES (continued)

End Competence: Participants should be able to develop their role as professional, specialised educators on the basis of their developing knowledge and appreciation of current educational trends and developments in education and training. This achievement signifies that the participant has:

STATEMENT OF COMPETENCE	SELF-ASSESSMENT	REFLECTIVE COMMENTS
Utilised the local environment, community or workplace as a learning site and resource.		
Participated in management and decision-making processes in education or training contexts.		
Identified and/or used the range of opportunities available to teachers for professional development.		
For Nurses (Compulsory): Participated in the management and decision-making process related to: • Clinical effectiveness • Clinical supervision • Internal validation.		

STANDARD OF PERFORMANCE STATEMENT: EXAMPLE 1

Focus: Communication

Under the supervision of a skilled practitioner the learner is given the opportunity to:

ELEMENTS OF COMPETENCE	RELATED PERFORMANCE CRITERIA	DATE	LEARNER'S SIGNATURE	COMMENTS	ASSESSOR'S SIGNATURE	COMMENTS
(a) The use of appropriate communication skills to enable the development of an effective, caring relationship. (b) The use of appropriate communication skills to initiate and conduct therapeutic relationships with clients and friends.	1 Discuss the rights of the individual to be involved in all aspects of his/her care. 2 Discuss the different methods of communications observed and experienced. 3 Communicate the observations made during client interactions. 4 Identify the client's usual forms of communication and social interaction. 5 Communicate effectively by talking and listening to the individual and his/her family or friends. 6 Identify the client's communication difficulties.					

Contract assignment: During concurrent clinical-placement learning in each clinical-placement environment, the learner will keep and produce a diary of notable incidents of communication witnessed.

259

STANDARD OF PERFORMANCE STATEMENT: EXAMPLE 2

Focus: Promotion and maintenance of health
Nature: Summative assessment

ELEMENTS OF COMPETENCE	PERFORMANCE CRITERIA	SIGNATURE OF LEARNER	NAME OF ASSESSOR	ACHIEVED	NOT ACHIEVED
The identification of health related learning needs of clients, their families and friends.	Identifies the methods used to teach a health education topic to a client and/or his/her family.				
	Recognises the ways in which the carer/practitioner helps an individual to accept his/her altered health status.				
	Identifies the factors which can influence the health of an individual.				
	Understands the social factors affecting the client's perception of health.				
	Identifies legislation, policies and practices designed to maintain a safe environment.				

Contract assignment: The learner will produce an assignment (approximately 1500 words) identifying strategies used to help a client promote and maintain his/her health.

ASSESSMENT CRITERIA: AN EXAMPLE

COMPETENCIES	COMPETENCE ACHIEVEMENT STRATEGY	RESOURCES	CRITERIA FOR ASSESSMENT AND EVALUATION
Ability to find, interpret and present material (in writing). Ability to assess, set goals and plan care using a problem-solving approach.	Client interview (with consent or parental consent). Interviews of relatives/friends (with client consent).	Chosen client and relatives/friends and significant others.	The completed study will contain an assessment, a plan of care (including goals) an in-depth evaluation of care and a critical appraisal. Possible alternative care strategies must be included when relevant (preferably research based).
Ability to analyse critically the care planned and/or implemented.	Study of other professions and/or significant other.		
Ability to question care and find and offer alternative care strategies based on research when possible.	Discussion with primary carer and/or significant other.		The data gathered will identify the client's strengths and weaknesses, his/her priorities for care and his/her contributions to the care (of parental contributions).
Has in depth knowledge of chosen client's social, psychological, physical and spiritual status and ability to relate these to his/her identified needs/care.	Taught theory and taught practice.

Discussion with other health professionals involved. | For example: college staff 'Learning Resources Centre', hospital libraries, journals, etc., personal tutor and clinical mentor. | The model on which the care was based should be defined and critically evaluated. |
| | Discussion with personal tutor. | | Record of:

● negotiated work

● negotiated dates

● negotiated marks

Tutor and learner meeting times agreed.

Application of taught theory to taught practice. |

APPENDIX 4   MISSION STATEMENT FOR A NURSING DEGREE COURSE: AN EXAMPLE

We believe that people are of central importance, have inherent dignity, are worthy of respect and care, and have the irrefutable freedom to make choices. Each is unique with potential for growth and development towards their own optimum levels of functioning, mediated by internal and external factors.

Individuals enter into reciprocal caring relationships that generate a reservoir of experience providing an ever growing resource for development towards social roles.

People are social beings; their nature derives from interaction, within their social context. Whilst contributing towards the creation of self and society they are, in turn, influenced by what they and others have created.

The process of growth and development is fostered by interpersonal exchanges between people, groups and organizations and will be influenced by the wider cultural context.

Individuals are in continuous dynamic interaction with their biological, psychological and spiritual environment. Within our pluralistic society political, economic and ecological factors contribute to, or detract from, a nurturing environment which reflects upon an individual's health status.

Health is not merely the absence of illness but a state of complete physical, social and psychological well being. It is a concept without fixed boundaries and implies forward movement towards a creative and constructive individual member of society. Health is a relative state and is affected by personal values, culture, society and political ideologies. It is determined by the ability of the person to set realistic and meaningful goals and to mobilize resources to attain this. Health, therefore, is the purpose of all nursing behaviours.

Nursing is a dynamic interpersonal process which aspires to promote, maintain, and restore health. It encompasses the care of a large variety of people of all ages and differing needs.

It is a unique enterprise whose practitioners are skilled in the assessment, planning, implementation and evaluation of health care.

The nursing process is dependent upon the relationship developed between the nurse and client. This relationship develops through the four sequential phases of orientation, identification, application and resolution. During these phases the nurse may adopt the roles of counsellor, leader, resource person, surrogate, teacher and technical expert.

Nursing is an essentially practice-based activity whose body of knowledge is grounded in the biological and social sciences. Increasing emphasis is placed on the use of research findings to support theory and practice.

The practitioners of nursing need to be innovative and offer creative responses to the changing pattern of health care demands, whilst working within ethical and legal frameworks.

This requires a broad knowledge and skill base in order to competently care within the hospital and wider community settings. Nursing practice must be concerned with health as well as disease thus enabling practitioners to enhance health knowledge, facilitate maximum independence, respect individual choices and comprehend the diversity of human needs.

These demands require a mature and confident practitioner who accepts responsibility, and is able to think analytically. The ability to recognize a need for further personal and professional development is of paramount importance.

Continuing self and professional development entails qualitative changes in thought structures in the direction of creative and critical thinking. This change is promoted through meaningful dialogue that facilitates enquiry, discovery, critical analysis, reflection and some evidence of synthesis.

The purpose of nurse education is to promote growth whilst enabling the person to obtain a qualification which provides eligibility for admission to the Council's Register and to assume the responsibilities and accountability that nursing registration confers.

This course seeks to achieve its stated purpose by utilizing a framework that exemplifies the notions and values contained within this mission statement.

The major concepts of person, environment and society, health and health care and nursing thread throughout the course and provide the structure for addressing the relevant knowledge and skills.

The contexts of self, group, locality, culture and globe within which the learner operates form the care that enables learners to illuminate and understand the concepts through their own experiences.

The course enables the concepts and context to relate in a meaningful way through the processes of orientation, identification, application and resolution.

The construction of this and subsequent mission statements has been influenced by the following classic texts:

Peplau, H.E. (1952) *Interpersonal Relations in Nursing*. Putnam & Sons
Dickoff, J.P. (1968) ' "A theory of theories": a position paper'. *Nursing Research* 17.

ORIENTATION

Mission statement for Part One

Part One of the course is concerned with the process of orientation. During this part the learner will adjust to and align themselves with the course, its contexts and concepts.

As a unique individual, the learner will bring to the course life experience which will enhance their own professional growth and also enrich the educational environment of their peers. Self-awareness and the addressing of interpersonal skills, therefore, provide a medium through which the individual begins to orient towards self.

Orientation towards the peer group is facilitated by an educational approach that values exploration, problem posing, dialogue and equality. This will produce a nurturing environment in which group members feel able to share in the responsibility for learning and to value the contribution made by peers.

Orientation to local, cultural and global issues will be assisted by planned exposure to selected aspects of the neighbourhood. Reflection upon these experiences will illuminate the central concepts.

During this part, orientation to the central concepts of Person, Environment, Health and Nursing will be established. The intention of this stage will be to enable the learner to isolate, define and describe those factors encompassed by the concepts. The learner's ability to recall information and identify its appropriateness will be enhanced by the fostering of critical and analytical thinking.

IDENTIFICATION

Mission statement for Part Two

The second part of the course focuses on the process of identification. During this period the learner will identify the relationship between previously addressed concepts and their relevance to nursing and health care provision.

The local and cultural contexts within which the learner will operate become increasingly health and health-care centred. They will incorporate both institutional and non-institutional settings; reflection on these experiences will enable identification and recognition of aspects of self and group that will enhance professional development. This process will be facilitated by dialogue and negotiation with the learners' academic and placement supervisors.

Previous orientation to the central concepts will enable ideas to be identified, related and adjusted through applying them to real experiences. This process will require the ability to practise, interpret and discuss techniques and knowledge. Answers to problems will result in a growth of knowledge and understanding, the acquisition of essential nursing skills and further development of analytical skills.

APPLICATION

Mission statement for Part Three

Part Three of the course is concerned with the process of application. In this part the learners will be able to utilize their increasing repertoire of knowledge and skills in relation to the care of a particular client group.

Within the context of hospital and community care, learners will engage in the process of nursing and demonstrate flexible responses to meeting an individual's health care needs.

The intention at this stage is to enable the learner to employ conceptual knowledge of health and dysfunction within the practical situation. This will require the learner to demonstrate the ability to distinguish and differentiate between care strategies, to be able to apply research findings and to critically analyse their relevance to the individual.

The use of research findings, analysis of specific practice situations and the specialized nature of knowledge input are central to the learner's professional development within a specified area of nursing endeavour.

RESOLUTION

Mission statement for Part Four

The final part of the course is concerned with the process of resolution. During this part, the learner will integrate theory and practice to a level whereby situations can be produced and outcomes determined.

The practical experiences at this stage will be within the context of rostered service in NHS hospital provision, enabling the learner to contribute in a skilled and meaningful way to the assessment, planning, implementation and evaluation of health care, demonstrating effective observational communication and caring skills. High-calibre role models, able to assist in disentangling dilemmas and removing uncertainty, will supervise the learner's movement towards becoming a registered practitioner able to be innovative and offer creative responses to the changing pattern of health-care demands whilst working within ethical and legal frameworks.

Elucidation of the four central concepts is at a level that will allow the learner to demonstrate creative and critical thinking within the activity of critical analysis and reflection.

Resolution will be attained through self and peer reflection, facilitated by the academic supervisor utilizing adult teaching and learning strategies established throughout the course.

During resolution, the learner will demonstrate competency in knowledgeably and skilfully meeting the nursing needs of individuals and groups in health and sickness, in a specified area of practice. They will be sufficiently prepared to obtain a qualification which provides eligibility for admission to the Council's Register and to assume the responsibilities and accountability that nursing registration confers.

ACADEMIC LEVELS

The course planning team recognizes that academic levels are a notion new to Nurse Education and, as such, is likely to be an area of continuing development. This will be enhanced by the proposed input from Polytechnic staff already well versed in teaching at Diploma level.

To ensure that the level is broadly appropriate from the commencement of the first course, evidence is given in a variety of forms.

- The quality of the course team evidenced by the curriculum vitae of teaching staff and details of how their expertise underpins the learning process.
- The suitability of the assessment process which identifies the criteria for assessing the development of critical and analytical nursing skills.
- Satisfactory resources and their appropriate utilization to enhance the achievement of learning outcomes evidenced by library facilities and innovative teaching and learning strategies.

The Diploma requires individuals to learn through a variety of techniques and procedures. As the course is particularly professionally orientated it includes significant components of work-based learning or clinical practice. The learning which is developed in this process is an integral part of the assessment package and contributes to the credit awarded in appropriate units.

Central to the issue of levels is the development of critical and analytical skills.

Nurse education, whilst requiring learners to perform competently in their chosen area according to current criteria, should lay down the foundation for continued growth and development as a professional.

This means that personal flexibility should be encouraged and emphasis placed on the capacity to reflect on and analyse current constructions of the role.

The nature of the course

The implementation of UKCC Project 2000 within the Health Authority is seen as a crucially important development in nurse education. It is part of the ongoing plans of the Authority to continue to meet the health care and nursing needs of the community which it serves. The BSc (Hons) Nursing course contains key features of English National Board (ENB) Project 2000, in particular the Common Foundation Programme (CFP) which is contained within the first 18 months of the course, and the Branch Programme (BP) (i.e. Adult nursing or Mental Health nursing) which is included in the last 18 months of the course.

This course is designed:

i.   to fulfil the requirements of the statutory bodies and to enable learners to achieve the outcomes stated in rule 18A (2) (Statutory Instrument 1989 No. 1456), and qualify as a profession practitioner

ii.   acknowledging that pre-registration courses represent the gateway to an integrated package of nursing education in which the emphasis is upon continuing education throughout the professional life of the practitioner

iii. to fulfil the academic requirements of the BSc (Hons) Nursing Course

iv.   recognizing the adult status of the learner

v.   acknowledging that the study of nursing should be embedded in health and research

vi.   acknowledging that nursing is a practice and research based profession and that theory and practice should be integrated into a meaningful whole.

Course philosophy

The following statement sets out the underlying beliefs that are held about nursing and provides a framework for the course.

Nursing in today's society is a dynamic interactive process which responds to states of health in a sensitive, skilled way. Nursing, therefore, provides for the physical, emotional and social needs of individuals and groups by applying skilled and conscientious assessment, planning, delivery and evaluation to their states of health.

Nursing care is based on concepts of health and the promotion of well being combining the unique synthesis of knowledge from the social and life sciences with the development of interpersonal skills.

Health is a state of mind of body and is more than a symptom-free existence. It is about being sensitive to the present, taking opportunities and responding creatively within the means and ability of the individual.

This Nursing Degree course seeks to combine these beliefs and values with educational parameters centred on learning as a creative process, a means of enhancing the professional and personal self. Emphasis is placed on education as a process for acquiring knowledge and developing abilities of analysis and synthesis using research critically and constructively. The roles of teacher and learners may be interchangeable and are dynamic. Value is placed on learners sharing responsibility for learning. Academic development, self-directed study and independent learning are supported and encouraged.

This Nursing Degree is based on beliefs which are intended to inspire learners to develop a critical and enquiring approach to the theory and practice of nursing. Nursing and health are the central themes of the course and provide the focus for the integration of social and life sciences with practice in institutional and non-institutional settings. Thus the art and science of nursing are studied in relation to states of health in ways which will develop abilities to critically analyse health-care approaches both during and beyond completion of the course.

It is envisaged that learners on graduating will make a significant contribution to the practice of professional nursing and strive for excellence.

Course aims

The course aims reflect the course philosophy and professional, statutory and academic requirements. They also reflect the way educational processes will enhance the personal and professional development of the learner.

The course sets out to develop in the learner:

i. abilities in the application of those disciplines which form a foundation for nursing in order for him/her to practise holistic nursing as a registered nurse in an institutional and non-institutional setting
ii. abilities to engage critically in information retrieval, problem solving, critical analysis and self-directed learning
iii. the ability to assess, plan, implement and evaluate nursing in its professional context using and applying knowledge from research in a critical manner
iv. abilities to promote health, to establish and maintain a sensitive and supportive helping relationship and insight into the parameters of nursing management in practice settings
v. the ability to form his/her philosophy of nursing care
vi. the process of personal growth, development and professional self-awareness. This will enable him/her to realize his/her potential with confidence as a reflective practitioner promoting excellence in the delivery of nursing care and realizing the place of ongoing education.

The learning outcomes as stated in the Statutory Instrument 1989 No. 1456 rule 18 A-2 are also requirements of the course as follows:

a. the identification of the social and health implications of pregnancy and child bearing, physical and mental handicap, disease, disability, or ageing of the individual, her or his friends, family and community

b. the recognition of common factors which contribute to, and those which adversely affect, physical, mental and social well being of patients and clients and take appropriate action

c. the use of relevant literature and research to inform the practice of nursing

d. the appreciation of the influence of social, political and cultural factors in relation to health care

e. an understanding of the requirements of legislation relevant to the practice of nursing

f. the use of appropriate communication skills to enable the development of helpful, caring relationships with patients and clients and their families and friends, and to initiate and conduct therapeutic relationships with patients and clients

g. the identification of health-related learning needs of patients and clients, families and friends and to participate in health promotion

h. an understanding of the ethics of health care and of the nursing profession and the responsibilities which these impose on the nurse's profession practice, etc.

COURSEWORK CHARTER

Coursework is an important component of all taught courses. It is set in all courses and invariably counts towards the final assessment. It is a means of continuous assessment which provides information to staff about the progress or otherwise of students. For these reasons the coursework procedures for all courses in the School of Informatics operate according to this charter.

Student rights

Coursework assessment

At the start of each year of your course you will be given the following information by the course director, in writing:

- The coursework weighting in the final assessment, for the year and/or course.
- Whether coursework has to be passed individually or collectively to pass and at what percentage level.
- The planned schedule for coursework overall which will allocate assignments evenly throughout the course/year.
- The schedule will include the latest date for setting the work, the deadline for its submission and the name of the tutor responsible for each assignment.
- The penalties for the submission of coursework copied, plagiarised or late.
- The office for the submission and collection of all assignments, and procedures for submission.
- The procedure for recording receipt of submitted work by the office and return of assessed work to students.
- The course director will see that the schedule is followed, that sufficient

work is set to enable a fair assessment and take corrective action when this is not the case.

The setting and marking of assignments

The tutor for each course module is responsible for adhering to the schedule and will carry out the following at or before the due time:

- Define the assignment to be completed, on a handout which may be delivered by email and will say clearly the work that is to be done and by when.
- Provide guidelines as to the amount of effort required for an assignment.
- Advise on the availability of books, journals and computer software necessary for its completion.
- Indicate the distribution of marks where the assignment has multiple parts and the quality standards for the assessment.
- Set work that reflects the progress of the module at that date giving any special guidance that is necessary.
- Provide reasonable help with interpretation and clarify any ambiguity on request.
- Assess assignments with due care, using the criteria indicated at the time of issue. Marking that has been carried out by anyone other than the setting tutor will be so indicated and the assessor identified.
- Indicate the grade prominently on the returned work showing clearly the scheme that has been used. The same scheme will be used on all scripts within an assignment submission.
- Provide feedback so you understand why the grade has been given. This will be in the form of comments on the script. A handout on the submissions as a whole, and/or a verbal statement in class/tutorial may also be given to cover general points.
- The marked and graded work will be returned to you either through the course office or through scheduled tutorials. Different arrangements may apply to courses within the Computer Science Department.
- Coursework that has been submitted on time will be returned not later than 5 term-time weeks after the deadline and in any case not later than 2 weeks before relevant examinations. If, exceptionally, this cannot be achieved for any reason you will be warned and an intended return date given.
- The relevant course office will maintain records of assessment grades and be able to inform you at any stage as to your current status. Students registered in the Computer Science Department can obtain this information from their tutors.
- The deadline for an assignment will not normally be less than 2 term-time weeks after the date of issue.
- The final assignment for the module will be set no later than 5 term-time weeks before the examination paper covering the related module.

Student obligations

You are personally responsible for ensuring:

Quality
- That submitted work is well presented, legible and, where appropriate, in

good standard English. The use of word processing and spell checking is always recommended and may be mandatory.

- That the submitted work is clearly seen to be your work done alone or the work of your group if the assignment was specifically set as a group project. You may nevertheless work with your colleagues in interpreting and working out the general approach to an assignment.
- That all quotations are in quotation marks or otherwise clearly and completely indicated. The source of any quotation must be given in full.
- That the use of other sources whether published, unpublished, paper or electronic is recorded in a bibliography and fully cross-referenced to the text.

Administration
- That work is submitted to the appropriate office on time with the cover sheet attached.
- That you sign the declaration on the cover sheet that the work is entirely your own.

Self-protection
- That when work is set you immediately ensure you clearly understand the requirements and resolve any problems with the tutor responsible.
- That to protect yourself against a missing assignment you keep a copy of the assignment for personal reference and replacing lost work.
- That if coursework cannot be submitted on time you discuss problems with your personal tutor or course director as soon as they become apparent. With good and exceptional cause such as sickness, personal or family crises, or, in the case of part-time students, changes in employment, special arrangements may be made given evidences of good faith. In certain cases of sickness a medical certificate may be required.
- That you plan your time and work allowing for problem situations. Sympathy is unlikely to be forthcoming where coursework is lost because of failure to keep security copies or delayed because of failure to allow sufficient time to cope with equipment failure.

Penalties and procedures

Copying and plagiarism
Coursework is about the extent of your knowledge and understanding. You, therefore, must present your work, your ideas and your discussion. Submitting work that is not your own is a serious offence. Action will be taken on its discovery.

- Submissions which show a very close likeness to each other will be treated as copying (i.e. cheating) and awarded 0%. Feedback on this work may be provided at the sole discretion of the tutor.
- Work submitted that has partly or substantially been done by someone else will be assessed at 0%.
- Plagiarism (copying or paraphrasing from any other source whether paper-based or electronic) will be treated as cheating and recorded at 0%. This offence is especially serious if the bibliography and cross-referencing are inadequate.

- Repeated copying and plagiarism will be reported to the Chairman of the Board of Examiners and may result in advice that you withdraw from the course or other disciplinary action.

Coursework failure

A very poor performance in overall coursework requirements will normally cause the Board of Examiners to deem the student to have failed or at least at best not to have taken the course and therefore be required to retake the entire course or year.

- Work that is submitted on time, demonstrating reasonable individual effort, but failing to achieve the pass mark, may, at the discretion of the tutor, be replaced by another piece of work that if satisfactorily completed will bring the grade to the pass level.
- If you fail to achieve the coursework pass level before the examinations you may subsequently be referred in the coursework by the Board of Examiners. You are warned that this will in general involve considerable extra work, may be invigilated and will not merely be a replacement for the shortfall.
- Referred work is assessed as either satisfactory or not (i.e. pass or fail). The original failed mark is used in the weightings for determination of the award of Degree or Diploma. Tutors at their own discretion may provide feedback.
- Failure to achieve the required pass(es) in referred coursework normally results in the Board of Examiners advising the student to withdraw from the course.

Lateness

Missed submission deadlines cause disruption to work schedules, confusion for office staff, variation in academic standards and resentment in those who observe the deadlines. Therefore late and missing coursework is penalised.

- Coursework that is not submitted will be recorded as not submitted and entered at 0%.
- Penalties for the late submissions will be on scales established for each course by the course director.
- These may be varied for good reason by the tutor at the time of issue of the assignment with the consent of the course director.

REFERENCES AND BIBLIOGRAPHY

Abercrombi, N. and Urry, J. (1983) *Capital, Labour and the Middle Class*. London, Allen and Unwin.

Allan, P. and Jolley, M. (eds) (1987) *The Curriculum in Nurse Education*. London, Croom Helm.

Anderson, D., Brown, S. and Race, P. (1997) *500 Tips for Further and Continuing Education Lecturers*. London: Kogan Page.

Anderson, G., Boud, D. and Sampson, J. (1996) *Learning Contracts: A Practical Guide*. London, Kogan Page.

Andrews, M. (1996) 'Using reflection to develop clinical expertise'. *British Journal of Nursing* 8(8): 508–13.

Andrusyszn, M.A. (1989) 'Clinical evaluation of the affective domain'. *Nurse Education Today* 9: 75–81.

Apple, M.W. (1975) *Ideology and Curriculum*. London, Routledge and Kegan Paul.

Apple, M.W. (1982) *Education and Power*. London, Routledge and Kegan Paul.

Apple, M.W. (1988) 'Facing the complexity of power: for a parallel list position in critical education studies'. In M. Cole (ed), *Bowles and Gintis Revisited*. Lewes, Falmer Press.

Argyris, C. and Schön, D. (1974) *Theory in Practice: Increasing Professional Effectiveness*. San Francisco, Jossey-Bass.

Armitage, A., Bryant, R., Dunnill, R. *et al.* (1999) *Teaching and Training in Post-Compulsory Education*. Milton Keynes, Open University Press.

Armitage, P. and Burnard, P. (1991) 'Mentors or preceptors? Narrowing the theory–practice gap'. *Nurse Education Today* 11: 225–9.

Ashcroft, K. and Foreman-Peck, L. (1994) *Managing Teaching and Learning in Further and Higher Education*. London, Falmer Press.

Ashworth, P. and Morrison, P. (1991) 'Problems of competence-based nurse education'. *Nurse Education Today* 11, 256–60. London, Longman.

Ashworth, P. and Saxton, J. (1990) 'On competence'. *Journal of Further and Higher Education* 14(2): 3–25.

Askrew, S. and Carnell, E. (1998) *Transforming Learning: Individual and Global Change*. London, Cassell.

Atherton, J. (2000a) *Assessment* (on-line). Leicester, De Montfort University. Available at *http://www.staff.dmu.ac.uk/~jamesa/teaching/assessment.htm* (accessed 7 February 2001)

Atherton, J. (2000b) *Marketing* (online). Leicester, De Montfort University. Available at *http://www.staff.dmu.ac.uk/~jamesa/teaching/marking.htm* (accessed 7 February 2001)

Atherton, J. (2000c) *The Problem of Assessment* (online). Leicester, De Montford University. Available at *hhtp://www.staff.dmu.ac.uk/~jamesa/teaching/assess_problem.htm* (accessed 7 February 2001)

Atkins, M.J. (1984) 'Pre-vocational courses: tensions and strategies'. *Journal of Curriculum Studies* 16: 403.

AUT (1999a) *Higher Education in the New Century*. London, AUT.

AUT (1999b) *Analysis of Labour Force Survey Data*. London, AUT.

AUT (2001a) 'Now is the time to spend on people' (Pay claim 2001–2), Table 3. Available at *http://www.aut.org/uk/pandp/index.html*

AUT (2001b) 'Now is the time to spend on people' (Pay claim 2001–2), Section 6. Available at *http://www.aut.org.uk/campaigns/index.html*

Ayres, J. (1989) *Evaluating Workshops and Institutes*. ERIC digest (online). Washington, US Department of Education. Available at *http://www.ed.gov/databases/ERIC_Digests/ed315427.html* (accessed 7 April 2001).

Ball, C. (1973) *Education for a Change: Community Action and the School*. London, Penguin.

Bantock, G.H. (ed.) (1977) *Towards a Theory of Popular Education in Curriculum Design*. London, Croom Helm.

Barber, M. (1996) *National Curriculum: A Study in Policy*. Keele, Keele University Press.

Barnes, D. (1982) *Practical Curriculum Study*. London, Routledge.

Barrow, R. (1984) *Giving Teaching Back to Teachers. A Critical Introduction to Curriculum Theory*. Brighton, Wheatsheaf Books.

Bates, L. and Riseborough, C. (1995) Special issues on Competence and the National Vocational Qualification Framework. *British Journal of Education* 8(1) and 8(2).

Bates, T. (1993) 'How external mentoring operates'. *Management Development Review* 6(4): 6–9.

Battersby, D. (1990) 'From andragogy to gerogogy'. In F. Glendenning and K. Percy (eds), *Ageing, Education and Society*. University of Keele, Association for Educational Gerontology.

Beaumont, G. (1995) *Review of 100 NVQs and SVQs*. A report submitted to the Department for Education and Employment. London, DFEE.

Bean, T.W. and Zulich, J. (1989) 'Using dialogue journals to foster reflective practice with pre-service, content-area teachers'. *Teacher Education Quarterly* 16(1): 33–40.

Becher, A. Eraut, M.R. and Knight, J. (1981) *Policies for Educational Accountability*. Heinemann. London.

Bees, M. and Swords, M. (eds) (1990) *National Vocational Qualifications and Further Education*. London, Kogan Page.

Benn, C. and Chitty, C.(1997) *Thirty Years On: Is Comprehensive Education Alive and Well or Struggling to Survive?* Harmondsworth, Penguin.

Benner, P. (1982) 'Issues in competency-based testing'. *Nursing Outlook* 30(5): 303–9.

Benner, P. (1984) *From Novice to Expert: Excellence and Power in Clinical Nursing Practice*. Menlo Park, California, Addison-Wesley.

Bennis, W.G., Benne, K.D. and Chin, R. (1985) *The Planning of Change*. New York, Holt.

Bernstein, B. (1975) *Class, Codes and Control. Vol. 1: Theoretical Studies towards a Sociology of Language*. London, Routledge and Kegan Paul.

Berte, N.R. (1975) *Individualising Education through Contract Learning*. University of Alabama Press.

Bett, Sir Michael (1999) *Independent Review of Higher Education, Pay and Conditions*. London, Stationery Office, para.21.

Bevis, E.O. (1982) *Curriculum Building in Nursing: A Process* (3rd edition). London, C.V. Mosby.

Biggs, J.B. (1999) *Teaching for Quality Learning at University: What the Student Does*. Buckingham, Society for Research into Higher Education and Open University Press.

Biggs, J. (2001) 'The reflective institution: assuring and enhancing the quality of teaching and learning'. *Higher Education* 41: 221–38.

Bines, H. (1992) 'Issues in course design'. In H. Bines and D. Watson (eds), *Developing Professional Education*. Buckingham, Society for Research into Higher Education and Open University Press.

Block, J.H. (1971) (ed.) *Mastery Learning: Theory and Practice*. New York, Rinehart, Winston and Holt.

Bloom, B.S. (1965) *Taxonomy of Educational Objectives*. London, Longman.

Bloom, B.S. (1970) 'Towards a theory of testing which includes measurement-evaluation-assessment' in M.C. Wiltnock and D.C. Wiley (eds), *The Evaluation of Instruction*. New York, Holt, Rinehart and Winston.

Blunkett, D. (n.d.) Foreword by the Secretary of State to *The Learning Age* (online). London, Department for Education and Employment. Available at *http://www.lifelonglearning.co.uk/greenpaper/ch-fore.htm* (accessed 17 April 2001)

Bobbit, F. (1918) *The Curriculum*. Boston, Houghton Mifflin.

Boone, E. (1985) *Developing Programmes in Adult Education*. Englewood Cliffs, New Jersey, Prentice Hall.

Boreham, N.C. (1978) 'Test-skill interaction errors in the assessment of nurses' clinical proficiency'. *Journal of Occupational Psychology* 51: 249–58.

Boss, L.A. (1985) 'Teaching for clinical competence'. *Nurse Educator* 10(4): 8–12.

Boud, D. (1981) *Developing Learner Autonomy in Learning*. Kogan Page, London.

Boud, D. Keogh, R. and Walker, D. (1985) *Reflection: Turning Experience into Learning*. London, Kogan Page.

Boud, D., Cohen, R. and Walker, D. (1993) *Using Experience for Learning*. Bristol, Open University Press.

Bourner, T., Martin, V. and Race, P. (eds) (1993) *Workshops that Work*. Maidenhead, McGraw-Hill.

Bowles, S. and Gintis, H. (1976) *Schooling in Capitalist America*. New York, Basic Books.

Boyd, E.M. and Fales, A.W. (1983) 'Reflective learning: key to learning from experience'. *Journal of Humanistic Psychology* 23(2): 99–117.

Boyd, R. (1989) *Improving Teacher Evaluations*. ERIC digest No. 111 (online). Washington, US Department of Education. Available at *http://www.ed.gov/databases/ERIC_Digests/ ed315431.html* (accessed 7 April 2001).

Boydell, T. (1976) *Experiential Learning*. Manchester Monographs.

Broadbent, J. (1977) 'The management of teaching'. *New Universities Quarterly*, Autumn: 421–57.

Brookfield, S. (1984a) 'The contribution of Eduard Linderman to the development of theory and philosophy in adult education'. *Adult Education Quarterly* 4(34): 185–96.

Brookfield, S. (1984b) 'Self-directed adult learning: a critical paradigm'. *Adult Education Quarterly* 2: 59–71.

Brookfield, S. (1986) *Understanding and Facilitating Adult Learning*. Milton Keynes, Open University Press.

Broome, A. (1990) *Managing Change*. London. Macmillan Education.

Brown, G. and Atkins, M. (1991) *Effective Teaching in Higher Education*. London, Routledge.

Brown, S. (1994) 'Assessment: a changing practice'. In B. Moon and A. Shelton Hayes (eds), *Teaching in the Secondary School*. London, Open University/Routledge.

Brown, S. and Knight, P. (1995) *Assessing Business in Higher Education*. London, Kogan Page.

Brundage, D.H. and Macheracher, D. (1980) *Adult Learning Principles and Their Application to Programme Planning*. Toronto, Ontario Institution for Studies in Education.

Bruner, J.S. (1971a) *The Process of Education*. Cambridge, Massachusetts, Harvard University Press.

Bruner, J.S. (1971b) *Towards a Theory of Instruction*. Cambridge, Massachusetts, Harvard University Press.

BTEC (1993) *Implementing BTEC GNVQs: A Guide for BTEC Centres*, Issue 1. London, BTEC.

Burgess, R.G. (1986) *Sociology, Education and Schools*. London, Batsford.

Burke, J. (1989) *Competency Based Education and Training*. Lewes, Farmer Press.

Burnard, P. (1990) 'The students' experience: adult learning and mentorship revisited'. *Nurse Education Today* 6(5): 349–54.

Burnard, P. (1991) 'The language of experiential learning'. *Journal of Advanced Nursing* 16: 873–9.

Burrell, T. (1988) *Curriculum Design and Development: A Practical Manual for Nurse Educators*. New York, Prentice Hall.

Calderhead, J. and Gates, P. (1993) *Conceptualizing Reflection in Teacher Development*. London, Falmer Press.

Cantor, L.M. and Roberts, I.F. (1986) *Further Education Today*. London, Routledge and Kegan Paul.

Capey, J. (1995) *GNVQ Assessment Review: Final Report of the Review Group*. London, NCVQ.

Carroll, E. (1988) 'The role of tacit knowledge in problem solving in clinical setting'. *Nurse Education Today* 8: 140–7.

Castling, A. (1996) *Competence-based Teaching and Training*. London, Macmillan.

CBI (1994) *Quality Assessed: The CBI. Review of NVQs and SVQs*. London, CBI.

Cell, E. (1984) *Learning to Learn from Experiences*. Albany, State University of New York Press.

Chickering, A.W. (1983) *Education, Work and Human Development: Making Sponsored Experiential Learning Standard Practice*. New Directions for Experiential Learning, No. 20. San Francisco, Jossey-Bass and Cael.

Childs, D. (1985) *Psychology and the Teacher* (4th edition). Eastbourne, Holt.

Chin, R. and Benne, K.D. (1976) 'General strategies for effecting changes in human systems'. In W.G. Bennis, K.D. Benne and R. Chin (1976) *The Planning of Change*. New York, Holt.

Clamp, C. (1980) 'Learning through incidents'. *Nursing Times* 76(40): 1755–8.

Clarke, A. (1995) 'Professional development in practicum settings: reflective practice under scrutiny'. *Teacher and Teacher Education* 11(3): 243–62.

Clutterbuck, D. (1985) *Everyone needs a mentor: how to foster talent within the organisation*. London, Institute of Personnel Management.

CNAA (1988) *Credit Accumulation and Transfer*. Information Services Digest 1(1): 6.

Coburn, L. (1984) *Student Evaluation of Teacher Performance* (online). Washington, US Department of Education. Available at *http://www.ed.gov/databases/ERIC_Digests/ed289887.html* {accessed 7 April 2001}.

Cohen, J.A. (1993) 'Caring perspectives in nursing education: liberation, transformation and meaning'. *Journal of Advance Nursing* 18: 621–6.

Cookson, C. (2001) 'UK scientists responsible for third of genome project'. *Financial Times* 13 February, p.2.

Copeland, U., Birmingham, C. and De La Cruz, E. (1993) 'The reflective practitioner in teaching: towards a research agenda'. *Teaching and Teacher Education* 9(4): 347–59.

Court, S. (1996) 'The use of time by academic and related staff'. *Higher Education Quarterly* 50(4): 237–60.

Courtney, S. (1992) *Why Adults Learn*. London, Routledge.

Coutts-Jarman, J. (1993) 'Using reflection and experience in nurse education'. *British Journal of Nursing* 2(1): 77–80.

Cox, A. (1996) 'Teacher as mentor: opportunities for professional development'. In J. Robson (ed.) *The Professional FE Teacher*. Aldershot, Avebury.

Cronbach, L.J. (1963) 'Course improvement through evaluation'. *Teacher's College Record* 64: 672–83.

Cross, K.P. (1981) 'Adults as learners: increasing participation and facilitating learning'. San Francisco, Jossey-Bass.

Curzon, L.B. (1997) *Teaching in Further Education: An Outline of Principles and Practice* (5th edition). London, Cassell.

Cusick, P. (1973) *Inside High School*. New York, Holt, Rinehart and Winston.

Dale, R. (1985) *Education, Employment and Training*. Oxford, Pergamon in association with the Open University.

Danines, J., Daines, C. and Graham, B. (1993) *Adult Learning, Adult Teaching* (3rd edition). Nottingham, Continuing Education Press.

Darbyshire, P. (1993) 'In defence of pedagogy: a critique of the notion of andragogy'. *Nurse Education Today* 13: 328–35.

Darbyshire, P., Stewart, B., Jamieson, L. and Tongue, C. (1990) 'New domains in nursing'. *Nursing Times* 86(27): 73–5.

Davenport, J. and Davenport, J.A. (1985) 'A chronology and analysis of the andragogy debate'. *Adult Education Quarterly* 35: 152–9.

Davies, I.K. (1981) *Instruction Technique*. New York, McGraw Hill.

Davies, W.B., Neary, M. and Phillips, R. (1994) *The Practitioner-Teacher. A Study in the Introduction of Mentors in the Pre-Registration Nurse Education Programme in Wales. Final Report*. Cardiff University Press.

Dearden, R.F. (1966) 'Instructions and learning by discovery'. In R.S. Peters (ed.), *Ethics and Education*. London, Allen and Unwin.

Dearden, R.F. (1968) *The Philosophy of Primary Education*. London, Routledge and Kegan Paul.

Dearden, R.F, Hirst, P.H. and Peters, R S. (eds) (1972) *A Critique of Current Educational Aims*. London, Routledge and Kegan Paul.

Dearing, R. (1997) *Higher Education in the Learning Society* (online). University of Leeds. Available at *http://www.leeds.ac.uk/educol/ncihe* (accessed 18 April 2001).

DES (1991) *Education and Training for the 21st Century*. Cmnd 1536. London, HMSO.

Dewey, J. (1916) *Democracy and Education*. New York, Macmillan.

Dewey, J. (1938) *Reflection: Turning Experience into Learning*. London, Kogan Page.

De Wit, P. (1992) *Quality Assurance in University Continuing Vocational Education*. London, HMSO.

DfEE/FEDA. (1995) *Mapping the FE Sector*, London, Further Education Development Agency.

DfEE/Scottish Office/Welsh Office (1995) *Lifetime Learning: A Consultation Document*. London, DfEE.

Diekelmann, N. (1990) 'Nursing education: caring, dialogue and practice'. *Journal of Nursing Education* 29(7): 300–5.

Dobl, R.C. (1970) *Curriculum Improvement*. Boston, Allyn.

Donabedian, A. (1980) *The Definition of Quality and Approaches to Its Assessment*. Ann Arbor, Michigan.

Donabedian, A. (1986) 'Criteria and standards for quality assessment'. *Quality Review Bulletin* 12(3): 99–100.

Downie, N.M. (1967) *Fundamentals of Measurement: Techniques and Practices*. New York, Oxford University Press.

Dreeben, R. (1968) *On What Is Learned in School*. Reading, Massachusetts, Addison Wesley.

Duke, C. (1992) *The Learning University*. Buckingham, Open University Press in association with the Society for Research in Higher Education.

Durkheim, E. (1964) *The Role of Sociological Methods*. New York, Free Press.

Ecclestone, K. (1995) *Understanding Assessment*. Leicester, National Institute of Adult Education.

Edexcel (1999) *The Foundation for Educational Excellence*. London, Edexcel.

Edwards, J. (1991) *Evaluation in Adult and Further Education*. London, Taylor and Francis.

Edwards, R. (1993) 'Multi-skilling the flexible workforce in post-compulsory education'. *Journal of Further and Higher Education* 17(1): 44–51.

Eisner, E.W. (1966) 'Educational objectives: help or hindrance'. *School Review* 75: 250–60.

Eisner, E.W. (1969) 'Instructional and expressive educational objectives: their formulation and use in the curriculum'. In W.J. Popham, H.J. Sullivan and L.L. Tyler (eds), *Instructional Objectives*. AERA Monograph No. 3. Chicago, Rand McNally.

Eisner, E.W. (1985) *The Art of Educational Evaluation: A Personal View*. London and Philadelphia, Falmer Press.

Elliott, J. (1981) *Action Research: A Framework for Self-Evaluation in Schools*. Cambridge Institute of Education.

Elliott, J. (1991) *Action Research for Educational Change*. Milton Keynes, Open University Press.

Entwistle, N. and Ramsden, P. (1983) *Understanding Learner Learning*. Beckenham, Kent: Croom Helm.

Eraut, M. (1982) *Curriculum Development in Further Education*. University of Sussex, Education Area Occasional Paper No. 11: 37.

Eraut, M. (1985) 'Knowledge creation and knowledge use in professional context', *Students in Higher Education* 10(2): 117–33.

Eraut, M. (1994) *Developing Professional Knowledge and Competence*. London, Falmer Press.

Eraut H, Goad, C. and Smith, G. (1982) *Handbook for the Analysis of Curriculum Material*. University of Sussex.

Everhart, R.B. (1983) *Reading, Writing and Resistance*. Boston, Routledge and Kegan Paul.

Fagan, E. (1984) 'Competence in educational practice: a rhetorical perspective'. In E. Short (ed.), *Competence: Inquiries into Its Meaning and Acquisition in Educational Settings*. New York, University of America Press.

FEFC (1996a) *Quality and Standards in Further Education in England. Chief Inspector's Annual Report 1995–96*. Coventry, FEFC.

FEFC (1996b) *Analysis of Institutions' Strategic Planning Information for the Period 1995–96 to 1997–98*. Circular 96/02. Coventry, FEFC.

FEFC (1996c) 'Student numbers at colleges in the further education sector and external institutions in England in 1995–96'. Press release, 17 December. Coventry, FEFC.

FEFC (1996d) *Inclusive Learning*. Coventry, FEFC.

FEFC (1996e) *Introduction to the Council*. Coventry, FEFC.

FEFC (1996f) *College Responsiveness: A National Survey Report*. Coventry, FEFC.

FEFC (1996g) *The Report of the Learning and Technology Committee*, chaired by Sir Gordon Higginson. Coventry, FEFC.

FENTO (2001) *Further Education Sector Workforce Development Plan*. Consultation version, April. London, FENTO.

FEU (1979a) *Active Learning: A Guide to Current Practice in Experiential and Participatory Learning*. London, FEU.

FEU (1979b) *A Basis for Choice*. London, FEU.

FEU (1981) *Vocational Preparation*. London, FEU.

FEU (1982) *Curriculum Styles and Strategies*. London, FEU.

FEU (1983) *College Based Course Evaluation* (ch. 11). London, FEU.

FEU (1989a) *Partnership in Continuing Education*. London, FEU.

FEU (1989b) *Planning the FE Curriculum: Implications of the 1988 Education Reform Act*. London, FEU.

FEU (1989c) *The Strategic Planning of FE*. London, FEU.

FEU (1989d) *Towards a Framework of Curriculum Entitlement*. London, FEU.

FEU (1989e) *Training for Curriculum Development*. London, FEU.

FEU (1991) *Flexible Colleges, Part I: Priorities for Action*. London, FEU.

FEU (1993) *Introducing General National Vocational Qualifications*. London, FEU.

FEU (1994) *Managing the Delivery of Guidance in Colleges*. London, FEU.

Fivars, G. and Gosnell, S. (1966) *Nursing Evaluation: The Problem and the Process*. New York, Macmillan

Fletcher, S. (1991) *NVQs: Standards and Competence*. London, Kogan Page.

Forsythe, G.B., Williams, C., McGuthrie, C. and Friedman, C.P. (1986) 'Construct validity of medical clinical competence measures: a multinational multimethod matrix study using confirmatory factor analysis'. *American Educational Research Journal* 23(1) (Summer): 315–36.

Francis, D. (1995) 'The reflective journal: a window to pre-service teachers' practical knowledge'. *Teacher and Teacher Education* 11(3): 229–42.

Freeman, R. and Lewis, R. (1998) *Planning and Implementing Assessment*. London, Kogan Page.

French, H.P. (1989) 'Educating the nurse practitioner: an assessment of the pre-registration preparation of nurses as an educational experience'. Unpublished Ph.D. dissertation, University of Durham.

Friere, P. (1974) *Pedagogy of the Oppressed*. Seabury Press, New York.

Fullan, M. (1996) *New Meaning of Educational Change*. London, Cassell.

Furlong, J. and Maynard, T. (1995) *Mentoring Student Teachers: The Growth of Professional Knowledge*. London, Routledge.

Gagné, R.M. (1967) 'Curriculum research and the promotion of learning'. In R. Tyler and R.M. Gagné, *Perspectives of Curriculum Evaluation*. AERA Monograph. Chicago, Rand McNally.

Gale, J. and O'Priory, M. (1981) 'The development and implications of frames of reference in curriculum evaluation programmes: the experience of a British school of medicine'. *British Journal of Educational Technology* 1: 49–63.

Gallagher, A. and Locke, M. (1992) *Mature Students in Higher Education: How Institutions Can Learn from Experience*. London, Centre for Institutional Studies.

Gibbs, G. and Habershaw, T. (1990) *253 Ideas for Your Teaching*. Bristol: Technical and Educational Services.

Giles, D.E.J. (1986) 'Getting students ready for the field'. *Experiential Education* 11(5): 1–8.

Gleeson, Dennis (ed.) (1990) *Training and Its Alternatives*. London, Oxford University Press (chs 7, 8 and 11).

Goddard, D. (1985) 'Assessing teachers: a critical response to the government's proposals'. *Journal of Evaluation in Education* 8: 35–8.

Golby, M., Greenwood, J. and West, R. (eds) (1975) *Curriculum Design*. London, Croom Helm.

Goldman, G. (1979) 'A contract for academic improvement'. In P.J. Hills (ed.), *Study Courses and Counselling*. London, Society for Research into Higher Education.

Goodson, I.F. and Ball, S. (1984) *Defining the Curriculum*. Lewes, Falmer Press.

Greater London Group (1996) 'Higher education productivity' (draft report), p.3.

Green, A. and Steadman, H. (1995) *Education Provision, Education Attainment and the Needs of Industry: A Review of the Research for Germany, France, Japan, the USA. and Britain*. London, National Institute for Economic and Social Research.

Gronlund, N.E. (1971) *Measurement and Evaluation in Teaching*. New York, Macmillan.

Guilbert, J.J. (1981) *Educational Handbook for Health Personnel*. Geneva, World Health Organisation.

Habershaw, S., Gibbs, G. and Habershaw, T. (1998) *53 Interesting Ways to Assess Your Students*. Technical and Education Services, Wiltshire, Cromwell Press.

Habershaw, T., Habershaw, S. and Gibbs, G. (1987) *53 Interesting Ways of Helping Your Students to Study*. Avon, Whitehall.

Haffenden, I. and Brown, A. (1989) *Implications of Competence-based Curricula*. London, FEU.

Haffer, A. (1986) 'Facilitating change'. *Journal of Nursing Administration* 16 (4): 18–22.

Hagerty, B. (1986) 'A second look at mentors'. *Nursing Outlook* 34 (1): 16–19.

Hall, V. (1991) *Maintained Further Education in the UK*. Blagdon, Bristol, FE Staff College.

Hamilton, D. (1976) *Curriculum Evaluation*. London, Open Books.

Hamilton D.D. (ed.) (1977) *Beyond the Numbers Game: A Reader in Education Evaluation*. London, Macmillan Education.

Hammersley, M. and Hargreaves, A. (1983) *Curriculum Practice: Some Sociological Case Studies*. Lewes, Falmer Press.

Hammersley, M., Scarth, J. and Webb, S. (1984) 'Developing and testing theory: the case for research on student learning and examination'. In R. Burgess (ed.), *Issues in Educational Research: Qualitative Methods*. Lewes, Falmer Press.

Handy, C. (1990) *The Age of Unreason*. Boston, Harvard Business School Press.

Harding, J.M., Kelly, L. and Nicodemus, R.B. (1976) 'The study of curriculum change'. *Studies in Science Education* 3: 1.

Hargreaves, A. (1989) *Curriculum and Assessment Reform: Modern Educational Thought*. Milton Keynes, Open University Press.

Hargreaves, D.H. (1978) 'Power and the para curriculum'. In C. Richards (ed.), *Power and the Curriculum: Issues in Curriculum Studies*. Duffield, Nafferton.

Harries A, Lawn, M. and Prescott, W. (eds) (1975) *Curriculum Evaluation*. London, Croom Helm.

Hartree, A. (1984) 'Malcolm Knowles' theory of andragogy: a critique'. *International Journal of Lifelong Education* 3(3) 203–10.

Hatton N. and Smith, D. (1995) 'Reflection in teacher education: towards definition and implementation'. *Teacher and Teacher Education* 11(1): 33–50.

Havelock, R.G. (1973) *Planning for Innovation through Examination and Utilisation of Knowledge* (4th edition). Centre for Research on Utilisation of Scientific Knowledge.

Havinghurst, R.J. and Orr, B. (1956) *Adult Education and Adult Needs*. Boston, Centre for the Study of Liberal Education for Adults..

Heath, H. (1998) 'Keeping a reflective practice diary: a practical guide'. *Nurse Education Today* 18: 592–8.

Heathcote, G, Kempa, R. and Roberts, L. (1982) *Curriculum Styles and Strategies*. London, FEU.

HESA (1999) *Higher Education Management Statistics: Sector Level 1997/98*. Cheltenham, HESA, p 23.

HESA (2000) *Learners in Higher Education Institutions 1998/99*. Cheltenham: HESA, Table A.

Higham, J., Sharp, P. and Yeomans, D. (1996) *The Emerging 16–19 Curriculum*. London, Fulton.

Hilt, P. (1992) *Enhancing Learning through Co-operation Learning*. London, College Press.

Hinett, K. and Weeden, P. (2000) 'How am i doing? developing critical self-evaluation in trainee teachers'. *Quality in Higher Education* 6(3) 245–57.

Hinman, J. (1987) 'From assessment to accreditation: reflections on the use of prior learning in further education'. In C. Griffin (ed.), *Assessing Prior Learning: Progress and Practices*. Conference report, June, London, Learning from Experience Trust.

Hirst, P. (1975) *Knowledge and the Curriculum*. London, Routledge and Kegan Paul.

Hirst, P. and Peters, R.S. (1970) *The Logic of Education*. London, Open University and Routledge and Kegan Paul.

Hodkinson, P. (1996) '"Careership": the individual, choices and markets in the transition into work'. In J. Avis, M. Bloomer, G. Esland *et al.* (eds) *Knowledge and Nationhood*. London, Cassell Education.

Hodkinson, P. and Issitt, M. (1995) *The Challenge of Competence*, London, Cassell Education.

Hodson, A. and Spours, K. (1997) *Beyond Dearing, 14–19: Qualifications, Frameworks and Systems*. London, Kogan Page.

Holt, M. (1980) *Schools and Curriculum Change*. London and New York, McGraw-Hill.

Holt, M. (1987) *Judgement, Planning and Educational Change*. London, Harper and Row.

Hoover, L. (1994) 'Reflective writing as a window on pre-service teachers' thought processes'. *Teacher and Teacher Education* 10(1): 83–93.

Houle, C.O. (1972) *The Design of Education*. San Francisco, Jossey-Bass.

Hoy, R.A., Moustafa, A.H. and Skeath, A. (1986) *Balancing the Nurse Curriculum*. Tunbridge Wells, Costello.

Hoyle, E.R. (1975) 'Innovation and the social organisation of the school'. In A. Harris, M. Lawn and W. Prescott (eds), *Curriculum Innovation*. London, Croom Helm.

Huddleston, P. and Unwin, L. (1997) *Teaching and Learning in Further Education: Diversity and Change*. London, Routledge.

Hutton, M. (1989) 'Learning from action: a conceptual framework'. In S.W. Weil and I. McGill (eds), *Making Sense of Experiential Learning*. Society for Research into Higher Education and Open University Press.

Hyland, T. (1991) 'Vocational studies that won't work'. *Times Educational Supplement*, 20 September.

Hyland, T. (1992) 'The vicissitudes of adult education: competence, epistemology and reflective practice'. *Education Today* 42(2): 7–12.

Hyland, T. (1993) 'Competence, knowledge and education'. *Journal of Philosophy of Education* 27(1): 55–66.

Imel, S. (1988) *Guidelines for Working with Adult Learners*. ERIC digest No. 77 (online). Washington, US Department of Education. Available at *http://www.ed.gov/databases/ERIC_Digests/ed299456.html* (accessed 7 April 2001).

Jackson, P.W. (1968) *Life in the Classroom*. New York, Holt, Rinehart and Winston.

James, M. (1983) 'Course evaluation and curriculum development'. *Nursing Times* 10(8): 83.

Jarvis, P. (1985) *The sociology of adult and continuing education*. London, Croom Helm.

Jarvis, P. (1995) *Adult and Continuing Education: Theory and Practice* (2nd edition) London, Routledge.

Jeeves, M. and Greer, B. (1983) *The Analysis of Structural Learning*. London, Academic Press.

Jeffocate, R. (1984) *Ethnic Minorities and Education*. London, Harper and Row.

Jenkins, D. and Shipman, M.D. (1976a) *Curriculum: An Introduction*. London, Open Books.

Jenkins, D. and Shipman, M.D. (1976b) *Curriculum Evaluation: An Introduction*. London, Open Books.

Jessup, G. (1989) Foreword to J.W. Burke (ed) *Competence Based Education and Training*. Lewes, Falmer Press.

Jessup, G. (1990) 'The evidence required to demonstrate competencies'. In H. Black and A.

Wolf (eds), *Knowledge and Competency: Current Issues in Training and Education.* Sheffield, COIC.

Jessup, G. (1991) *Outcomes: National Council for Vocational Qualifications and the Emerging Model of Education and Training.* London, Falmer Press.

Jessup, G. (1994) *GNVQ: An Alternative Curriculum Model.* London, NCVQ.

Johns, C. (1994) 'Nuances of reflection'. *Journal of Clinical Nursing* 3(2): 71–5.

Johnson, C.E. (1974) 'Competency-based and traditional education practices compared'. *Journal of Teacher Education* (Winter): 335–6.

Jones, J.E. and Woodcock, M. (1985) *Manual of Management Development.* Aldershot, Gower.

Jowett V. (1995) 'Mentoring the "Working for a Degree" project'. Leeds Metropolitan University.

Keeton, M. (1981) 'Assessing and credentialing prior experience'. In A.W. Chickering (ed.), *The Modern American College.* San Francisco, Jossey-Bass.

Kelly, A.V. (1986) *Knowledge and Curriculum Planning.* London, Harper Education Series.

Kelly, A.V. (1989) *The Curriculum: Theory and Practice* (3rd edition). London, Paul Chapman.

Kember, D. (2000) *Action Learning and Action Research: Improving the Quality of Teaching and Learning.* London, Kogan Page.

Kember, D. and Kelly, M. (1993) *Improving Teaching through Action Research.* Green Guide No.14. HERDSA, New South Wales.

Kember, D., Jones, A., Yuenloke, A. *et al.* (2001) *Reflective Teaching and Learning in the Health Professions.* Oxford, Blackwell Science UK.

Kemmis, S. (1985) 'Action research and the politics of reflection'. In D. Boud, R. Keogh and D. Walker (1985) *Reflection: Turning Experience into Learning.* London, Kogan Page.

Kenworthy, N. and Nicklin, P. (1989) *Teaching and Assessing in Nursing Practice.* London, Scutari.

Kerr, J.F. (1968) *Changing the Curriculum.* London, University Press.

Keyzer, D.M. (1986) 'Using contracts'. *Nurse Education Today* 6: 103–6.

Kirby, C. and Slevin, O. (1992) 'A new curriculum for care'. in O. Slevin and H. Buckenbarn (eds), *Project 2000: The Teachers Speak.* Edinburgh, Campion Press.

Kirkpatrick, D. (1994) *Evaluating Training Programs: The Four Levels.* San Francisco, Barrett-Kjoehler.

Knowles, M.S. (1975) *Self-Directed Learning: A Guide for Teachers.* New York, Associated Press.

Knowles M.S. (1980) *The Modern Practice of Adult Education, from Pedagogy to Andragogy.* Cambridge, Adult Education Company New York.

Knowles, M.S. (1984) *Andragogy in Action.* San Francisco, Jossey-Bass.

Knowles, M.S. (1990) *The Adult Learner: A Neglected Species* (4th edition). Houston, Texas, Gulf Publishing.

Kolb, D.A. and Fry, R. (1975) 'Towards an applied theory of experiential learning'. In *Theories of Group Process*, Chichester, John Wiley.

Kolb, D.A. (1978) *Learning Style Inventory: Technical Manual.* Boston: McBeri.

Kolb, D.A. (1984) *Experiential Learning: Experience as the Source of Learning and Development.* Englewood Cliffs, New Jersey, Prentice-Hall.

Kyriacou, C. (1991) *Essential Teaching Skills.* Cheltenham, Stanley Thornes.

Lambert, P. (1987) 'The assessment of prior learning: curriculum duplication'. In C. Griffin (ed.), *Assessing Prior Learning: Progress and Practices.* Conference report, June. London, Learning from Experience Trust.

Last, J. and Crown, A. (1993) 'Teacher training in adult education'. *Adult Learning* 4(9): 2344–6.

Lawn, M. and Barton, L. (eds) (1981) *Rethinking Curriculum Studies.* London, Croom Helm.

Lawton, D. (1973) *Social Change: Educational Theory and Curriculum Planning.* University of London Press.

Lawton, D. (1979) *The End of the Secret Garden?* Inaugural lecture, University of London Institute of Education.

Lawton, D. (1978) *Theory and Practice of Curriculum Studies*. London, Routledge and Kegan Paul.

Lewin, K. (1958) 'The group reason and social change'. In E. Maccoby (ed.), *Reading in Social Psychology*. London, Holt, Rinehart and Winston.

Lindblom, C. (1964) 'The science of muddling through'. In W.J. Gore and J. Dyson (eds), *The Making of Decisions*. Glencoe, Scotland, Free Press.

Linderman, E.C. (1926) *The Meaning of Adult Education*. New York, New Republic. Republished in 1989 by Oklahoma Research Center for Continuing Professional and Higher Education.

Link, F. (1972) 'The unfinished curriculum'. From a working draft of seminars for leadership personnel curriculum development. Washington, Associate.

Long, J. (1997) 'Mentoring for school-based teachers in education in Australia'. *Mentoring and Tutoring* 4(3): 11–17.

Long, P. (1976) 'Judging and reporting on student nurse clinical performance: some problems for the ward sister'. *International Journal of Nursing Studies* 13: 115–21.

Lynch, K. (1989) *The Hidden Curriculum. Reproduction in Education: An Appraisal*. Lewes, Falmer Press.

McAleavey, M. and McAleer, J. (1991) 'Competence-based training'. *British Journal of In-service Education* 17(1): 19–23.

Maccia, E.S. (1972) 'Conceptual structures for curriculum inquiry'. Paper presented at a meeting of the American Educational Research Association, Chicago, April.

McCoy, S. (1990) *Towards a Framework for Curriculum Development*. London, FEU.

Macdonald, B. and Walker, R. (1976a) *Changing the Curriculum*. London, Open Books.

MacDonald, B. and Walker, R. (1976b) *College Based Courses Evaluation*. London, FEU.

MacDonald-Ross, M. (1973) 'Behavioural objectives: a critical review'. *Instructional Science* 2: 1–52, 58.

McGagaghie, W.C., Miller, G.E., Sajid, A.W. and Telder, T.V. (1978) *Competency-based Curriculum Development in Medical Education: An Introduction*. Geneva: World Health Organisation.

McKenzie, L. (1977) 'The issue of andragogy'. *Adult Education* 27(4): 225–9.

McKernan, J. (1991) *Curriculum Action Research*. London, Kogan Page.

McRobbie, A. (1978) 'Working-class girls and the culture of femininity'. In Women's Studies Group *Women Take Issue* London, Hutchinson.

Mager, R.F. (1962) *Preparing Instructional Objectives*. Palo Alto, California, Feason.

Mansell, E. (1987) 'The way ahead: priorities for the future'. In C. Griffin (ed.), *Assessing Prior Learning Progress and Practices*. Conference report, June. London, Learning from Experience Trust.

Marshall, K. (1991) 'NVQs: an assessment of the outcomes approach in education and training'. *Journal of Further and Higher Education* 15(3): 56–64.

Martins, K. (1981) 'Self-directed learning: an option for nurse education'. *Nursing Outlook* 29: 472–7.

Matthews, R. and Viens, D. (1988) 'Evaluating basic nursing skills through group video testing'. *Journal of Nursing Education* 1: 44–6.

Maxwell, R. (1984) 'Quality assessment in health'. *British Medical Journal* 12 May: 1470–2.

Messick, S. (1975) 'The standard problem: meaning and values in measurement and evaluation'. *American Psychologist* October: 955–66.

Messick, S. (1982) *Abilities and Knowledge in Educational Achievement Testing: The Assessment of Dynamic Cognitive Structure*. Princeton, New Jersey: Education Testing Service.

Miller, C., Hoggan, J., Pringle, S. and West, C. (1988) *Credit Where Credit's Due*. Report of the Accreditation of Work-based Learning Project. Glasgow, SCOTVEC.

Milligan, F. (1995) 'In defence of andragogy'. *Nurse Education Today* 15: 22–7.

Minton, D. (1991) *Teaching Skills in Further and Adult Education*. London, Macmillan Education.

Molyneux, F. (1992) 'The learning society: rhetoric and reality'. In N. Small (ed.) *The Learning Society: Political Rhetoric and Electoral Reality*. Association of Lifelong Learning, University of Nottingham.

Moon, J. (1999) *Reflection for Professional Development*. London, Kogan Page.

Moore, C. (1984) 'TEC programmes evaluated'. *Educational Research* 26: 111.

Morle, K.M. (1984) 'The problems in evaluating student nurses'. *Nurse Education Today* 4(4): 80–5.

Morle, K.M. (1990) Mentoring: is it a case of the Emperor's new clothes or a rose by any other name?' *Nurse Education Today* 10: 66–9.

Mosher, B. Darline, L. and Fike, E. (1996) *Training for Results: Teaching Adults to be Independent, Assertive Learners*. New York, Ziff-Davis.

Mowatt, I. and Siann, G. (1998) 'Learning in small groups'. In P. Sutherland (ed.), *Adult Learning: A Reader*. London, Kogan Page.

MSC/DES (1986) *Review of Vocational Qualifications in England and Wales: A Report by the Working Group* (chaired by H.C. Deville). London, MSC/DES.

Muller, D. and Funnell, P. (eds) (1991) *Delivering Quality in Vocational Education*. London, Kogan Page.

Murry M. and Owen, M. (1991) *Beyond the Myths and Magic of Mentoring*. San Francisco, Jossey-Bass.

NACETT (1995) *Report on Progress towards the National Targets*. London, NACETT.

Neary, M. (1992a) 'Contract assignments: an integral part of adult learning and continuous assessment'. *Senior Nurse* 12(4): 14–17.

Neary, M. (1992b) 'Planning, designing and development of an assessment tool'. *Nurse Education Today* 12: 357–67.

Neary, M. (1996a) 'Preparation for assessing clinical competences: Project 2000. An investigation'. PhD dissertation. School of Education, University of Wales, Cardiff.

Neary, M. (1996b) 'The introduction of mentorship to Project 2000 in Wales'. *Nursing Standard* 10(25): 37–9.

Neary, M. (1997a) 'Defining the role of assessors, mentors and supervisors', Part 1. *Nursing Standard* 11(42): 34–9.

Neary, M. (1997b) 'Defining the role of assessors, mentors and supervisors', Part 2. *Nursing Standard* 11(43): 34–8.

Neary, M. (1998) 'Contract assignments: change in teaching, learning and assessment strategies'. *Educational Practice and Theory* 20(1): 43–58.

Neary, M. (2000) *Teaching, Assessing and Evaluation for Clinical Competence: A Practical Guide for Teachers and Practitioners*. Cheltenham, Stanley Thornes.

Neary, M. (2001a) 'Assessing the clinical competence of students in nurse education'. *Welsh Journal of Education* 10(1): 46–58.

Neary, M. (2001b) 'Responsive assessment: assessing student nurses' clinical competence'. *Nurse Education Today* 21: 3–17.

Nicholls, A. and Nicholls, H. (1978) *Developing a Curriculum*. London, Allen and Unwin.

Nottingham Andragogy Group (1983) *Towards a Developmental Theory of Andragogy*. University of Nottingham Department of Adult Education.

Oakeshott, M. (1991) *Educational Guidance for Adults: Identifying Competences*. London, FEU.

Oakland, J.S. (1989) *Total Quality Management*. Oxford, Heinemann.

OECD (1998) *Education at a Glance*. Paris: OECD, p.198.

O'Neill, E., Morrison, H. and McEwen, A. (1993) *Professional Socialisation and Nurse Education: An Evaluation*. Belfast: Queens' University Press.

Parlett, M. (1981) *Illuminative Evaluation in Human Inquiry* (eds) P. Reason, J. Rowan. John Wiley.

Parlett, M. and Hamilton, D. (1972) *Evaluation as Illumination: A New Approach to the Study of Innovatory Programmes*. Occasional Paper No. 9. Centre of Research in the Educational Sciences, University of Edinburgh.

Payne, J. (1995) *Routes beyond Compulsory Schooling*. England and Wales Youth Cohort Study. Sheffield, Employment Department.

Peters, R.S. (ed.) (1966) *Ethics and Education*. London, Allen and Unwin.

Petter, G.S.V. (1970) 'Coherent secondary education'. *Trends in Education* 19: 38–43.

Petty, G. (1998) *Teaching Today* (2nd edition). Cheltenham, Stanley Thornes.

Philips R, Neary, M. and Davies, B. (1996) 'The practitioner-teacher: a study in the introduction of mentors in the pre-registration nurse education programme in Wales'. *Journal of Advanced Nursing* 23. Part 1: 1037–44; Part 2: 1080–8.

Pick, C. and Walker, R. (eds) (1976) *Other Rooms, Other Voices*. Centre for Applied Research in Education, University of East Anglia.

Popham, W.J. and Baker, E.L. (1970) *Systematic Instruction*. Englewood Cliffs, New Jersey, Prentice-Hall.

Pring, R. (1992) 'Liberal education and vocational preparation'. In H. William (ed.) *Continuing the Education Debate*. London, Cassell.

Pring, R. (1997) *Affirming the Comprehensive Ideal*. London, Falmer Press.

Pring, R., Barrow, R. and White, R. (eds) (1993) *Beyond Liberal Education: Liberal Education and Vocational Preparation*. London, Routledge.

Quicke, J. (1996) 'The reflective practitioner and teacher education: an answer to critics'. *Teaching and Teaching: Theory and Practice* 2(1): 11–12.

Quinn, F.M. (1988) *The Principles and Practice of Nurse Education* (2nd edition). London, Chapman and Hall.

Race, P. (1982) 'Help yourself to success: improving polytechnic students' study skills'. In F. Percival and H. Ellington (eds), *Aspects of Educational Technology XV: Distance Learning and Evaluation*. London, Kogan-Page.

Race, P. (1989a) *The Open Learning Handbook*. London, Kogan Page.

Race, P. (1989b) *Forward Thinking: How Do We Learn? Why Are You at College?* Teaching and Learning Higher Education Series 13, Aberdeen, CICED.

Race, P. (1991) 'Learning through feedback'. In *Putting Students First*. Paper 64, SCED.

Race, P. (1993) 'Never mind the teaching – feel the learning'. SEDA Paper No. 80, ch. 1, Birmingham: SEDA Publications. Summarised at *http://www.lgu.ac.uk/deliberations/eff.learning/happen.html* (accessed 5 February 2001).

Race, P. and Brown, S. (1995) *500 Tips for Tutors*. London, Kogan Page.

Radford, J. and Govier, E. (1980) *A Textbook of Psychology*. New York, Sheldon Press.

Raht, P. (1971) 'Criteria for a process model'. In R.A. Hoy, A.H. Moustafa and A. Skeath (eds), *Balancing the Nurse Curriculum*. Tonbridge Wells, Costello.

RCN (1989) *Standard Setting*. London, Royal College of Nursing.

Reece, L. and Walker, S. (1992) *Teaching, Training and Learning: A Practical Guide*. Sunderland, Business Education Publishers.

Reid, W.A. and Walker, D.F. (1975) *Case Studies in Curriculum Change*. London, Routledge and Kegan Paul.

Richardson, S. (1987) 'Implementing contract learning in a senior nursing practicum'. *Journal of Advanced Nursing* 12: 201–6.

Richardson, W., Woolhouse, J. and Finegold, D. (1993) *The Reform of Post-16 Education and Training in England and Wales*. Harlow, Longman.

Rick, A. (1972) 'When the dead awaken: writing as revision'. *College English* 34(1) 18–25.

Roberts, J. and Norman, G. (1990) 'Reliability and learning from the OSCE'. *Medical Evaluation* 24: 219–23.

Robinson, J.E., Such, S, Walters, C. *et al.* (1996) 'Researching in further education: an illustrative study from Suffolk College'. In M. Young *et al.* (eds), *Colleges as Learning Organisations: The Role of Research*. Unified 16+ Curriculum Series No. 12. London, Institute of Education

Robson, J., Cox, A., Bailey, B. *et al.* (1995) 'A new approach to teacher training: an evaluation of a further and higher education partnership'. *Journal of Further and Higher Education* 19(2): 79–91.

Rogers, C. (1983) 'The process of the encounter group'. In M. Tight (ed.), *Adult Learning and Education*. Milton Keynes. Open University Press.

Ross, M., Carroll, G., Knight, J., Chamberlain, M. *et al.* (1988) 'Using the OSCE. to measure clinical skills performance in nursing'. *Journal of Advanced Nursing* 13: 45–56.

Rowntree, D. (1981) *Developing Courses for Students*. Maidenhead, McGraw-Hill.

Rowntree, D. (1982) *Educational Technology in Curriculum Development* (2nd edition). London, Harper and Row.

Runciman, P. (1990) *Competency-based Education and the Assessment and Accreditation of Work-based Learning in the Context of Project 2000 Programmes of Nurse Education: A Literature Review*. National Board for Nursing, Midwifery and Health Visiting for Scotland.

Sainsbury, Lord (Minister for Science) (1998) Speech at the British Association Festival of Science, Cardiff University, 7 September.

Sandberg, J.A. (1994) 'Educational paradigms: issues and trends'. In R. Lewis and P. Mendelsohn (eds), *Lessons From Learning*. IFIP TC3/WG3.3 Working Conference 1993, Amsterdam, pp. 13–22.

Scheffler, I. (1965) *Conditions of Knowledge*. Chicago, Scott Foresman.

Schneider, D.K. and Block, K. (1995) *The Learning and Teaching Environment: in the World-Wide Web in Education*. ANDREA. (A Network for Distance Education Reporting from European Activities), Vol. 2, No. 5, 12 June. Available at *http://tecfa.unige.ch/tecfa/research/CMC/andrea95/andrea.html* (accessed 10 February 2001).

Schofield, H. (1972) *The Philosophy of Education* (chs 3 and 9). London, Unwin.

Schön, D.A. (1971) *Beyond the Stable State: Public and Private Learning in a Changing Society*. New York, Norton.

Schön, D. (1987) *Educating the Reflective Practitioner*. San Francisco, Jossey-Bass.

Schön, D. (1991) *The Reflective Practitioner: How Professionals Think in Action* (2nd edition). San Francisco, Jossey-Bass.

Schools Council Research Studies (1973) *Evaluation in Curriculum Development: Twelve Case Studies*. London, Schools Council.

Scriven, M. (1973) *Methodology of Evaluation*. AERA Monograph Series on Curriculum Education. Chicago, Rand McNally.

Searight, M.W. (1976) *Preceptorship Study: Contracting for Learning*. Philadelphia, F.A. Davies.

Sheehan, J. (1979) 'Measurement in nursing education'. *Journal of Advanced Nursing* 4(1): 47–56.

Smith, A. and Russell, J. (1991) 'Using critical learning incidents in nurse education'. *Nurse Education Today* 11: 284–91.

Smith, E. (2001) *Assessment in Adult Education* (online). New York, Hudson River Center for Program Development. Available at *http://www.nyadulted.org/prodevg2.htm* (accessed 7 February 2001).

Smith, G. (1993) *BTEC GNVQs and Development in Vocational Education*. Adults Learning (5). Leicester NIACE.

Smyth, W. (1986) *Reflection in Action*. Victoria, Australia, Deakin University Press.

Snow, R.E., Frederico, P. and Montague, W.E. (eds) *Aptitude Learning and Instruction*. Hillsdale, New Jersey, Lawrence Erlbaum Associates.

Sockett, H. (1976) *Designing the Curriculum*. London, Open Books.

Spender, D. and Spender, E. (eds) (1980) *Learning to Lose: Sexism and Education*. London, Women's Press.

Spooner, A. (1993) 'Mentoring and flexible training'. *Management Development Review* 6(2): 21–5. Bradford, MCB University Press.

Squires, G. (1987) *The Curriculum Beyond School*. Sevenoaks, Hodder and Stoughton.

Squires, G. (1993) 'Education for adults'. In M. Thorpe, R. Edwards and A. Hanson (eds), *Culture and Processes of Adult Learning*. London, Routledge.

Stake, R.E. (1973) *Evaluating the Arts in Education: A Responsive Approach*. Columbus, Ohio, Merrill.

Stake, R.E. (1977) 'The countenance of educational evaluation'. In D.D. Hamilton (ed.), *Beyond the Numbers Game: A Reader in Education Evaluation*. London, Macmillan Education.

Stake, R.E. (1980) 'Program evaluation, particularly responsive evaluation'. In W.B. Dockrell and D. Hamilton (eds), *Rethinking Educational Research*. London, Hodder and Stoughton.

Stake, R.E. (1986) 'Program evaluation, particularly responsive evaluation', in G.F. Madaus, M. Scriven and D.C. Stufflebeam (eds), *Evaluation Models: Viewpoints in Educational and Human Services Evaluation*. Boston: Kluwer-Nijoff.

Steinaker, N.W. and Bell, R. (1979) *The Experiential Taxonomy: A New Approach to Teaching and Learning*. New York, Academic Press.

Stenhouse, L. (1971) 'Some limitations on the use of objectives in curriculum research and planning'. *Pedagogica Europaea*: 45.

Stenhouse, L. (1975) *An Introduction to Curriculum Research and Development*. London, Heinemann.

Stenhouse, L. (1980) *Curriculum Research and Development in Action*. London, Heinemann.

Stephenson, J. (1988) 'The experience of independent study at North East London Polytechnic'. In D. Boud (ed.) *Developing Students' Autonomy in Learning*. London. Kogan Page.

Stephenson, J. and Laycock, M. (1993) *Using Learning Contracts in Higher Education*. London, Kogan Page, pp.57–62.

Stephenson, M.E. (1986) 'Curriculum development in action'. *Nurse Education Today* 6: 263–9.

Sternberg, R.J. (1986) *Beyond IQ: A Triarchic Theory of Human Intelligence*. New York, Cambridge University Press.

Stufflebeam, D. (1971) *Educational Evaluation and Decision Making*. Itasca, Minnesota, Peacock.

Sutcliffe, J. (1990) *Adults with Learning Difficulties: Curriculum, Choice and Empowerment. A Handbook of Good Practice*. Leicester, NIACE.

Sutherland, P. (ed.) (1998) *Adult Learning: A Reader*. London, Kogan Page.

SWAP (2000) *SWAP News*, Issue 2. University of Southampton. Available at *http://www.swap.ac.uk*

Taba, H. (1962) *Curriculum Development: Theory and Practice*. New York, Harcourt Brace and World.

Tawney, D. (ed.) (1976) *Curriculum Evaluation Today: Trends and Implications*. London, Macmillan.

Taylor, P. (1993) *The Texts of Paulo Freire*. Buckingham: Open University Press.

Taylor, W. (1968) *Towards a Policy for the Education of Teachers*. Colston Papers. London, Butterworth.

Taylor, W. (ed.) (1973) *Research Perspectives in Education*. London, Routledge and Kegan Paul.

Teenant, M. (1996) *Psychology and Adult Learning*. London, Routledge.

Thompson, G. (1989) 'The complete adult educator: a reconceptualisation of andragogy and pedagogy'. *Canadian Journal of University Continuing Education* 15(1): 1–13.

Thorpe, M., Edwards, R. and Hanson, A. (eds) (1993) *Culture and Processes of Adult Learning*. London, Routledge.

Thwaites, B. and Wysock-Wright, C. (1983) *Education 2000: A Consultative Document on a Hypothesis for Education in AD 2000*. Conference 1–8 July, Queen Mary and Westfield College, London.

Training Agency (1989) *Development of Accessible Standards for National Certification Guidance: Note No. 1*. Sheffield Employment Department/Training Agency.

Tripp, D.H. (1990) 'Socially critical action research'. *Theory into Practice* 24(3): 158–73.

Tutworth, E. (1985) 'Competence-based education and training: background and origins'. In J.W. Burke (ed.), *Competency-Based Education and Training*. Lewes: Falmer Press.

Tyler, R.W. (1949) *Basic Principles of Curriculum and Instruction*. Chicago, University of Chicago Press.

UDACE (1991) *What Can Graduates Do?* Consultation Document. Leicester, UDACE.

UKCC (1999) *Fitness for Practice*. London, UKCC.

UNESCO. (1990) *Evaluating Educational Programmes and Projects*. Paris, UNESCO.

Vallance, E. (1974) *Conflicting Conception of Curriculum*, Berkeley, California, McCutchan.

Veale, D.J. and Wachtel, J.M. (1996) 'Mentoring and coaching as part of a human resource development strategy'. *Management Development Review* 9(6): 19–24. Bradford, MCB University Press.

Wagenaar, T.C. (1984) 'Using students' journals in sociology courses'. *Teaching Sociology* 11(4): 419–37.

Walker, R. (1985) *Doing Research: A Handbook for Teachers*. London, Methuen.

Walklin, L. (1990) *Teaching and Learning in Further and Adult Education*. Cheltenham, Stanley Thornes.

Walklin, L. (1991) *The Assessment of Performance and Competence: A Handbook for Teachers and Trainers*. Cheltenham, Stanley Thornes.

Walklin, L. (1995) *Teaching Today*. Cheltenham: Stanley Thornes.

Waterhouse, P. (1991) *Tutoring*. Stafford Network Educational Press.

Watson, S.J. (1991) 'An analysis of the concept of experience'. *Journal of Advanced Nursing* 16(99): 1117–21.

Weil, S.W. and McGill, I. (eds) (1989) *Making Sense of Experiential Learning: Diversity in Theory and Practice*. Society for Research into Higher Education and Open University Press.

West, L. (1998) 'Implications of recent research for improving secondary school science learning'. In P. Ramsden (ed.), *Improving Learning: New Perspectives*. London, Kogan Page.

Wheeler, D.K. (1967) *Curriculum Process*. London, University of London Press.

White, J.P. (1971) 'The concept of curriculum evaluation'. *Journal of Curriculum Studies* 2(2): 102–12, 41, 54.

White, J.P. (1973) *Towards a Compulsory Curriculum*. London. Routledge.

Whittington, D. and Boore, J. (1988) 'Competence in nursing', In R. Ellis (ed.), *Professional Competence and Quality Assurance in the Caring Profession*. London, Chapman and Hall.

Wildemeersch, D. (1989) 'The principal meaning of dialogue for the construction and transformation of reality'. In S.W. Weil and I. McGill (eds), *Making Sense of Experiential Learning*. Society for Research into Higher Education and Open University Press.

Wilson, J. (1967) *Introduction to Moral Education*. Harmondsworth, Penguin.

Wilson, J. (1969) *Thinking with Concepts*. Cambridge, Cambridge University Press.

Winfrey, E. (2001) *Kirkpatrick's Four Levels of Evaluation* (online). College of Education, San Diego State University. Available at *http://coe.sdsu.edu/eet/articles/k4levels/start.html* (accessed 7 April 2001).

Wolf, A. (1989) 'Can competence and knowledge mix?' In J.W. Burke (ed.), *Competency-based Education and Training*. Lewes, Falmer Press.

Wood, E. (1985) 'Problem-based learning and problem-solving'. In D. Boud (ed.) *Problem-based Learning in Education for the Professions*. Sydney Higher Education Research and Development Society of Australia (HERDSA).

Wood, V. (1982) 'Evaluation of student nurse clinical performance: a continuing performance'. *International Nursing Review* 29(1): 11–18.

Wray, M.J. (1980) 'UVP: an evaluation of the pilot programme'. *Educational Research* 23: 34.

Young, M.F.D. (ed.) (1971) *Knowledge and Control*. London, Collier-Macmillan.

Young, M. *et al.* (1996) *Colleges as Learning Organisations. The Role of Research*. Unified 16+ Curriculum Series No. 12. London, Institute of Education.

Zuber-Skerrit, O. (1992) *Action Research in Higher Education: Examples and Reflections*. London, Kogan Page.

Zwolski, K. (1982) *Preceptors for Clinical Care*. FOCUS 10: 7–11.

Useful websites

Department for Education and Skills (DfES)
http://www.dfes.gov.co.uk

Further Education National Training Organisation (FENTO)
www.FENTO.org

Further Education Development Agency (FEDA)
http://www.feda.ac.uk

Further Education Funding Council (FEFC)
http://www.fefc.ac.uk

The Guardian
http://www.guardianunlimited.co.uk

Institute of Learning and Teaching (ILT)
http://www.ilt.ac.uk

Quality Assurance Agency (QAA)
http://www.qaa.ac.uk

Qualifications and Curriculum Authority (QCA)
http://www.qca.ac.uk

Times Educational Supplement
http://www.tes.co.uk

University Colleges and Admissions Service (UCAS)
http://www.ucas.co.uk

Social Policy and Social Work Leaning and Teaching Support Network (SWAPltsn)
www.swap.ac.uk
(Includes examples of programme specifications for social policy and social work and a range
of other materials relevant to the QAA and Subject Review. See also the QAA website.)

INDEX

Page references in italics indicate figures

157442